QUEER THEATRE

STEFAN BRECHT

**The original theatre
of the City of New York.
From the mid-60s
to the mid-70s.
Book 2**

QUEER THEATRE

Methuen Drama

METHUEN DRAMA

First published in this edition in 1986 by Methuen London Ltd,

Originally published by Suhrkamp Verlag,
Frankfurt am Main, West Germany in 1978

Copyright © Stefan Brecht   New York 1978

ISBN 0-413-49600-7

»Three stages of the disease are distinguished, *primary, secondary and tertiary s.*: the first characterized by chancre in the part affected, the second by affections of the skin and mucous membranes, the third involving the bones, muscles and brain.«

Contents

Preface 9

Jack Smith, 1961-71. The sheer beauty of junk. With a poem by Stuart Sherman and a footnote by Charles Ludlam on Mr. T. . . 10

Family of the f. p. Notes of 1968 on the theatre of the ridiculous, 1965-8. 28

The *Conquest of the Universe* (1967). Vaccaro staging Ludlam. Followed by a poem on Mary Woronow. 56

John Vaccaro, 1968-77. The gesture of hatred. 60

Charles Ludlam, 1967-77. The gesture of compassion. Introduced by an excerpt from a story by George Dennison and followed by a poem. 76

Ronald Tavel, 1967-73. Cleverness, the disgusting use of language. 107

Centola, the Hot Peaches, 1973. Dialectic of the ambition to be beautiful. 112

Centola, the Hot Peaches. Appendix I. Warhol's *Nude Restaurant*. 125

Centola, the Hot Peaches. Appendix II. The N. Y. Dolls. 129

Ridiculous ballet. Larry Ree's Original Trockadero Gloxinia Ballet Company and Les Ballets Trockadero de Monte Carlo. Poetry of the illusion of perfection vs. the indignity of failure. . . 133

Ridiculous movies. John Waters, 1968-75. The joys of transgression, the morality of filth. 137

Jack Smith, 1975-77. The horror of sex. 157

Queer theatre

»Call me a freakish man. What
more was there to do? She call me
a freakish man: What more was
there to do? Just cause she said I
was strange, that did not make it
true. I sent her to the mill to have
her coffee ground (repeat) cause
my wheel was broke and my grinder could not be found .... Had a
strange feeling this morning. Well,
I've had it all day (repeat). I wake
up one of these mornings, that
feeling will be here to stay.«

George Hannah, *Freakish Man
Blues*.

Preface

Queer theatre is derisive low comedy and burlesque, disdainfully (without compassion) and gleefully (instead of tragically, and rather than merely comically or satirically), and thus, as is logical, without pretense of its makers being otherwise, – not from a moral viewpoint, but amorally, by no standard or rule, – yet with a core or nuance of despair and dejection, as tho the universal comedy were tragic, – portraying mankind as low (lecherous and depraved), evil (malevolent and vicious) and ridiculous (preposterously pretentious, foolish and devoid of dignity and stature), and love as the supreme lie, but upholding the aesthetic ideal, aspiring to invest itself, – performers, language and performance, – with beauty, viz; the beauty possible under these conditions, the beauty of the low, the evil and the ridiculous, low, evil and ridiculous beauty, in no way natural, but artifice only, or art.

Its sense of tragedy, tho perhaps arising from self pity, is a touching inconsistency; its devotion to truth, tho perhaps an expression of anger, an arbitrary admirable choice; its love of beauty, tho perhaps rooted in despairing vanity, a heroic paradox. This inconsistency, choice and paradox make it queer.

Since the queer artist, having no justification for it, cannot allow himself the disfigurement of care, his art is entirely dependent on energy. But since his energy is entirely dependent on an exuberance of rage, his art, an active rebellion, is prone to degenerate into good-humored comedy and unthinking repetition, and to fall apart.

Jack Smith, 1961-71. The sheer beauty of junk.

Time passes
and we are absent.
Jack takes time
between thumb and forefinger of each hand, manages
to suspend it, a slightly soiled handkerchief,
as backdrop. Suddenly
you see yourself APPEARing
on the stage. Of course,
you are pleasantly surprised.
I fade out.
The hard-core refuse up there sits quietly:
glittering.

June 21, 1970

Jack Smith does not advertise his *Withdrawal from Orchid Lagoon,*
but the off-off-B'way column of the Village Voice has been listing it
for weeks, – »presented by Reptilian Theatrical Company on Saturdays at midnight at Plaster Foundation, 36 Greene Street at Grand
(free).« I do not know who the other members of the Reptilian
Theatrical Company might be. 36 Greene is Smith's loft.
There was nobody on the streets and the street door was locked when
I arrived shortly after midnight. I tentatively rang some bells on a
nearby elevator- street-door type of door. Just then three young
fellows and a boy arrived, bells were rung again, Smith opened the
door, we walked in, – he knew the others, they walked on up ahead.
Smith, a tall, thin man with a low hesitant high voice explained as
we walked up that it had been a queer intellectual day so nobody had
come – no actors, no audience. He did not know what he should do.
When he and I walked in, the others were seated and talking idly.
The loft was not too large for a loft, perhaps 15 by 50 foot, with the
stage at one end, stove, refrigerator, table at the other. It is double
height, the ceiling has been broken through to another loft, with a
balcony left above the kitchen for sleeping, storage . . . It was quiet,
Smith put on some records – sentimental mood music, mostly Spanish,
Christmas songs, patriotic tunes . . . pretty music. Some couples walked
in, hardly discernible in the half-dark. Smith explained, more or less
mumbling, that there were no actors, put it up to us if perhaps we
should just listen to some records, but gradually seemed to decide,

walking about, puttering, to go ahead, asked for volunteers for acting, finally two of the boys, of whom I knew one, Mr. T.,* grud-

* *Mr. T. or El Pato in the Gilded Summer Palace of Czarina-Tatlina*, by Charles
Ludlam, a fairy tale:
»Once upon a time there was a little boy whose mommy made him go to mass
every Sunday and to Catholic School during the week. On Saturdays when the
other children were out playing Tag, Hopscotch and Doctor, this little boy was on
his knees in front of the priest confessing his sins and doing penance. One day
the little boy ran away to the Big City. At first he felt very lost and alone. He
had no money and no place to stay. But he soon discovered that certain older men
in the Port Authority Bus Terminal would give him money if he let them suck on
his pee pee. So he did.
»One day the little boy, whose name is Mr. T. found a home in the ghetto at 266
E. 4th Street. Here he met Puerto Rican boys who were Catholics like himself.
They peed in the hall and made him get down on his knees in front of them and
suck on their pee pees. This reminded him of the confessional. He liked it very
much. ›I never want to leave the ghetto,‹ said Mr. T. ›This is where I live.‹ Then
the junkies robbed him of the money he had just gotten from the older man in The
Port Authority Bus Terminal.
»Mr. T. got tired of living on the gratitude of older men (›Besides they're not that
grateful,‹ he said.) and got welfare. Now he hardly knew how to express his gratitude to the City of New York. Yet with all these things, a railroad flat on the
fourth floor of a tenement, the companionship of the queens on Christopher Street,
and the Welfare grant, Mr. T. was not happy. He felt a longing in his heart, a
nostalgia to hear the Mass prayed in a language he did not understand. The reforms
of the Ecumenical Councils made him feel disinherited. If only he could combine
his taste for botanicas, gypsy store fronts and Puerto Rican boys with the grandeur
that was Rome . . . . the grandeur that was St. Petersburg. He prayed to St.
Catherine for a sign. And the sign came. He would build the Artorama, a genre
more queer than Mexican folk art and a thousand times more detailed than Macy's
Christmas windows. The artorama would be the apotheosis of the Catholic religious
holidays, Christmas and Easter rolled into one, an electric train, tin foil Wonder
City where jewel encrusted rats in ecclesiastical garb murmur novenas in detailed
replicas of Fabergé Easter Eggs. The heart of Christ bleeds rubies into a levitating
grail. Silver stars hang about the head of a life-sized statue of St. Francis from
the painted blue sky above your head. Forgeries of the crown jewels of the Imperial Family of Russia serve as harbingers of the *new* orthodoxy of Queer Catholi-
cism. Rome and the Pope have become too liberal. They are heretics in the sacristy
of the Slum Goddess. Mr. T. begins the seventies with an invocation of the muse
and a clarion call to return to the tradition of high art. Reincarnate the nineteenth
century! The glamor of the Baroque will be revived by renegade Catholics. Fig
leaves will fall from the crotches of Roman Statues painted in fashion colors. Mr.
T's dream is to build a chapel to the martyred saints in a store front on East 4th
Street. Perhaps he would paint frescoes. But his Public Assistance Grant from the
Department of Welfare does not permit the undertaking of so ambitious a project.
Attendance at his art exhibits (he shows in his apartment only) has been limited
to a small coterie of people in the know and Puerto Rican children in the neigh-
borhood. They love Mr. T because he has entered their world and crystalized the
Puerto Rican Mystique. Last week Mr. T gave Mario Montez a large fake leopard

gingly agreed, they vanished in the stage-area, behind a tall, indistinct structure which I later found was a kind of teepee made of eight-or-ten-foot-long, thick planks leaning together. I smoked something, Smith asked if anybody had anything to smoke for him, and somebody had. I relaxed to the music, found a saggy couch over the back of which I might watch the stage area if I sat up. The others grouped themselves similarly on another couch, some chairs. I dozed off. At one point, coming out of it, raising myself above the back of the couch, I groggily noticed that one of the two boys, not Mr. T, the other, had assumed a giant wild wig of all flowers, it seemed, that just about hid her face, – he/she was sitting half behind that dark vertical structure. – In the forefront, a junk heap – metallic and plastic street refuse measuring in the inches and feet, broken, and bottles. A minor votive screen in the background, with empty bottles in the niches. A toilet with junk in it, including a crippled, perhaps headless doll. Old, small Christmas trees with hardly any needles left. Feathers, wire netting, a string of colored lights. A huge ladder with a net suspended from it goes up to the sleeping balcony. Smith ascends and descends several times purposefully, he arranges for some illumination of the junk heap. The assembly of reject artifacts is tawdry. Even with some glitter from the light there is no glamor, even momentary. Nor any kind of beauty, nor the interest of the concrete.

handbag which she now carries as Leopard Women in Bluebeard. ›She's the first Puerto Rican artist who knew she was Puerto Rican and used it.‹ he said. › I never want to leave the ghetto. This is where I live.‹ Mr. T is influenced by the Ukrainian religious art around Avenue A too. ›Polish and Ukrainian kids have big dicks, but they're too mean.‹ ›It's a cop out to fall in love with someone. It's just an attempt to lose yourself. I think it's better to make things. Don't you?‹ The things that Mr. T makes are not made to last. His is a transitory art that creates an illusion and then disappears. For this reason it might be called theatrical. The images seem to dissolve before your eyes. Now it is an exquisite piece of jewelry or a relic of the true cross encased in a richness unmatched outside the Vatican. Then suddenly you realize that it is made of Saran Wrap or Wondafoil, packaging materials symbolic of the octopus that has us in its inky clutches, the present regime. The item appears worthless if seen from behind or from its ›bad‹ side. We turn it and it becomes exquisite again. This is Queen Art transformed by the genius of Mr. T into a metaphysical mockery. Profanation of the Mother and the sacred religious relics becomes the veneration of the invert. To have a new idea is as gauche as being seen in a new suit. Heresy is for heterosexuals. Says Mr. T, ›Heterosexuals can't understand camp because everything they do is camp.‹
Mr. T's new show can be seen at 266 E. 4th Street, Apt. 17 (4th floor) Tuesdays, Wednesdays and Thursdays from 2 PM to 4 PM Saturdays from 1 PM to 5 PM. Wait at the street level door until someone opens the door for you.‹ (© Charles Ludlam, May 1970.)

There is some very slight arrangement – order – in it, a sensitively restrained encroachment on a chance disorder which has been allowed to affirm itself. Smith seems to have picked up these things by an attraction to the definitely squalid, a sentiment for orphanage among the merest means. The disruption of function defines the heap. –

It is very late. Mr. T wants to go home, but Jack wants to finish the play. Almost everybodys has left. I volunteer to help Mr. T bury the child. We are to bring the little coffin (some box or carton) very slowly into the plank structure, – a mausoleum. Smith corrects our acting often. We are doing it too fast. Finally I am processioning so slow Smith has to ask me to speed my steps up a little. I am worried he will shut us up inside the heavy planks, so try to bypass the structure. But he directs us inside.

January 2, 1971

»*Claptailism of Palmola Christmas Spectacle*,« by Jack Smith, presented on Saturdays at midnight at the Plaster Foundation, 36 Greene Street (free).

Smith does this with somebody introducing himself as Abby.* I arrive a little before Abby who drives up in his car, calls up to the window. Abby is of Jewish appearance – business suit, little black hat. Arrived up in Smith's loft, we are the only arrivees so far. I sit on the couch, watch the tv, Smith turns off the sound, it's a George Raft Foreign Legion movie. The cat jumps on my lap. Abby thinks maybe 5 or 10 more people will come. Smith doesn't think anybody will, – so soon after New Year and with that much snow on the ground. But a few people – 7 or so – come, some leave after a while, some more come. We are seated or are lying – on the couch, on the floor, on a scaffolding that goes up to the ceiling, but as yet is mostly just the two-by-fours, with only one plank, in one section, to sit on. I am the only one that stays to the end, apart from a woman that knows Smith, wears dark glasses, seems stoned. He served us some chocolate cake out of the refrigerator when the show was over.

Smith puts on a record that starts the mood, thus the performance. He climbs up on his bedroom half-loft, projects a picture on the screen – it is pale, indistinct, – seems a shot of an Oriental marketplace with four people, two couples, posing, might be something

* Dear Abby answers the letters of troubled readers in, I believe, the New York Post.

vastly else. It stays on, very effective, the white-suited figures poised, until the final part of the performance when another image is projected – a formal garden, French style, with water jet, I would say.

Abby and Smith dress up in costumes – vaguely Semitic – draped kimonos with large patterns, burnouses, they are glimpsed as wearing brassieres under the kaftans, over their other clothes (it is cold in the loft, people who have shed their outer clothes put them back on again after a while), – skull caps. Magis ... The center stage is filled with junk as before, partly the same items, – plastic fish, signs, bottles ... Jumbled, stuffed in. The needle-less branches-only Christmas tree, heeling, is there from before, I believe. But much of the display is new. Notably something which in the dark – it is rather dark for most of the evening – looks like suspended bottles, but might be plastic. It glitters in the light that comes from the end of the room, »behind« the »stage.« It is féerique.

Abby and Smith busy themselves with things, arranging ...

Abby approaches us and asks for money. For 50 cents this time, rather than a dollar, – in a little speech, a subdued mumble in which he repeatedly stresses that the show is free, but that we have to pay 50 cents because food is needed, and ... The effect is slightly humorous, but mostly sincere.

Abby sits down on a chair center-left, a little table in front of him, draped in his burnouse, his beard and glasses barely showing, writing carefully on some sheets of paper. Now and then he and Smith consult. Smith is still busy, in fact keeps on being continuously busy, adjusting things in a nervous way.

Behind the suspended glass or whatever, there is a red light, other things I can't make out. One sinks down into this atmosphere, hypnotised. There is a wooden cross in the back of the stage. The wigwam from the last show is gone.

Smith announces that Abby will advise us. We are to tell him our most important problem, his answer will solve it. This will cost an additional dime. Various members of the audience successively go up there, most in a spirit of fun. They sit down across from Abby. The exchanges are inaudible. I tell him my problem is the rush of time. He tells me there is no time. I express my disagreement. His breath is bad.

Jack Smith, *Gas Stations of the Cross Religious Spectacle.*
36 Greene St.
I did not stay for the whole show, but its first sequence at least and most of the junk in the middle of the floor seemed the same as in the Christmas program. The record exhorting us to give ourselves to Mary was played again. The first act was again Abby – this time you were supposed to look in his eyes and you would see the solution to your problems. Externally viewed, Abby's task (his name this time was not Abby but Nogood) had been made easier. This act was introduced by Jack in not quite flowing but at least loosely hanging robe and some make-up around the eyebrows. He read from a sheet ⅓ covered in large scribbled, corrected writing: read as awkwardly as possible, stumbling, inexpressively, dully, with an admonition not to engage in a fucking staring contest. The point seemed to be that one's problems were illusory and/or insignificant anyhow, and that anything done putting them in this light would solve them as well as any other action or better. Jack wore a bra over his clothes from the beginning, later put on a Mongolian skull cap. Abby gradually got into togs Jack found for him, a feather-, ruffle- or puff-compounded, semi-spherical brief toga around neck and shoulders, white, and a light blue flat, flouncy ladies' hat. His bespectacled Jewish-smart face with an occasional smile or laugh on it, was barely visible between them. His girl friend was the first to go up. Jack stood there with his battered Quaker Oats box receiving the dimes, after a while he also held a purloined sign saying »File Early.« In the foreground of the junk a sign was suspended saying »For the Birds,« – an advertising of something, perhaps bird seed. Among the junk leaned at least two of the bare Christmas trees with a little silver paper streamers on them. Abby and Jack part of the time acted serious, like carny-fakers, part of the time laughed, giggled or smiled as though »breaking up«: making the put-on explicit, more than trying to escape the ridicule of identification with the act, – daring the audience (half a dozen or more, kids, friends, a Negro junkie...) not to take the act serious. The second act was again Jack sitting sifting sand, Abby kneeling in Prayer, with a Jewish skull-cap on his head, minus the previous costume.
Jack occasionally sweetened the air with something like Aerosol, from a spray can.
Bill Stewart and Mary Peer dropped in, left again.

Abby's girl friend was there. She saw the message as being »nothing is anything.« Personally, she did not buy this, but, though sometimes bored, she enjoyed the shows.

All of Smith's gestures are hesitant. The simplest lifting of an object or securing of a string is a serious task which he will accomplish, but which he does not seem quite to know how to go about. He tries various approaches – in front of you – perhaps gives up some lines of approach too quickly. He is figuring out how to do it while doing it. Changing one slide for another, he stops pulling the first one while a corner of the image is still (dimly) on the screen, then pulls it out. Perhaps he is not sure he is doing the right thing. Any performance of his contains many such episodes of change of approach to a simple practical task.

He is continually busy with simple practical tasks. It's not that the show has not been carefully prepared. E.g. the bottles, containers, old Xmas trees, signs, broken toys, baby carriages that compound his stage setting – a central object taking up 80 percent or more of the area set aside for performance, – have all been carefully arranged and this has taken him a long time because many minute rearrangements were needed. But much remains to be done nevertheless and he is continually busy with it during the show, in fact so much so that only very little time is left over for anything like mere appearance or performance. For one thing, his arrangements are precarious. Also, like Robert Wilson, he seems concerned with the subliminal impression: this demands an (ineffable) exactitude. The effect is vaguely comic. Much of his time is spent directing his assistants who tend in fact to be the major performers. He is apt to get seriously irritated – is said sometimes to resort to physical violence (no act): people don't seem to be able to follow the simplest instructions. (This is true, incidentally: to follow not quite the simplest instructions is easier.) Also they have no (adequate) sense of responsibility – their responsibility being considerable because of the importance of the whole thing. They think it can be done any old way. Also his cooperants tend to confer with him about the proper next step. The audience apparently is mostly sparse. There is a good percentage of jokers. Of young couples (or trios). Not noticeably a queer audience. Mainly hippie – long hairs with blue jeans, leather jackets, big fur coats. The audience gradually thins out, by 3 or 4 in the morning there are rarely – I would say – more than one to three people left to see the end (such as: the death, perhaps of consumption, of the beautiful nun of Noa-Noa). Sleepiness, boredom – in the case of many probably irritation or anger – alternate with mild hilarity and a trancelike appreciation of the beauty of the form of time displayed as object, – this last feeling strengthening in intensity as this object is progressively constituted. The only real feeling of objection that I have noticed in myself might be put: why the fuck am I not fucking instead?

Jack does not in these shows move as slowly as he did as Mister X in Charles' *Big Hotel* or as he did as Magician in Wilson's *Deafman Glance*. He is not brisk, he is puttering about with an unambitious competence in the performance of a job. He is slow, but not super-slow (as in the sand-pouring). The show as a whole is slow – the same thing is done for a long long while each time, there are long waits with Jack fetching something up on the upper-level loft or adjusting the spotlight or putting a new slide in or disappearing behind the altar-like wooden screen (a cross in front of it) to the rear of the stage, doing something, presumably.

To see the death of the beautiful nun from close up, you have to pay two bits extra. Jack played her, just lay there.

I run into Jack at a screening of Hilary Harris' *The Nuer*.* He is with a girl named Marie. He asks me do I want to do the part of Plodius in a film he is going to shoot of *Hamlet*. I immediately say yes. They don't have the *Nuer*, so after watching an old documentary of Harris', a hymn to ship-building on the Clyde, we leave. He is going to shoot the film in his loft, wants me to see the scenery, – maybe we can work on it a little. He is hungry, so after a pastrami sandwich at the Smith's on University Place, we go to have some soup at Marie's and Leon's, up on the top floor of 18 Mercer, a loft building just above Canal, where Jack, – having been evicted from his last loft, – he couldn't pay the $150 a month, – has his new studio. He has brought over everything that was really valuable. On the way down, Jack talks about landlordism. He thinks rent is magic, doesn't understand it, – the fact that you have to keep paying: you are paying for time itself, for your very life. Landlordism in his view

* To George and Hilary

The fashionably old encyclopedia opened tells
of men like riverbirds in shape and habits, –
the river glints and moves beneath
the few in sum contemptuous lines
as from afar the new imperial city strains
a distant lensëd eye upon the sun-dark creatures moving.

is the origin of all the current crimes and troubles. A previous landlord of his had sneaked around to take the notice notifying Jack of the court hearing on the eviction charges off his door! Not knowing he was to show up, Jack was evicted. At the moment he is doing OK. He is finally on welfare and every time one of his old movies is shown, he makes a hundred dollars or so. Marie has some of the pop-art collage paintings she was doing until 3 or 4 years ago up on her walls. Waiting for the soup that Leon, her boyish-looking Negro boy friend is heating up, we have 3-5 joints. Leon puts free form jazz on the phonograph, he has Shepp's latest French record, – also some marvellous drumming by the Master Players of Morocco. But Jack takes over, puts on a concert of lush romantic music, obscure Russians etc., also show tunes, Latin music . . . A while after eating the soup (I'm floating, reclining in a swing), Jack transfers the party to his studio in the cellar. It is long and narrow, its walls, scattered scabby irruptions creeping down them, peeling in the most opulent manner imaginable, brittle slats sticking through the soft plaster here and there. A heater dispenses scant heat from up near the ceiling. The place is darkish and very, very crowded. Access to its inner two-thirds is barred by a rusty pipe-structure of an industrial sort, something like a giant-sized garment-rusher's rack, – not that there are that many pipes making it up, but their arrangement is such that you have to step over some, duck under others, plus do the same but not quite the same thing again. It annoys – and tires – Jack a great deal. The junk has been set up in that inner part of the cellar against the rear wall. Here is the stage. Jack rolls some more joints.*

Jack has for years been talking of doing *Hamlet* on stage, – say at La Mama. He feels the play is very badly written, no structure, more like a radio or tv series, but can be salvaged by much cutting. Only the good lines are to be retained. It will be in the family: just Hamlet

* Richard Foreman on the 1960s: »I didn't think I've ever talked at length about how much of my stuff comes out of all the drug-oriented art of that period, even though I did not take any drugs to speak of. The art that I was seeing in the days I was hanging around the Cinematheque, which seemed to me the truest and the most provocative, was made by people under the influence of drugs, pure and simple. Now what does that mean? I don't think it *means* much – it means the drugs stopped them from moving their fingers in the way habit had taught them so other energies would start bleeding through. It is strange to me, to think of it, especially since a lot of these people made very beautiful things, most of which are now lost, and many of them are burned out. They really destroyed themselves. And here am I benefitting from all of it. I mean, how many people who are now so-called leaders of the American experimental theatre owe volumes to Jack Smith? (interview in the Village Voice, January 2, 1978.)«

(Jack Smith), Gertrude (Marie-Antoinette, one of Vaccaro's actresses), Ophelia (Silva, – a drag-queen I don't know), and Plodius (Polonius + Clodius, – to be played by myself). It will be Jack's first talking movie, in lush colors. The UP film studio will help with the sound. The whole family will be landlords, – modern royalty. E.g. Plodius is to be a pear-shaped, grey-skinned, white haired, jovial and reptilian criminal age 50, the age at which depravity breaks out in people, the criminal age. Jack will take me along when he next pays his rent, – it will be very instructive. He is looking for 20 pounds of white glitter, he will color it himself, some of it grey for my part. The action will take place under water, – Plodius will also be an octopus. Jack already has some octopus legs, – the setting will be Middle Western, – Jack is looking for some corn stalks. It will be done Arabian Nights style, – Jack is still looking for a picture of the desert, – sand dunes, – that's one of the things that have been holding up the production, – i.e. it will be Universal Pictures 1940s exotic. (Jack figures that the fact that Universal was run by a bunch of Jews might have had something to do with their specialising in the exotic, a terrifically artistic thing to do, – not in money or sex, the two more usual topics.) He doesn't have Silva's current address: another thing holding up the production.

To our left, once we are past the obstruction, along the north wall, there is nothing much, – a sink is set leaning on the floor. This is Gertrude's playing area. The glamorous section runs along the east wall. The southeast corner is Plodius', the junk builds up toward it for five or six feet along the south wall, in the corner rising on and next to a kind of stair-structure, most precarious, made of old weak boards, crates, etc., leading to a platform behind a string-suspended light-blue rag of a curtain. Behind the curtain stands a chair, my throne. Jack points to a hole in the ceiling high above, saying the set-up is not finished at all yet: the refuse will be tumbling out of that hole. Next to this elevation there is a structure made of heavy wooden beams coming out of the middle of the wall, that Jack refers to as a wharf, quoting:

> And duller shouldst thou be than the fat weed
> That rots itself in ease on Lethe's wharf,
> Wouldst thou not stir in this, –

Ghost, act 1, sc. v. Jack plans to grow a marijuana plant in some dirt on top of this. This is Hamlet's platform. Hamlet is an art student, – Jack fears he is too old for Hamlet now, he wasn't 3 or 4 years ago when he first thought of doing the play, but close to 40 one ages so quickly, – one is suddenly all gone. He aims to play him as a fop, and very very queer, – why otherwise would he have turned on both his mother and Ophelia? – there are a few hints in the text, but not many ... Ophelia will come out of the northeast corner, that will be her area, – it's the john. Jack chuckles.

He is going to work on Plodius' area now. He puts on his Hamlet costume – slightly Harlequin, stage-renaissance, black and white checkered, striped and ruffled – for working, – also worn pigskin gloves: showing me my royal robe at the same time, and making me try it and a paper crown on before a mirror. I am not obese, but that can be arranged. He puts on some records, – sentimental stuff rather than the lush, gorgeous brassy tone-paintings he played upstairs, and apparently the essential stuff as far as he is concerned: more directly emotional, i. e. pastiche-emotional. Marie goes upstairs.

Jack is rearranging Plodius' stair-display. He is holding an artificial leg, splintered off at the hip. He places it in slightly different ways many times in the same place, in between stepping back to study the effect from a slight distance. His handsome face (blonde moustache, – on some old stills he just showed me, he looked very much the movie star) looks young, but he is very thin, often sways as though from weakness. Of course, it's difficult working on those junk-crowded pseudo-stairs. He does not want the leg so dominant, – one won't be able to see anything else. On the other hand, he does not want to blend it in – he definitely does not want to create a harmony. – There is a bunch of artificial roses. Many of the things are christmassy, little plastic Xmas trees f. inst. All the stuff clearly and definitely comes off the street. – He turns to an artificial palm with a twisted lower trunk twisting around a slim green barrel made of carton or the like. He wants the palm to stand up in some certain way or other. He asks for advice. Leon gives an opinion on how it should be, and illustrates, holding the palm. It needs to be supported, so Jack wanders off for string, but gets involved in putting on more records. Leon is still holding the palm. I locate a piece of string. Leon and I tie up the palm. But the barrel does not look quite right. Jack wants it to look like part of a fallen column, which it doesn't. He saws off part of its top with a light Japanese saw-knife, rearranges the column under the twisted palm leg. Then there is a little altar-like cave near the top, a doll lying on her back in its entrance. Jack rearranges her, pulling her wispy blue dress down over her crotch, but spreading her legs more, – she looks like a dead raped girl-child, – covers her with a red and yellow dime store flower garland. She is now just about invisible. He rearranges the garland in many ways, quite prettily, but finally rather sort of throws it on her.

In the meantime I am nailing three little respectively green, red and blue plaster fish to the wall. They are to swim behind their mother who is already up there. For a while we are all three on top of two contiguous small crates, working at the same time at different things. Jack has loaded me down with the fish, a handful of nails, a hammer. I pick a spot for the first fish just behind the mother fish, a little lower down, – sort of sniffing after her, playing merrily on his own in a cautious way. Jack makes me pull the nail out again, shows me where he wants the little fish, scratches an outline in the plaster: in line with the mother, behind her. Also he wants the pink fish there, not the blue one. The next little fish is too close to the first one, he wants me to deplace it further back, at a regular distance, the same as between the mother and the first baby. The plaster is coming off catastrophically, there are very hard spots in some places under it, Jack brings me masking tape which I put up. The jagged strips of tape traverse the cracks and the areas where the plaster is crumbling away. I am now able to place the next fish where he wants it. I put up the third fish without further consultation. They are all in line now, swimming in perfect artificiality along the wall. This looks just right. Jack nails two tinny, bronze-colored flat lions to one of the ziggurat steps, wonders if it is too much, but decides it's OK, – it's a very very ornate temple. He nails an Easter palm cross to the wall further up, – the dry cross crumbles under the big nail head, he puts the nail somewhere else. All his handicraft work is impatient, rough, fast. (Putting on records, stooping, his arm movements are very rapid, he is in a hurry. But he walks slowly.) He sighs, the work is drudgery. He foresees where nights and nights will be soaked up by nailing and taping everything in place. He asks me to bring an intelligent helper.

The heap glitters melodiously. It is clearly exotic, a landscape of desire. The fact that the material is with puritanical strictness, in demonic purity junk, – in substance, shape and monetarily of absolutely no value, – isolates this longing into its form of pure sentiment. But this is no dream world, it is not even the world of daydreams, tho' that is closer: it is the world of art, a formally artificial arrangement. Its artificiality is explicitly part of its form, and that what it is an arrangement of, its matter, doesn't matter, is also part of its form.

It is no dream world because the ambiguities between the purity of sentiments that are popular, everybody's and their obvious insane vulgarity (insane because they are far removed from the realities of conceivable pleasure) – an ambiguity operative in Smith's salvaging jetsam infecundated with the big city's desires, – and between the maker's 100 percent artistic devotion and the total humor of it are complete. Except where the art elevates that preciousness of material into epiphany of the natural world's capacity for glory, the purity of art is adulterated by precious substances, as those in certain visions of paradise, and by admonitory signs of the work's importance, as where the materials are of good quality. I take leave – he is loathe not to keep working. When I get out on the streets the bars are all closed, there are only late-night people. It is around 4 a. m. I have learned more about art than on any other day or night of my life. Jack takes you on a trip, but it turns out not an ego-trip of his but like the love-offering that in the 60s a flower-child

> ›child of Orpheus,
> called by the dove,‹

might have made her up-tight lover, saying, ›it's pure stuff, you don't have to worry‹, in a pretty box no bigger than a walnut, prettily wrapped, and containing just enough acid for 2. My friend Stuart Sherman on one of these evenings noticed a teddy bear in a toilet bowl. He wrote the following poem entitled:

Teddy Bear Is Dead, Long Live Jack Smith!

Teddy Bear is dead,
Accidentally? killed by Jack's favorite friend,
Whom Jack can't kill because
His favorite friend was Teddy Bear.

Jack holds his breath.
We suffocate.
Jack releases his breath
Into harmless air.

Safe,
Jack speaks every word, sings every song.
Words and songs, echoless, expire.
Jack sighs soap-bubbles.

Unsolicited, colors cloak his naked body.
Jack sheds his skin.
Affrighted by the absence of a skeleton,
The importunate colors pale, fade, disappear.

Charnel things are visible – –
Relics preserved in abject memory – –
Arranged in unmanifest design,
Minutiae of Jack's providence.

His arms signal:
His legs move.
His arms stop signalling:
His legs stand still.

Falling stars graze the silence,
Streaking a circle round it.
Sparks sizzle our rotting flesh,
The silence thickens and rises.

Inside, Jack sleeps to
Dream of Teddy Bear and himself
When Teddy Bear was old and
Jack was young.

Jack Smith's *Scotch Tape* of 1961. For 3 minutes or so various faggots
cavort in a dense, three-dimensional lattice of curving, namely bent
and twisted steel girders, – or did I see the fibrous strands of rigid
cables? – locally encumbered by cracked cement blocks, between
which the curving girders snake, the blatantly de-functionalised flower
of what indubitably at one time previous to 1961 had had because
it had been given the form of a useful construct, i.e. of an obnoxious
synthesis serving an execrable purpose. If he shot it as a whole, he
did not include the shot in the film. In one shot at the beginning we
see Jack Smith, serious and businesslike, surveying or supervising.
There is a shot toward the end, through this environment, of a small
group, presumably the same people, moving about in a distance far
below, on what appears rubble-strewn ground, a texture known to
us from a work-phase of de Kooning's not long before he got involved
with his Monstrous flesh-colored Women as that of the Vacant Lot,
as well as from Dubuffet's close-on and in-depth portrayals of urban

surfaces. The cavortings are partly the lady-like posturing gestures of inverts, partly jungle gym gamboling in some game of Tarzan, horizontal positions and displacements playfully and a little awkwardly suggesting a spiderish dream-transcendence of gravity, but the shaking hand-held camera's erring has created a ballet.

Bob Fleischner, who much later came to be the nebbich hero of Richard Foreman's autobiographical comedies, by the mid-70s giving splendidly sure and powerful performances of him, and who in 1965 directed and shot the 25-minute *Grandma's House*, with Barbara Kahn and starring Mr. Jerry Sims, portrait of a piteous man lost in distrust, a moving and beautiful love story in the French manner of around 1930, in or about 1959 photographed and together with its star, Jack Smith, – Jerry Sims, the other actor, comes in at the edges, in a sinister vein, – co-conceived a film that under the title *Blonde Cobra* ended up 25 minutes in length also, but which, having quarreled with Jack Smith, which is easy, he abandoned and gave to Ken Jacobs to make something out of. Fleischner's shots show Smith playing a madly sinful infant and also the Middle Eastern femme fatale of his dreams. The camera, sometimes ostentatiously dwelling on some texture, light/shadow, light effect, is pointed somewhere, people move in and out of the frame, heads, feet are cut off. Smith's face is alternately arch and horrible, desire to please, pain of pleasure. Sims' forehead is deeply furrowed vertically, he seems a Depressive. He has been told to play with his tongue out. Jacobs, adding a little footage of his own, for sound getting Smith to provide pet phrases of his, quasi-songs, short discourses (the screen going blank when Smith's voice goes on), and editorially liberalising into phony pity for genius stymied* what Smith had evidently conceived grandiosely as glorification of perverse child-man, lost in the Lord's enormous (10-room) mansion, – a Lord not dead, but with his will divided against itself, – by 1963 had made an exploitation of Jack Smith out of it. It is a powerfully unpleasant, inept movie: but its disgustingness and ineptness would merely have been material, and the movie mov-

---

* »*Blonde Cobra* ... is a look in on an exploding life, on a man of imagination suffering pre-fashionable lower East Side deprivation and consumed with American 1950s, 40s, 30s disgust. Silly, self-pitying, guilt-strictured and yet triumphing – on one level – over the situation with style, because he's unapologetically gifted, has a genius for courage, knows that a state of indignity can serve to show his character in sharpest relief. He . . . does all he can to draw out our condemnation . . . enticing us into an absurd moral posture the better to dismiss us with a regal ›screw-off‹.« (Ken Jacobs, Note for a February 1975 showing at the Whitney Museum.)

ing and beautiful, at least possibly, had Fleischner and Smith finished it, had not Jacobs turned it into an exposure of Smith.

Jack Smith's *Flaming Creatures* of 1962/3 shows the ball that a bunch of transvestites are having in some most disorderly room, dressed up in women's party- or going-out-finery and having been given, for the orgy, an early culmination recrudescing later, a voluptuous little Jewish girl-woman (I am not sure if the beautiful soft Semitic woman's face, aristocratically fine and simple as an animal's which the lens swings to ever so often is always that of the girl) to mock-rape* endlessly, and as context for their gropings and friggings of themselves and one another. The manipulation of her right breast, brought out of her black evening dress, a soft white perfect semisphere, is, – followed in second place by the anchor-image of a swaying lead- or iron-framed, unlit rhomboid substitute for a grandiose crystal chandelier, – the (sustained and repeated) key-image of this social event and moving gallery of plastic sculptures: a hand indents it below the nipple, making the nipple, never erect, protrude, a hand jiggles it, imparting to it a jigging motion, an automotion, more harmonious and more powerful than anything My Sister Kate could ever do, and which, during the last musical accompaniment, a rock number, is in time with the beat. Many of the shots are of a confused assemblage of glorious rags and male limbs, a tight collage on the floor. Twice, if not more often, we see a hand rapidly shaking a limp prick grasped between thumb and forefinger, the arm at a nearly right angle across the hose-clad shanks revealed under the hoisted shirt, the executor of the perfunctory gesture invisible. The queers preen themselves. This involves on the one hand the mock-coy, mock-shocked, mock-anxious, mock-sorrowful swivellings of their eyeballs, a soulful itinerary through the movies, with the camera moving in under in complementary, opposite curves, on the other, lip-gymnastics, a mock-sensuality derived from the pout, demonstrating the lips' flexibility, humifiability and suction-power, a visual paean to cocksucking, grand rivalry for the cock of mouth with cunt, culminating in the second of the movie's grand Scenes, a universal elaborate putting on of lipstick, dark and glistening, the extreme close-ups

* That it is a mock-rape is made *clear:* by the metronomic, loose swinging of the girl's free right arm, a visually invalidated gesture of helpless warding off. After the collective violation of her, the girl is consoled on a divan in a draped niche by a blonde, billed in the credits as The Fascinating Woman, – Judith Malina. The girl finds relief in Lesbian love. This is the only discernible story-element in the film.

revealing the grainy skin, stubble, bad teeth, epidermal pouches of these not-so-young queens: to the accompaniment of a woman's commercial recorded lecture on why and how to put on lipstick. Only one of the preening figurants has talent as female impersonator. The camera catches the others getting into their acts. Toward the end of the movie, Mario Montez comes on as a Spanish gypsy, all in black, rose between his teeth, his long bony face extraordinarily appealing, boyish, innocent: a moment of pathetic human beauty. The camera does not bear down on him, but catches him in glimpses, tenderly, discreetly, or as though Jack wanted to go easy on *simple* beauty. For though the entire film is of considerable beauty to the eye,* the beauty of the texture of the seen, of smoke, mist, chiffon, a poetic beauty, the images, – scarfs, dead leaves, artificial flowers, gowned sentimental beauties, – are all cast in the artwork's searing gesture of irony,** an adoration neither of the tawdry, nor of beauty, but of the aspiration toward beauty, the purer for its immersion in the tawdry, a more fond, defiant and compassionate respect for this aspiration, than an adoration of it. Of this aspiration toward beauty, the wish to be like a woman would be the first sign. The photographed scene bears the mark of arrangement, like some sitting room carefully furnished in good taste: the photography supervenes on the arrangement, registering it, – all detail, here, and no good taste, – with an evident approval bordering on delectation, and, shoddy,*** but very much alive, visibly seeking the objects and angles, partakes

* »What I am urging is that there is not only moral space, by whose laws *Flaming Creatures* would indeed come off badly; there is also aesthetic space, the space of pleasure. Here Smith's film moves and has its being.« (Susan Sontag in The Nation)
** »I have been ... processed and recycled into the Mekas column as confirmation of all the beanbaggery it has contained over the last 10 years; since my film, »Flaming Creatures,« designed – like John Waters' *Pink Flamingos* – as a comedy, had riotously laughing audiences at its first screenings, right up to the time the media lesbians began to write their spicy, orchid hothouse, deviee description and turned my film into a sex issue of the Cocktail World, giving rise to the speculation, understandable in their case, that a real brassiere-dyke may not be able, professionally or otherwise, to recognise any difference whatsoever between comedy and sex.« (Jack Smith on *Pink Flamingos*, in the Village Voice, 1973)
*** Cf. Susan Sontag's intelligent and perceptive essay on the film. Her beautiful clear voice, except when she is making movies out in the open, is muffled by the heavy concrete walls of the underground shelter she speaks from, – culture (in Dubuffet's sense in the days when he spoke of *crude art*). She uses such words as »a different aesthetic«, »visual material« and »sensibility,« tho' she *knows* that art is life.

of that aspiration in tawdry toward beauty, honoring it by its allusions (e.g. the overhead shot of a dancing couple) to the shooting devices of the romantic branch of the film industry.

Jack's defiant aesthetic lower-depthism, proud self-affirmation of the lower depths, and his defiant lower depths' aestheticism, his proud self-affirmation against the lower depths define ridiculous theatre, theatre of the sons and daughters of the hard hat Ethnics, frozen in adolescent rebellion, queer and renegade Roman Catholics on welfare.

Family of the f. p. The theatre of the ridiculous, 1965-68.*

> »Jack is the daddy of us all.«
>
> *Charles Ludlam, 1971*

> »(Vaccaro.) December 26, 1961 is when I got to NYC. I met Jack Smith, and I was acting in his films. He was an incredible influence on my life. Probably the biggest influence. (Interviewer.) Were you a star in any of them? (V.) Oh, sure. (I.) You want to name one? (V.) *Normal Love, Normal Love.* We had mummies and a cobra woman and bats and mermaids and werewolves. We made love to each other. It was very normal..... Jack is pretty much the pure artist, *the* pure artist of our day.« (Confronting the Ridiculous / A Theatrical Review with John Vaccaro, ... 12/8/75 and 1/20 /76 Interviewer: Playwright Kenneth Bernard. In: Confrontations, Spring/Summer 76.)

This theatre has attracted little but unfavorable notice: it is slovenly, amateurish, silly, just boring; a put-on, really an actors's lark; not art, certainly not serious art; a coterie occasion for a pariah in-group; by and for queers (not the nice kind, but drag queens and dykes and leather/motorbike/S and M hard trade); a display case for transvestites, pure camp, devoted to movie fetishism; anyhow just adolescent pornography; ritual enactment of an impotent humiliation of women (vicious, loveless); pointless, emotionally impactless, untheatrical; certainly devoid of social relevance; in sum, *stupid* and *immoral.*

The theatre of the ridiculous is an important theatre and theatre form.

* Article of 1968.

I want to interpret here my impression* of the theatre's theatrical impact, in the light of interviews with John Vaccaro, Charles Ludlam, Mary Woronow and some written pieces of Ronald Tavel's

* Calvin Tompkins, a competent and gentlemanly journalist, in a New Yorker piece of Nov. 15, 1976, gleaned the following early history of this theatre: Edie Sedgwick, a Warhol star, refusing to star in it, Ronald Tavel took the script of *Shower*, written for Warhol, to Vaccaro, »who had acted with the American Poets' Theatre and in Jack Smith films,« and Vaccaro and he put it on at the Coda Gallery in July of 1965, together with *The Life of Juanita Castro*, another Warhol script of Tavel's, Vaccaro directing. Tavel, in his literate way feeling they were taking theatre beyond the absurd, – picking up on the appreciative comment on what they were doing of Yvette Hawkins (then in the 2nd Ave. production of *The Blacks*; helping out Vaccaro with the two Tavel plays), »it's ridiculous,« – named the enterprise The Play-House of the Ridiculous. *Shower* running for 2 months, Vaccaro, Tavel, Tavel's brother and the lighting man for *Shower*, Bill Walters, rented a loft on 17th St. off 5th Ave, and in the spring of 66 did Tavel's *The Life of Lady Godiva* there, a »full-length play«, Vaccaro getting Ludlam, a recent graduate of Hofstra University, where he had majored in drama, to do one of the characters, Peeping Tom, and in September of 1966 Tavel's *Indira Gandhi's Daring Device* and »a Tavel curtain-raiser called« *Screen Test* (another Warhol script), in which Vaccaro did the cruel director torturing Mario Montez as would-be star, and which Ludlam, at Montez' request, to ease Vaccaro's pressure on him, joined in a Norma Desmond improvisation, – *Screen Test* due to Ludlam's advent expanding from 30 minutes to 2 hours. Ludlam also played Kamaraj, empress Gandhi's stud-prime minister in *Indira Gandhi*, – »it was clear to everyone that Ludlam had become the star of the company, and it was becoming clear to Ronald and Harvey Tavel, at least, that he wanted to take over the Play-House of the Ridiculous.« One way or another, tho the company started rehearsing Tavel's next play, *Gorilla Queen*, or at least a truncated version of it acceptable to Vaccaro, the Tavels cut loose and did it themselves a number of times – a month? – at the Judson Poets' Theatre instead (spring of 1967), Vaccaro instead opening (February 67) – and almost immediately closing – with Ludlam's first play, *Big Hotel*, instead, the now-remembered reason for the closing relating to State Department and NYC Fire Department pressures in revenge for *Indira Gandhi's* offenses to India. The theatre and company had been or were rehearsing Ludlam's 2nd play,– *Conquest of the Universe*, – but now Vaccaro fired Ludlam from the cast, and 7 others, – Montez, Brockmeyer, Vehr, Black-Eyed Susan. Lola Pashalinski, Jeannie Phillips and Eleven, – left the cast in protest, in Mario Montez' apartment forming the Ridiculous Theatrical Company, so named at Jack Smith's suggestion – Smith was there, but did not join till later: Vaccaro could be the Playhouse, Ludlam explained to Tompkins, but they were the Company. Vaccaro had the rights to *Conquest* and with a Warholite company staged it on the Bowery in the fall of 1967, the Ridiculous Theatrical Company opening with it (renamed *When Queens Collide*) and *Big Hotel*, done in alternation, Friday and Saturday midnights at the Gate Theatre, a month later. *Queens* ran for 6 months, was not reviewed; Vehr's *Whores of Babylon* replaced *Big Hotel*. – All of this history I have also myself gotten from the principals, but I never trusted any information of theirs qua history.

and Jack Smith's – keeping Freud, Sartre, Artaud, de Sade, Genet, Warhol and *la pataphysique* out of it.

Essentially, I think this theatre proposes a certain ideal life-style or attitude, doing theatre as part of living that way, which it conveys by its style on stage and which it defends in its plays by ridiculing its opposite and *in no other way* because that life-style is rigorously indefensible (being incompatible with such an impersonal approach as an appeal to reason and values). It only shows the style in action and the action chosen is public ridicule of all authority.

The life-style adopted is that of a *free person* as distinct from an *authoritarian phony*, the civilized adult.

The f.p. is erotic, socially self-assertive, playful and imaginative. His erotic and self-assertive inclinations are social and coincide – two facets of his love/hate, selfish/other-oriented, life-affirming/life-destroying interest in the personality and reactions of others – facets of the same natural propensity to relate *personally* to others, physically and mentally, thereby *to come to be* somebody. Personal identity comes into being by imposing it on another; it does not pre-exist privately. The f.p.'s erotic inclination fuses with his inclination to impress his personality on another's, hence his ends are not simply to fuck and/or kill but to establish *families*, somewhat enduring groups structured by erotic relations and relations of self-imposition (domination/subjugation).

His world is thus a universal erotic imperialist war, open or momentarily stabilized between physical persons, with the aim of moving, penetrating, dominating the other. Non-human nature and all economics are mere background.

This battle is *play*. For the f.p. at all times (even in subjugation) feels free, feels creatively spontaneous – not just as regards supervening choise, preference, decision, abstention on the basis of given inclinations: he experiences inclinations not as drives but as his own freely conceived arbitrary ideas for something to do. His psyche is as he makes it.

Personality-creation is effected by *imagination*; interests and inclinations spring from imagination, not instinct or culture. His personality is like the make-believe identity a child assumes in play with others or an actor assumes in the theatre and is as real as these – accepted (felt by him and projected outward in activity), real not in the sense of corresponding to any true given nature but as being his free product expressed in action. This expressive action is *theatre*, not poetry: erotic imperialism, the familial life (strife) for and in which the f.p. creates himself.

The f.p. has no values. Standards and principles of conduct are freely convened rules of the game within freely constituted families – without objective validity, in no sense rational. His purposes are imaginary play-objectives grounded in equally imaginary motivations assumed for the purpose of play. Thus, no course of action is more rational than any other, though some may be more likely to achieve chosen erotic and other ego-gratifications.

The luck of war in conventional family life, however, is apt to produce robots. For subjugation in erotic personality-conflict is a conditioning of will and imagination, destroys spontaneous creativity, and is achieved when the victim accepts a programmed will and imagination as his own objective reality, as what he is. He then acts out a role-identity not his at all. He participates in an institutional »theatre« with prepared scripts, mistakes the play for reality, his part for himself and the action assigned to it for his life.

The *authoritarian phony* takes things seriously, attributes meaning to life, is value- and achievement-oriented (i.e., anxious and compulsive), in conformity and even in rebellion accepts standards of conduct as objectively valid (ascribing value to rationality). He thus judges himself and others impersonally: what one *should* do. But since his values and reason are as arbitrary as the f.p.'s self-dramatizations, the phony's judgments and order are chaos.

The pretentious maniac has governed the human family so far.

The theatre of the ridiculous is produced by a family or families of approximately free persons as part of their family life. Its members adopt and act roles as the f.p. playfully assumes his identity – without identifying and only for the sake of playing them. This freedom is conveyed by the de-illusionistic »action« style of the roles: fantastic, romantic and heroic dream-identities like those produced by the f.p.'s imagination, engaged in the erotic and imperialist activities of the f.p. The patent non-seriousness of these plays is underlined by a farcical and ironic performance style. This theatre relates to the audience in the playfully erotic self-assertive manner of an f.p. Its effect is a corrosion of make-believe identity – i.e. phoniness. The theatre of the ridiculous sabotages internalized and institutionalized authority. Somebody ridiculous is either a clown or a fool – somebody without the control to act properly, somebody without the intelligence to do or say the right thing.

That's exactly what the f.p. is in the eyes of the a.p. (authoritarian phony) and what he will cheerfully admit to being – reinterpreting the terms for himself. So this theatre is ostentatiously both clownish and foolish. But that's also exactly what the a.p. is (*vide* the world), so this is what the theatre is about: the utter ridiculousness of institutionalized society in such clashing contrast to its obnoxious pretense of values and rationality. The theatre's relaxed pose of ridiculousness – infinitely unpretentious – is the safeguard against its coming on as the a.p. in turn, and transforming us into the same (cf. *The Balcony*). It's not just a pose. It is the a-rational, valueless life-style of the f.p.

The first essential point about the theatre of the ridiculous is that it's *de-illusionistic* as *conditio sine qua non* both for its life-style and for getting that life-style across to us. This is obligatory if the make-believe society represented by imitation (which is theatre) is to be utterly ridiculous. It suggests the fictions to which illusion might attach itself, but systematically prevents our escape into illusion by disorganizing both the representational mode and the fiction itself.

The tickets (club-memberships, contributions) all cost the same relatively little, the seats are not numbered, there are usually no ushers: thus the visitor is left autonomous mobility and self-possession, is not *assigned his* place in the theatre, remains sovereign, uncommitted. Most salles and stages used are dilapidated and do not represent an investment. No sumptuous comforts to make an occasion. The place is too small to feel lost in, big enough for a choice of seat; you are close to the actors. No curtain, no backdrop, no artificial clean bareness – a slightly cluttered small elevated space with a few items indicating a stage. Not enough to turn you on to fictions; enough to turn you on to fictionalizing.

A rabble of actors moves into, through, out of this space. They look bizarre and shoddy. Their faces are apt to be highly made up (masklike, grotesque) in strong colors and bold streaks. Generally they appear dressed in rags (not picturesquely, not to make a point): underwear, torn shirts; or garish finery with a hint of the lovely, reds, sequins, nettings, trains, huge wigs, tiaras – a dream of courts, some handsome fellow in princely attire – parodies on stage costumes, inappropriately put together – clownish clothes, baggy pants – much nudity – now and then a symbolic item (leather) – codpieces, merkins, fake pricks, boas, veils, fans, swords, guns and whips (Ludlam, as »Emerald Empress« in *Whores*, uses a flyswatter as whip), secret weapons, the paraphernalia of romance and adventure. The stage remains in view and unchanged throughout. The performance is continuous, which enforces relaxation, strengthens the company-audience relationship, fosters familiarity. (Intermissions would allow the audience to retreat into make-believe social identities.) Occasional taped or phonograph music (tinny, raucous, dated), musical set-pieces: chorus lines, tangos, voice and guitar.

Blatantly theatrical devices, daring and lovely, cheap. Dance, magic, acrobatics, clownery-skilled, mangled, inept. Like the decor, the lighting is for effects, not illusion. Often the stage is quite dark; light focuses on action. Light-source and operator are usually visible, part of the performance. Actors double as light-men, musicians, stagehands. Props are moved and removed ostentatiously. Occasionally costumes and makeup are changed onstage. The dictation and repetition of lines (*Screen Test, Juanita Castro*) – incorporating rehearsal into performance, making clear that the characters are puppets – puts the director onstage: this is all shockingly de-illusionistic.

Though burlesque and melodrama predominate, a great variety of acting styles brings out the acting and stylization, the variety emphasizes that the performers are developing their own styles according to personal relevance. Under- or perfunctory action in a drugged state, with few, slow, set and inexpressive expressions, a blase tone (notably Ondine); flamboyant hamming in oddly slow or quick cadences, with exaggerated expressiveness – operatic, melodramatic, filmstar romantic (e.g. Ludlam); expressionist, forced, pathological, assertive (e.g. Woronow); rarely naturalistic sentimental clichés misrepresenting real-life clichés; walk-ons posing as fashion models; some of the actors going through ebb-tides of non-acting.

The many de Mille mass-scenes, orgies, huddles, ceremonies, banquets and dances are social get-togethers of performers competitively camping up mock-similes of luxury and elegance. The most energetic physical interactions (fights, couplings) are the most stimulated. Removal of cadavers, necessitated by the high onstage death-rate, is done with exaggerated clumsiness, the corpse does not cooperate – but mostly the dead just sit up after a while, walk off, reparticipate in the action. So many of the female parts are played by males and vice versa that it strikes one as peculiar when an actor plays his own sex. The men play women with on irony directed at their own and/or the other sex. Irony directed at the fact of acting is a component of most of the acting styles.

The characters in these plays are stereotypes from other entertainment media and daily life: stock fantasy figures (rather than schemata of classes), figments we know already. Yet the actors' appearance, speech and action continually clash with their stereotypical lineaments. They are without personality in the sense that nothing they do or say would make us attribute to them a decision-making psyche. (Ludlam: »Psychology must be banished from the theatre.«) Intuition and anticipation are frustrated. No social or psychological subtlety is employed in their sabotage: they are mishandled in silly and/or symbolic ways (e.g. the cowardly lisping hero Cosroe; the pious, masochistic tyrant Tamburlaine in *Queens*). The spectator cannot anchor his attention in their minds, cannot enter and move within the fiction, but is constrained to watch what the theatre does with them. (Vaccaro claims to have studied and been influenced by Bunraku puppet theatre.) The characters do not relate much or well: because of attitudes conventionally intrinsic to their schematic natures (Tavel) or by shifting ill-defined ambiguous attitudes (Ludlam). Motivations are fragmentary, outside characters wander in, the main plot is ill-related to ill-explained sub-plots and both are disrupted by actions apparently unrelated to either. The dialogue sabotages the characters and illusion by dadaist travesty. They *quote*: from dramatic and other classics, political heroes and movie vamps, advertisements. They speak in quotational styles: the emotional evocation of universal truths or sentiments, smart-alecky comebacks, loud »presentational« delivery of burlesque dialogues. Tavel's characters tend to stilted banalities (excessively stilted and excessively banal), the trite small-change of conversation, quick-but-feeble-witted repartee, dumb quips: parodies of the trivial and the smart, further distorted by constant smutty punning, language quoting language, inconsistent with either the banal or the smart. Bill Vehr (*Whores of Babylon*) parodies tragic-romantic poetry.

The form is that of combat in cartoon serials or the hardboiled detective story – picaresque – though much of the action (especially in Tavel's plays) is just back and forth talk: much turmoil and confusion without direction. The story line (if there is one) is simple (though Ludlam loves to hint at sub-plots): Ludlam's plots are silly, Tavel's innocently foolish. The stories are not so much implausible as too trite for the effort of either belief or disbelief, pointless . . . like gossip. No effort has been taken with these mockingly minimal tales: the worn patterns of adventure, romance, heroism and tragedy. Hardly even stringing-strings, the plots are merely accretions of the scenes on which audiences' attention (taking the relaxed form of »What are they – the performers – going to do next?«) is successively thrown. Not carried by action, characters or story, each scene takes the form of a contest between the characters, conducted by the actors – like a cock fight with the bird-owners in the pit. But themes and motifs emerge obscurely, with a certain emotional impact and a musical rather than literary structure – romantic, developmentless. Illusion, concern with the fiction, are beside the point, are discouraged, foiled. The literary work's foolishness and clownishness obtrude – ridiculously ill-made plays reflecting an ill-made world. Their organization is left to the spectator.

Nor does the theatre distract from performance by *entertainment*.

You are entertained when you are made to enjoy *yourself* by a confirmation of your values and role-identity or status in terms of familiar and agreeable sentiments and sensa. The theatre of the ridiculous does not entertain by splendor of spectacle, by playing up to romantic or heroic preconditionings of sentiment, or by confirming moral stances. The productions are not only not costly (sumptuous) enough but have little poetic or sensual appeal (beauty) not vitiated by irony. Irony on sentimentality is intrinsically ambiguous: attacking fake-trite expressions implies corresponding genuine emotion. And though a code of personal liberty and integrity is conveyed (the life-style of the f.p.), the ridicule and rejection of conventional values predominate. The fabulosity of the costumes and the science, spy and crime adventure themes do not excite the escapist mechanisms of make-believe socialized existence for they are systematically undercut by the grotesque or mundane.

Though the shows may entertain some determined queers who can swallow the fact that their camp is corny, a normal not-queer homosexual will have seen it all at many parties. Nor are the plentiful nudity, dirty language and sexual acts and references very entertaining: we live amidst hard-core pornography these days. The sex and »obscenity« in these shows are done off-handedly, perfunctorily – anti-erotically according to the make-believe rotes of eroticism. They clear the air.

Of course if you insist (having come and paid) on enjoying yourself or if you enjoy enjoying the way-out as certification of your independence, you will be entertained.

The humor while not black has only a limited appeal because it is not only sick but low. Neither subtle nor mordant, it is innocently adolescent and vulgar, without much attraction either for women or for those who take their culture seriously. It is offensive because unredeemed by any underlying earnestness of social or moral concern, so pointless that it is disturbing (as nihilism), unrefined and hardly even clever – it is not intellectually stimulating.

These negative qualities add up to the vast gaiety of the low popular comedy of all times, of course, but the strong appeal to a limited audience – the pure appeal of the ridiculous – is weakened because this theatre draws attention to the performance in a manner which debilitates sheer fun. The theatre (especially Ludlam) works for laughs, but as psychosomatic spasms in an unclenching process marking breakdowns of resistance to ridiculousness on the therapeutic way toward a state of reckless identity: the embarrassed, shocked or spiteful, gleeful rather than self-satisfied or superior laugh (which it aberrationally solicits from and obtains from queers: in-group complicity), laughs rather than laughter, from the throat, not the belly. This theatre's techniques cut laughter short; unlike commercial comedy, it does not solicit appreciation of its wit. Its jokes are parodies on humor (Vaccaro used canned laughter in one production), destroying the innocent quality by not indicating that it is done in order to entertain – thus the sinister, irrationalist, valueless nihilism again.

Although humiliation (which always makes the victim seem ridiculous) is the essence of all comedy – no matter how harmless, innocent, good-natured, or well-meaning – the universal humiliation of all characters in this theatre gives it a repulsive air of viciousness, even cruelty, because it is absolute: the victims are accorded no basic dignity, no saving graces. We are not reassured of worthy or innocent motives, of underlying rational seriousness. The characters are not just clownish or foolish but clowns and fools. They are not exactly funny. Isolated clown scenes, jokes and parodies that at first seem pure fun trouble us by their implications of profound ridiculousness. Some important, often protracted, actions are specifically and formally cruel humiliations: Bajazeth's enslavement in *Queens/Conquest,* the entire action of *Screen Test,* Lady Godiva's undressing (according to Vaccaro) in *Lady Godiva,* Victor's re-education in *Vinyl.* These humiliations bring this close to a theatre of the terrible. It takes a strong stomach to participate in their fun; they color the other action.

The performances are not taken nor offered as statements: they present their makers in an unserious and irresponsible posture. Because the characters and events are familiar fantasies though ridiculed, the question of »meaning« scarcely arises. (Vaccaro holds that Ludlam's plays are perfectly meaningless.) We may take from them the message that the world as it is – a world of a.p.'s – is ridiculous or that freely to be a fool and a clown is glorious. But these messages preclude the earnest proclamation of them. Ludlam condemns Tavel for organizing plays to convey messages: the meaning of a theatrical event ought to be uniquely and purely theatrical – you have to go to the theatre to get it.

This theatre is resolutely opposed to art. It rejects the ideal of a formal integrity of the art-work in abstraction from the artist and his activity; it rejects the ideal of subordination of the artist's personality to his artistry; it intends aesthetic appreciation of its work only (if at all) as instrument to more important affective personal reactions; it invites reaction to its activity rather than to its product; it considers established and recognized conventions of its medium part of the culture's technique for artists and customers to escape authentic actuality, and therefore would allow the artist to employ them only in a destructive manner – i.e., destroying the effect of tranquilized impersonality – hence insists on sabotage – of effects – at all points.

However, sabotage becomes an artistic device and art as social sabotage in a social order as anti-artistic as ours is not precisely sabotage of art. In any event, the theatre of the ridiculous does not come on as art.

It's a ridiculous company: the opprobrium of the characters and plays they act attaches to the actors because they do not hide inside/behind the characters and yet (in hearty and not ostensibly motivated performance) assume responsibility for them. The typical performer in this theatre is neither particularly handsome or sexy (though Blackeyed Susan is both): even when they are, the zany spectacle hardly lets them cash in. The suppression of the habitual gestures of professionalism makes them seem amateurish – yet they accrue no credit for sincerity or for being »interesting« personalities because of the total investment of personality in the histrionic mode which makes this »action« theatre. The plays and the style not only continually involve the characters and actors in indecorous conduct and seeming foolishness and indignities/degradations/exposures in conflict with others; they also throw the actors qua performers into an analogous real conflict with one another, entailing analogous real degradations for them (in one another's eyes and in the public's). Their very engagement in public in such personal conflict is apt to render them ridiculous.

Without reaching or even aiming at poetic quality (Vehr may be in *Whores*) or metaphysical profundity (Tavel may be), not intended to hypnotize or excite as incantation (Ludlam claims otherwise), not striving for the special effects of total meaninglessness, the language is in all ways deliberately low, cheap and second-rate, its predominant banalities set in relief only by plagiarisms. (Vaccaro makes contempt for text and comprehensibility a directorial principle.) If it works out as a generic parody of American dialogue, this does not redeem its ridiculous quality. In vocabulary, syntax and delivery it relates to that of burlesque, nightclub and radio comedians. The wit is undergraduate and queer, a weapon for fake personal combat – catty, bitchy, unsubtle, and not really wounding (e.g., the use of »comic« ethnic accents). The language is further degraded by being dirty – so much and routinely so that titillation is transcended if not by-passed, as in the army. These vulgarities shatter the cultural aura by which the theatre stands off from the movies.

In making fools of themselves as authors, Ludlam, Tavel, and Vehr ridicule the making of well-made plays. The act of making a well-made play – even one proclaiming lack of meaning – testifies to the author's conviction that life has meaning. By the ridiculous form of their plays, Ludlam *et al.* promote the feeling that it does not. Frustrating illusion, entertainment, edification, instruction, the theatre retains us with the performance. We remain in the theatre, in front of the grubby stage, the interminable nonsense on it. We are offered the spectacle of a theatrical performance. Of this one. What is it?

The company's style projects with emotional impact the image of a family of f.p.'s: erotic beings intent on self-affirmation. This does not imply a show of generalized promiscuity – no odor of sperm, no display of specific personal relationships – but only that we feel the performers define themselves as they act and as erotic (rather than economic, moral, etc.). There is a feeling of play and comradeship, personal concern for the other, but also of conflict (not antagonism).

Their performances seem relevant to the actors not as expressions – of ideas, personality, values – but as projective self-assertions in interaction. Their styles are adapted to making the actuality of the performing person forcibly felt by the other performing persons (self-affirmative projections of will of a generically physical sort and thence generically erotic). There is a self-consciously purposive handling of bodies as the actors (by their special »business,« rhythmic patterns, stresses and pauses, eye-regards, displacements) charm, stun, scare, seduce, harass, disorient, shame, embarrass, carry away, move, hypnotize, amuse, distract one another, using their imagination within the rough confines of play and character as weapon of their will. This generally cool, even relaxed, combat determines the particular mood or feel of a scene or an evening's performance. Even when the performance does not convey actual conflict, we experience it as a stage in a family-life generally consisting in such conflicts, a barnyard with a momentarily settled pecking hierarchy.

But in fact all this has an air not only of will but of willedness (unlike Warhol's products), of unserious undesperate playfulness, and the means employed, the imaginative creation of action – of a manifestly make-believe fantasy-identity – contributes to the theatrical experience its perhaps most pervasive, sustained quality – that of the creative life of the imagination.

Any »permanent company« in fact approximates a family – but not of free persons. They are value- (culture-) and/or profit-oriented institutions and bureaucracies, authoritarian, bound to furnish a paying public with values, operating under rigid divisions of labor (their familial life is grafted onto such economic and professional association, rather than vice versa and ipso facto is to be kept out of their art). Free personal association and the personal meaningfulness and creativity of a collective art such as theatre are mutually interdependent: if the family is not free, its projection onto and from the stage is phony.

While the framework of reference of conventional theatre experience is the individual presentation of »the« play, in this theatre it is the production of the play – the series of presentations, rehearsals, composition of the script: its making in development defines the individual evening's experience. The composition of the script appears as mere preparation of the *mise-en-scene,* almost incidental. Script and set are essentially by-products of the developing performance, collapsing into the activity of making the play. The performance gives a glimpse into a process of personal interactions within a continuing community, everyone contributing personally. That the evening's performance is a meaningful event in, and a product of, their ongoing family life and history is a central part of the spectator's impression. The acting personalities extend beyond the performance: we are seeing an epoch in the history of the family defined by this play. Everything keeps changing: scripts, titles, the name of the company, its leadership its membership (though a nucleus has been maintained for three years), the stage names, the interpretations, who plays which part, the special effects, props and decor, costumes, the beginning and end of the play. Yet the impression is not of inartistic irresponsibility but of fanatic insistence on self-assertion by many individuals, of rampant creativity and a presumed passionate, anarchic private family life which corresponds to fact: thefts in the dressing room, lovers' quarrels about who shared a joint with who, burglaries of the director of which he suspects cast members (his pot stolen, his doll, a gift from his mother burned), actors fighting, knifings, temper tantrums, an actor institutionalized by his father, sexual advances, rejections and disputes. This life emerges into the play (e.g., *Screen Test*).

Each production is a three-way fight between the acting dramatist, the acting director and the cast. Productions take the form of combat because onstage are *persons*, not actors. No abstract or generic identity is projected, nor any private identity (»what I really am«). The performers project their personality by their parts. Whereas actors acting by empathy with the character give the impression of executing an internal compulsion – a zombie quality that is often thought of as naturalness – the actors in this theatre, having no viable stage personality to identify with, seem alive and themselves. The plays are so designed.

»Scripts« are apt to be decided upon by the dominant members of the company before finished or even written, in some accord with the company's prevailing mood (dissenting members are constantly splitting and the company may fission on the point), and are then written or provisionally finished. To a considerable extent, parts are composed for specific members of the company, who may themselves contribute lines and scenes; room is left for extemporization; actors ad lib in any case. A realistic psychological androgynism prevalent in the company allows the playing of many of the characters not only by but as either males or females. What in conventional view would be unequivocally defeats, dominations, or inferiority may become their opposites in terms of the interpersonal psychological conflict structuring the performance. In this sense, the plays often leave it open who wins, who is strong.

The parts are conceived as schemata for wish fulfillment, as opportunities for will, imagination, voice and costuming: fantastic creatures, colorful, sparkling, flaming. When not romantic or glamorous, they can still be played as extreme, with a touch of the adventurous or heroic: or can be so played for there is no unity to disrupt and it is up to the star to prove himself the stronger personality. But in every play several parts are designed for strutting glory, utmost nobility, unimaginable cruelty, what have you. Such fantasied high living is essential to the f.p.; it is of the essence to the members of this theatre; the glory of it emotionally affects the audience even while it

40

censors out the effect by concentrating on the ridiculous; and of course the heroes of Homer and of the bards of Iceland and Ireland and of all fairy tales are equally glorious and equally ridiculous.

We here perceive theatre, the collective elaboration of fictitious identities convened and projected in interaction, as a natural activity and a basic mode of existence. Not a perverse misrepresentation of true identity; not a special pleasure, art, or evocation – not natural and basic just to *these* people because of how they are. It is as obvious that the specific performance they give onstage is not the one they give offstage as it is that they play-act offstage. Yet clearly their stage life relates intimately to their real-life projections of imagined self-identities. And in fact they severally play the same diverse kinds of parts in private life. But the *form* glorified by this theatre is of its kind: spontaneous, autonomous, personal, familial, and aware – not the repressive theatre constituting institutionalized society.

The performers' attitude toward the audience at first seems to be indifference – no warmth or projection. An occasional address to the audience has the effect of an aside. This self-centeredness sets the tone for a subsidiary intent to charm the audience. (Woronow: »I want to take the audience on a trip – as one might a small kid by telling it a story which fascinates it even though perhaps it does not understand or like the story.«) This tentative domination relates to a relatively inoffensive vanity and runs the gamut from intents to be attractive to ideas of being offensive (by imposing a repulsive or aggressive personality). This approach combines unfocused eroticism (flirtatiousness) with unfocused social self-assertion.

The audience is made to feel that it's not in the family but might be.

In paradoxical correlation with its familial aspect, this theatre has an aspect of *action* – defined as *activity engaged in for its own sake*. I previously remarked that its activity seemed natural, a basic mode of familial existence and a free realization of personality. This is action *in fact*, but there is also the appearance of action – it is the *style* of the theatre of the ridiculous – and the audience experiences it as such. Action, being absolutely non-instrumental, is *non-expressive* and *non-technical*.

Activity styled as action neither explains nor justifies itself. Its style need not make these points: it is simply shorn of value-orientation. But though such activity need not proclaim itself either fortuitous, gratuitous, or spontaneous, being human it will impress one as spontaneous and interested in itself and to this extent not gratuitous. It is *ridiculous* because its ostensible lack of purpose makes it seem foolish. And it is *intensive* – concentrated in the agent, the activity, and the particular – because the lack of outside reference inhibits both agent and spectator from conceptualizing it as a whole.

The performers (though somewhat detached and without gravity) appear seriously committed to what they are doing: relating in the histrionic mode. Each performer seems animated by (1) an active personal interest in what he is doing and how he is to do it and (2) a personal commitment to sociability with the others, to play the game (as defined by the play) so that the others may do their thing. Some are of course more intent than others, but there is rarely a sense of obligation or job. What they are doing seems to make no sense. They are not trying to make fictions real. Their evocation of fictions seems in-turned and gratuitous: a silly, self-contained fantasy. The essence of this impression is that we are seeing an activity as such – a doing, perhaps a making – rather than the doing or making of something. We are not so much seeing a play as the making of a play. We know of course that actors are not extemporizing the play as they perform. Our impression is ultimately grounded in the fact that the authors actually composed the *script* in the self-purposing manner of action: non-expressively, non-technically, foolishly and with intensity, and that the actors perform it in the same manner. So the structure of the performance reflects the play-making activity. We seem to be watching the representation of the creative process. This sense would be destroyed if we experienced the play or any part of the performance as expression of personality. We don't.

In practice, this impression of action depends on the disintegration of the play; I called this de-illusionism. The systematized, continuous work of art is experienced in independence from its creation, at most »in relation to« it. In the theatre of the ridiculous, the experience is intensional rather than extensional.

The disintegration of the play disintegrates the theatrical experience: play, characters and situations are shattered shifting images – reference-frames rather than objects. Concentration focuses on elements, momentary events, motifs, themes. Instead of grasping fable, character, situation, or confrontation as a whole and starting from that, the mind stops and goes – from present particular to present particular. Nor can the mind pass from the simultaneous manifold to a formula, apparent meaning, effect, or tendency; it is forced to stick with divergent, perhaps incompatible, constituents. Nor is the mind oriented along the time-axis of the fable – caught up in the flow of action – but operates discontinuously. We *accompany* the action; the play adds up. It is foolish: apperception has to dive from moment to moment. The play's action originates with each character – a vital principle of plot-construction. The result in this theatre is a mare's nest of crossed actions that we can cope with only by the sort of scattered, multiple concentration needed to play several opponents in chess simultaneously. Never able to stash away a character as such and so, we don't know what they are driving at, cannot take them for granted. The various characters rarely share an understanding of what's going on, so we can't borrow their interpretation. Each line and act must be dealt with on its own terms: we are given no perspective on the series.

Withal, we obviously still relate and interpret; but as supplemental effort and free contribution.

Fiction *not* turning into illusion – the act of buggery or fellatio merely indicated – our mind oscillates between the action of the performers and its significance to the fiction: the two never quite coincide. We cannot withdraw into the timeless meaning of the fiction. Each time we might, we are drawn back to this evening in this theatre – for since we oscillate *within* the intrinsic duality of an observation of role-adoption, the actual activity in actual time and space is our base-reference. Furthermore, each performer attracts attention to what *he* is doing. We experience it as original, not only relative to script, *mise-en-scene* and his own prior performances but to what the other actors are doing. He concentrates on *it*, projects the intensity of a star, an intensity transmitted to our watching of him. Apperception goes from this to that actor and has to start out anew from each: a flickering of attention continually reset. Familial interaction is to gear-meshed *ensemble* acting as the movement of an animal is to that of a machine.

Each performer concentrates on the business at hand with the intensity of circus and vaudeville performers, magicians and acrobats, the intensity of doing a trick. He is not acting *out* anything. Words and gestures have not been polished to mere expressions, but stand out freshly against the expressive functions we may attribute to them. Actions speak for themselves. We see what he does before or while we see what it means.

The familial and action aspects combine to affect our time-sense. We are not only barred from the eternity of fictions and held to the present time and within it to the successive moments of the performance. We have an *instantaneous* impression of the action. We feel that we are seeing not what has just been done but what is being done. In other theatre, in spite of empathy and anticipation and regardless of the span of attention-focus, the action onstage and the play continually seem in the past. With the theatre of the ridiculous, we focus on the now; each act and image stands out in physical immediacy: colors and groupings are vivid, pitch and rhythm strike us, we inspect costumes and props, the actor is there as a physical being. We not only see him looking like or doing *this*; we see him *looking* or *doing* it. The physical stands over against its significations: not reduced to a mere symbol of the spiritual: we grope for the meaning of *this*. Nor are the individual sensa absorbed into larger physical patterns aesthetically prominent.

I am leaving aside certain major tendencies of this theatre: to assimilate speech to other sound effects, suppressing meaning and reducing communication to direct physical signals of emotion and intent; to subordinate aural to visual effects; to think of groupings and scenes as tableaux; to promote in costuming the stunning at the expense of the intriguing; to think of theatre as spectacle; to stress (in acting and *mise-en-scene*) rhythmic variation; to think of theatrical experience as sensory exposure to images; and by some or all of these means, primarily to aim at a direct (physical) stimulation of primary emotions. So far, these multi-media notions are incidental to what this theatre is and do not define it as it comes across.

Though we may describe this theatre-experience as »a bundle of series of intensive image-explosions« (Ludlam's term), each explosion that of a present identity (the acting actor's), into a make-believe fantastic role-identity, the manifold intentionality induces not so much an atomized experience as *mobile attention* in the dimensions of space (stage-space, play-space), time (performance-time, story-time), and impersonation. There is continual refocusing. We are apt as a matter of subjective choice to attend to any kind of performance (even a picture) with some such scanning, but it is integral and essential to this theatre-experience. The multiplicity of perspectives is not subordinate to the whole nor does it yield any single intuition or continuous comprehension of the whole. But it is adequate to the ambiguities and inconsistencies of the art object − theatrical action.

All this is apt to get *boring* from time to time. Not just because of the failures of talent, skill or effort but because the action-style of the play and performance so sharpen our awareness of the passage of time and the problem of its use that we become resentful of the foolishness and sterility as wasteful.

We are confronted with time by: lack of drive and direction; the absence of a sense of progress or continuity or development or achievement; inarticulation (no well-marked sub-sections or changes of direction in the line of action); deliberately slow-motion or speeded-up passages; frequent changes of rhythm and speed. The capricious creativity of play and show makes one feel they – and almost anything in them – could go on indefinitely. If the story does have an end, its arbitrariness is evidenced by its conventionality (the wholesale slaughter of tragedy, the happy end of romance); the unseriousness of projects prevents their definite abortion or success from feeling conclusive. There are no unique epochs in the life of the phantom hero – anything might repeat, with neither more nor less meaningfulness.

The basis of such boredom is anxiety, compulsiveness, the frenzy to keep busy so as not to face oneself, the habit of allocating time to particular purposes (tangible gains), tension or frustration, a general sense that one is wasting one's life – in short, an inability to play.

Two special devices exacerbate this temporal vacuum: unvaried repetition of an image and prolongation of its exposure. Their common objective is to destroy meaning. Encountering the image, the spectator copes with it intellectually, imaginatively and emotionally in terms of its context in the play, a first absorption of meaning. He can maintain his interest during some further exposure or repetition by additional exploitation of the image. Then comes a point when he is done with it, but it still keeps at him. He can tolerate it for a while longer, quietly recognizing it for what he has made of it; he is coasting on past meaning. But with continuing bombardment, at some point a reversal sets in: the image now loses its meaning for him; he is no longer able to react to it intellectually, imaginatively or emotionally. He is now face-to-face with the image itself, some sensum, a physical thing, his ego emptied. He is thinking/feeling/etc. nothing – i.e., he is aware of time only, empty time with a fact rattling about in it. This is an extremely valuable condition, a point of departure sought by mystics, but it irritates the average man: he feels threatened by this state of free self-identity, He is bored.

It is in terms of original authorship that most theatre presents itself as expression and contribution. We are supposed to appreciate the invention of themes and characters. We experience the play as treatment of them. But this appreciation and form of experience are incompatible with its action-style. The theatre of the ridiculous foregoes the claim to original authorship.

The plays are pop art. They draw on the mythologizing popular imagination reflected in and interacting with the folk art of vulgar commercial entertainment – the stereotyped imagination of the big city and small town poor, young and male – lower and lower middle class urban boys. They are *improvisations* on this material refracted through the alienating subcultures of queerdom and collegiate humanism which corrode the wild clichés of those oppressed, rebellious but brought-to-hell dreamers, imbue them with irony but preserve their sweet poetry.

Scenarist, actors and director all participate in this dream life. So do the audience. This makes it possible for the scenario to be a mere score for the actors and the spectacle similarly material for improvisation for the audience. The basic situation is that of Greek drama or of any religious folk art. Not just because of the nature of the source but because the style of the theatre is to admit it, shamelessly.

The plays have no author – an inventive individual deploying his private imagination within the discipline of a literary tradition on personal themes – though the writers and directors are vulnerable to literature.* Only a scenarist decomposing and recomposing

*SOURCES: BIG HOTEL

According to Ludlam, »Big Hotel« started out as a random piece, composed of cut-outs from literature, was not meant to be performed, but was expanded to fill a »Royal Vernon Line« school composition book at John Vaccaro's instigation, to be done instead of »Gorilla Queen.« The film »Grand Hotel« provided major inspiration – e.g., the figure of Birdshitskaya. Sources: »Cobra Woman« (film); »Salome« (film); Bela Bartok's »Miraculous Mandarin«; a Spanish translation of »Midsummer Night's Dream«; Ben Jonson's »Epicene«; »Coconuts« (a Marx Bros. film) (the characters and lines of Mr. X and Chocha Caliente); »Macbeth« (some lines); Tennyson or was it Byron; the Stations of the Cross (Ludlam was a very religious boy); some cowboy-vampire film (the character of Drago Robles); the name of a company on Delancey St. (»Port Now Trusses«); »Sunset Boulevard« (film) (the character of Norma Desmond – some of whose lines are from the film »Shanghai Express«); Joyce, »Ulysses« (»Like her I was, these sloping shoulders...«) »Dinner at Eight« (a scene); »Red Shoes« (film); an ad in »Woman's Wear Daily« (the madly sheik Norma Desmond?); »Chicago Confidential« (film) (police interrogation scene); Tormenta D'Lago contributed the Mata Hari lines; »Trilby« (film) (the Svengali scene); some O'Casey play with a river in it (the character of Mrs Madigan); »The Merchant of Venice«; a Spanish-language comic book with a character called Santo or El Enmascarado de Plata (these are long books with sepia photographs with drawn-in pictures) (some of the Chicago Assassination talk); »The Taming of the Shrew«; a first-year French grammar (the available figments into the form of a play, improvising on a scattering of traits, accents, figures, and themes alive in a collective inner world of day-dreaming. (In America, this cooperation of a popular imagination and vulgar commercial entertainment has remained fertile and the artistic imagination freer to participate in the former

dialogue with the apache dance); »Chinatown My Chinatown« (song); Strindberg, »Swan-white«; T. Hatigan, »Haunted House«; »Sunset Boulevard« again,» Niagara« (Marilyn Monroe film) (the Blondine Blondell sequence); Phillip Morris cigarette ad; Rimbaud (»Of Human Suffrage, of Human Aspiring . . .«); Wilde, »My Voice« (poem) (»Within this restless world . . . Therefore my cheeks before their time are wan«); »Wonder Woman« (comic book); Joyce, »Ulysses« (»Touch me, touch me, soft hands . . .«); an »Introduction to Yoga«; McLuhan (»All meaning alters with acceleration . . .«); »King Lear« (»Like flies to wanton boys . . .«); a cartoon from »Playboy« (»You dance divinely, Miss Montez«); »Shakuntala« (the final speech); some TV commercial (»I had . . . for breakfast . . . for lunch . . .«); T. Rattigan, »Separate Tables« (»I see the little lines and wrinkles . . .«).

SOURCES: CONQUEST OF THE UNIVERSE/WHEN QUEENS COLLIDE
According to Ludlam, »Conquest« derives from a previous play made with lines from Life's »Photography Issue«; Artaud's plan to do a »Conquest of Mexico« may have been relevant to its making; it has an obvious but unintended similarity to »Ubu Roi.« To my mind, the influence of Shakespeare's history plays on the plot, atmosphere, and main characters is evident, but the chief source is obviously Marlow's »Tamburlaine.« The figure of Hitler furnished many of Tamburlaine's lines; LBJ, like Tamburlaine, was unable to spawn male issue. Other sources: »Challengers of the Unknown,« a comic book (»Save yourselves, save yourselves . . .«); some sado-masochist pornography (»petty-coats over your heads«); »Shakespeare's Bawdy« (the Venus scene); the brand name »Magnavox« of a TV set; »Gorboduc« (Natolia's first speech); »The Damask Drum,« a Noh-play (some of Ebea's lines as she turns into a demon); some Strindberg play, possibly »The Great Highway«; »Wonder Woman« comic books; the librettos of »Fidelio« and »Tosca« and comic books furnish lines for the scene between Cosroe and the witch; Joyce, »Ulysses«; a TV commercial (»Six nights out of seven, Tamburlaine prefers Bajazeth for bed«); Brecht, »The Elephant Calf« (or »Man Is Man«?) (Tamburlaine and Alice in bed); Brecht, »Private Life of the Master Race«; Chaucer, »Wife of Bath's Tale« (almost all of Natolia's lines); Strindberg, »Crimes and Crimes«; some comic book (the robot scene); Shakespeare, »Julius Caesar« (»My wife is troubled . . .«); »Macbeth« (»Think not too deeply . . .«); N. .Y Times Want Ads; Christmastime ad in Life (»Let us pray that strength and courage . . .«); some comic book (»A giant enemy cargo is lying concealed . . .«); Cervantes, »Siege of Numantia«; some Joke Book (all of Bajazeth's jokes); a play that Ludlam wrote at the age of 16 (»When I die . . .«); »Midsummer Night's Dream«; »Richard the Third« (My boa, my boa . . .«); a Marlene Dietrich film; »The Mad Woman of Chaillot,« »Skin of our Teeth,« and some other plays in a volume that Ludlam leafed through in a book store; Shaw's »Major Barbara,« »The Haunted House,« and Brecht's »The Jewish Wife« all contributed to the conspiracy scene; »Poor Richard's Almanac«; »King Lear«; Wilde, »Salome; the Loretta Young Show (TV) (Mario Montez' entrance as Alice); »Cobra Woman« (film);« »Hamlet« (the prayer scene).

and to respond to both.) This theatre is not a comment (nostalgic, ironic, adoring or patronizing) on mass culture but it borrows from and imitates mass culture as fellow product of the popular imagination: its crude and fantastic figures, situations and actions; its direct unmannered (neither status-claiming nor status-bestowing) relationship to the audience; its simple strong effects. Like vulgar entertainment, this theatre dispenses with the gestures of instructing and improving, concentrates on sex and violence, glamour and romance, heroism and adventure (even lets in simple moral opposition: Tamburlaine vs. Cosroe in *Conquest/Queens*) – though in a debunking manner. It appeals to elemental emotions, conscious that those emotions have been arrested into social masks of repressive aggression; it seeks to destroy not to animate these artifices. In this respect, ridiculous theatre approaches the effects if not the status of a popular revolutionary art.

The fantasies that the popular-lore industry sells are those of the frustrated urbanized masses who (as is customary) buy back what they produce. These are not »free persons«; their position prevents them from freely assuming and enacting chosen role-identities as their real existence. But since even the real-life facsimilies of fantasy ambitions (careers, achievements) are relatively unavailable to these masses, since therefore their fantasy life has not been channeled into real-life perspectives, and since they have in this country (at least until recently) escaped subjective domestication by middle class rationality and values, the masses have kept up a peculiarly free and wild, grandiose and aggressive fantasy life. They have expressed it in industrialized commercial entertainment, have stimulated these industries to express it and sell it to them. They even act it out, not in terms of social and economic achievement, but in personal modes of conduct, manners – barroom supermen, Bowery cowboys, department store Juliets. The content of this fantasy life is erotic (and other) self-assertion. Insofar as this fantasy life is devorced from action, is socially regulated, and is industrially stereotyped, it is not the f.p.'s. It is in just (and only) these regards that the theatre of the ridiculous mocks and corrodes popular fantasy life. The theatre's baptism in the refractory media of queerdom and undergraduate humanism, far from alienating it idiosyncratically from »the people,« corrects the distortive censorship of institutionalized power and genteel entertainment by substituting irony for morality. This theatre sabotages the qualities of alienation of mass culture and of the popular dream life.

Indira Gandhi (in Tavel's play) is the Oriental Queen, the Lady from Welfare, the Voluptuous Jewess on her Boudoir Couch; her aide is the Up and Coming treacherously capable Sweet Man, the Technical Expert; Tamburlaine (in *Conquest*) the Space Conqueror, Lone Ranger, the Commanding General, the Football Hero, John Wayne, Hitler and Stalin. Magic Mandarin (in *Big Hotel*) is Fu Manchu, Confucious Say, Charlie Chan, the Soulful Chinee and Wise Oriental, the Tricky Gook, the Carnie Con Man. *Kitchenette* americanizes Wesker not only by Albee: its characters are from the comic strips' or soap opera's portrayal of lower middle class home life, its mother a dream of Mistress-Motherhood. The characters of *Vinyl* are out of Brando/Dean/Presley movies, the street corner gang's self-dramatizations – Doc is the sadistic, brain-washing, patient-molesting, heiress-committing psychiatrist, the charity ward brutalizer; the conflicts are out of the Westerns, Eastside Kids. Chicago is the background of *Big Hotel*; science fiction paperbacks and Amazon Queen comic books furnish the imagery of *Conquest* and (with the Bible) of *Whores*. The themes of *Shower* are out of James Bond, popular romance stories, spy fiction.

The romantic and/or dramatic, innocent and/or lewd bellboy and the blasé and/or all-seeing supersmooth vicious desk clerk are no less mythological characters in *Big Hotel* than the Great Film Star or Artist or the Voodoo Priestess. The transformation of the lowly Irish charwoman into high priestess is out of the same antique and modern realm of popular fantasy. The cheap big hotel is prime symbol of the Big City (as well as of International High Living) for the rural immigrant.

At the core of this American Dreamlife there once was the American Dream conditioned by Calvinism and free enterprise, its central figure the Puritan Yankee: a righteous free individual, man among men, proving himself in the combat of competition, vaguely provided with females. During the period of urbanization (after the frontier closed), this figure emerged in popular imagination and vulgar art as the violent loner doomed to extinction in the twin guise of cowboy fighting bad men and gangster fighting the cops, with heroines thrown in, rising but still minor figures – supporting, judging, bones of contention (desired property), rewards.

This rancid version of the American Dream survived wwii in popular imagination, but in an enfeebled state, crowded out by a mythology reversing it, in which the powerful self-contained woman triumphs over a weak male locked in combat for her with other males: the male-female (mother-son, husband-wife) relationship re-placed male competition at the center of things. The male has been deballed – the woman is the loner.

The early version is not totally absent from this theatre's repertory but, in terms of emotional impact, the dominant figure in these plays as performed is the dominant woman. As I've just argued, this is not an alien (freudian, queer) perversion of the popular imagination and arts – though here exposed to ridicule. Because of the plasticity of this theatre's form and style, the dominant woman need not be the same part in different productions or performances and it need not be a female part played by an actress. To dominate the action, it must be a part of some importance, acted by a strong personality, male (Ludlam, Montez) or female (Woronow, Phillips) – strong in the sense of either outgoing aggression (Ludlam, Woronow, Phillips) or quietly powerful concentration on itself (Montez, Ultraviolet), two quite different possibilities. If it's an actress, she projects her female personality into or through her part, male or female; if it's an actor, he either impersonates a woman of strong personality, projecting his own strength, or represents her as his fictional identity. The schema is weakened or breaks down when strong male personalities play strong male parts (Ludlam, Ondine, sometimes Vehr, Jack Smith, Vaccaro), or when the actress, whether in a male or female part, is not sufficiently strong. These cases are especially interesting because then we observe the theatre *trying* to impose the schema – trying to tone down the strong male acting or part, or pushing the weak female acting or part.

Big Hotel is conceived (perhaps subconsciously) to show female domi-nation: the underground kingdom, the Firepit Restaurant, is devoted to the female Martok's (Jeanne Phillips) cult of the Cobra Woman, the passively powerful center (Montez): they take over. Ludlam's Norma Desmond in effect rules the stage »aboveground«; the life of the lobby revolves around this female figure and those (»Lupe Ve-lez,« »Mata Hari«) also played by males, exemplifying the power of compelling female self-concern. Cramwell and Magic Mandarin, male parts male-played, project weakly (though the play would allow otherwise). The central action is carried by Magic Mandarin – weakly. Birdshitskaya rejects him for insufficient virility, and Martok finally picks him as a mate.

Mary Woronow's strong personality dominated *Conquest*. In *Queens*, Ludlam's staging of the same (his) play, Tamburlaine was played weakly by a man, dominated by his wife Alice (Montez). Ludlam's

Zabina was the strong personality of the production, an aggressive female figure complementing Montez' inert power. When Ludlam abandoned the part to the weak D'Lago, his Cosroe emerged as the stronger figure, contrary to the schema.

The plot of Tavel's *Shower* scarcely conforms to the schema, but the dialogue may. In the revival of the play, Marti Whitehead almost succeeded in imposing her Terrine as the dominant figure in spite of Ondine's coolly compelling Mark. She succeeded in subsequent performances when Harvey Tavel replaced Ondine. *Vinyl* was dominated by the clearly female Doc (Woronow again), in spite of the play's primary concern with what happens to Victor. The major impact was provided by the female's subjugation of the male. In *Indira Gandhi*, the rule of women (Phillips), her demands on her male aide, her interest in a heavy-hung commoner, rather than her »daring device,« provided the emotional impact of the play. *Kitchenette* centers around the prick-teasing mother's (Woronow's) domination of her son. In *Screen Test*, Ludlam's Norma Desmond was the dominant female figure, humiliating Montez (persistently male in this contrast) as the tested starlet. The theme of *Whores* is female treachery and its central purpose of emasculation: Delilah's (Montez') treatment of Samson (played as a pretty, well-hung, but weak boy) is presented as archetypal.

The theatre's farce is sexual and pervert: cunnilingus, sodomy, sadism, masochism, incest, lesbianism (in the scripts, but rarely acted out), male homosexuality of all variants, coprophagia, the antique cult of the big prick, masturbation, not much fellatio. Untold copulations.

It only verges on the pornographic: Woronow offering her arse for penetration (*Vinyl*), tantalizing her son and us with her legs (*Kitchenette*), Vaccaro's Venus with the flower above her cunt (*Conquest*). Eisenhower's big breasts, Marti Whitehead in her panties (*Shower*), Black-Eyed Susan's belly (*Whores*) – all simple like corn belt striptease, mocking. There is a marginal sexual – heterosexual – impact; no pandering, no lewdness, just the polymorphous play of the id in the best antique and primitive pre-Christian popular tradition.

The sex is comic because of its flat guiltless naturalness: the characters don't beat around the bush. This directness makes it seem shallow but also administers a special shock of self-recognition: *ecce homo*. It's nothing special, just the bare essence of sociability – playful, unserious, unurgent: the opposite of D. H. Lawrence, Casanova, Genet ... It is not a call for sexual freedom a la Henry Miller or naturalness a la Wedekind but mockery of the contemporary religion of this country: *pervert heterosexuality*. For ours is a historically unique culture dominated by a cult of sex to which it devotes the preponderance of its vast cultural efforts (advertising, films, advertising, musical comedies, advertising): a non-materialist and yet secular religion for corporation employees, who are bereft of opportunities for free enterprise and so identify as consumers. All is bawdry, but pervert and sterile bawdry. This theatre's bawdry opposes stereotypical role-identification, phoniness, authoritarianism.

The cult of the clitoris has replaced Christian and Platonic love by sexual love as condition of human fulfillment, and has replaced God by Woman, to whom it preaches service from all the communication media. Women are to adore themselves, men are to adore them. Its ideal (variously enshrined by the movie industry) is neither the mother nor the virgin but the prickteasing bitch – self-possessed, egocentric, eternally youthful, beautiful; simple or mysterious; flirt or lady; bounteous or withholding; frigid or insatiable – dissatisfied, demanding, commanding or just in command, but always task and challenge for the man. Her cult demands of woman only that her image be projected – youth, loveliness, desirability – by beautification; it demands of men that they pay homage by providing the consumption goods needed for this beautification, that they implement an assiduous but unobtrusive virility by earning capacity in competition with one another. Both their sex and business lives are service to Woman, of value not in themselves, but as tokens of faith in and love for Her.

In the face of this scandalous perversity of our culture it is preposterous to subsume the mock-erotics of this theatre under the category of queer camp. Rather, the peculiarly American forms of homosexuality are themselves reactions and protests against the dominant perversion – as well as forms of victimization by it. It is a matter both of male and civic rectitude to honor it in the former regard, pity it in the latter.

Male homosexuality in feudal and post-feudal Asia and Europe has taken two forms: gentlemanly platonism (Wilde) and lower-class companionship (Genet). In neither form has it precluded corresponding forms of heterosexuality; in both forms it not only has not precluded but has been most intimately associated with all the conventional modes of manliness and masculinity. Both types still exist in America, but under the pressure of the same social conditions resulting in the perverse cult which here has all but replaced christianity, the American 20th-century homosexual who is queer (freakish) came to predominate. It is his special characteristic to adore women – helplessly, to the point of imitation. He shares the clitoris-cult view of her absolute superiority, he wishes he were a woman, tries to be one, offering his mouth as a substitute for her cunt. He despises himself and yet – to withdraw from the ordained life of service to her and to hate her and her cult – he turns his life into a ritualistic inversion of her liturgy. The wish to be a woman – the fearful hatred of women are the *natural* consequences of a man's life under the cult's system.

To view the theatre of the ridiculous as the flaunting tool of pervert coteries – demeaning manliness, humiliating women, expressing self-hatred and alienation by a snide attack on culture, values, reason, »life itself« – is contemptibly facile. The essential point is that they are exposing and by their mockery opposing a perverse culture.

The theatre venomously reproduces the central image of the cult, the dominant female catered to by clownishly feeble males, and peppers it with various minor humiliations of women. That the sexes are essentially such is the cult's not so esoteric doctrine. But to portray them as such, and to present this as ridiculous, is protest. That this form of protest is perhaps a heretical allegiance to the cult is a secondary consideration.

The drag queen is the central figure in these spectacles: not as character in the play nor in terms of plot, but by his costuming and deportment on the stage – alone (in disdainful rejoinders, in careful entrances and exits) or en masse (as chorus when there is an excuse for a mass scene, a huddle of negligently draped snidely quipping queens). The perfect female impersonator, the would-be-beautiful but clearly male transvestite, the definitely male (cigar-smoking, beer-drinking) androgynous transvestite, the woman-mocking ugly male in female dress, the male in romantically elegant male costume affecting occasional or sustained female intonations or gestures ... playing the star, the high priestess, the haughty lady, the coy innocent, the slut ...

The drag queen on the street or in this theatre acts out in one the male and female characters of the inverted American Dream, the contemporary cult of heterosexuality – not, of course, as presented by dream and cult but as they turn out: the woman-adoring silly male, despising himself; the strong, self-contained woman, indifferent to but overpowering the male, radiating charm and/or sexuality –

and that male's envious resentment of that woman. He is not a homosexual, he is a frustrated homosexual – a motherlover and cocksucker. His pose combines a dreamt invalidation of his disgust for himself and a mockery of slavish male heterosexuality. He doesn't like himself and he just loves women. He poses not as a woman but as a man impersonating a woman.

He poses the problem of psycho-sexual identity: to what extent male and female conduct, masculinity and feminity, are social role-identities, cultural artifacts, what they are, might be, should be – how valid these roles are, how natural. Beyond both his enactment of the contemporary role-conceptions and his mockery of them, he poses the ideal of a freely and playfully polymorphous sexuality. Or, more generally, the ideal of a free and playful assumption not only of this but of all forms of personal identity and social role.

If in this theatre we are at all times watching the *making of a play* (i.e., the *subject matter* is play-acting, intercourse based on convened fictions, the adoption of role identities, the transformation of an f.p. into an a.p. by himself) then the plays are plays within the play. The theatre itself is what we are made to reflect on – not in the sense of self-expression, profession, or entertainment, but as ambiguous exemplar of the enterprise of civilization or of the games of »free personality.«

The theme of role-playing is emphasized by the *manner* of performance. Attention is focused on role-playing as an activity of taking on a role, the actors making of themselves what they become. And the theme of role-playing is crucial in the plays. It is the subject of *Screen Test* and (since The Director is in the play) of *Juanita Castro*; of *Vinyl*, thematically the inverse of Brecht's *Man Is Man*, the education of a victimizer into a victim; of *Shower*, in which spies (imposters) are played as movie actors (imitators), the information sought is who plays what part, the plot is a quest for the identity of the spy-seducer Mark; and it is a theme in *Big Hotel* in the theatricality of Desmond, Velez, and Birdshitskaya, but mainly because of the dual nature of *Big Hotel*, the world of routine, squalor, glamour, and romance, which turns out to be the hell of humiliations of the Firepit Restaurant; and in *Conquest/Queens*, the relations and contrast between Tamburlaine's private and public life is *the* theme.

The public/private role theme is political and recurs in *Conquest, Indira Gandhi, Juanita Castro* and marginally even in *Whores* (the Mano/Emerald Empress plot for world conquest). Affairs of state, history, the politics of the great arise out of private family affairs –

erotic, antagonistic, personal relations. The public roles of statesmen by which societies are formed and run are the make-believe misrepresentations of *real* private endeavors: the role-identities decisive in human affairs are make-believe. The implication: history and society are irrational: so that all social(ized) role-identities are not rational (functional) but ridiculous.

The ambiguity of sexual identity is the basic variant of the theme of role-playing. Whether the male is defined as active principle (fucker) or by his genitals, the plays repeatedly point up the make-believe, free, role-playing character of sexual identity. By their grotesque display of male and female genitalia and secondary sexual characteristics, the productions starkly emphasize biological sexual identity. Then by their equally stark and repetitious exposure of suxual overtures and of acts of physical coercion paint a picture of a world in which an androgynous psycho-sexuality gives biologically male *or* female creatures a challenging choice between playing male or female roles.

The theatre leaves us with an image of social life in its most basic and most salient aspects: the relations between the sexes and political life or organized state power. It presents both of these as the playing of roles. And after showing us the arbitrariness of all role-playing, it points out that the actual roles played (especially those basic and salient ones which between them control the playing of all others) are both evil and ridiculous. Furthermore, they are ridiculous not only by the actual way in which they are played but especially (more basically) in being imposed role-identities, strait-jackets put on us in the bosom of the family and by the power of the state and so transmitted from generation to generation – the inauthentic self-perpetuating variants of one and the same figure, the authoritarian phony.

The theatre of the ridiculous is radical social satire and protest-anarchist . . . possibly nihilist.

The Conquest of the Universe (1967)*

The playhouse of the Ridiculous has been for a year or two now
(winter 67/68) the first and only good theatre in New York since
the Living Theatre was exiled by the Federal authorities. Assorted
egomanias and mad squabbles explode such groups,** which do not
exist except by the cunning tyranny of egomaniacs and the ties of
personal animosity. The great thing about the Playhouse of the
Ridiculous is they don't go in for art.

Charles Ludlam's *Conquest of the Universe*: some great little monologues, replicas, cameos from the great dramatists: a firesale of theatrical properties. The genre is studiedly unambitious, Ludlam does not
claim to be a playwright. It's a crude entertainment: the stuff that
in the good old days of the republic crafty semites democratically
cooked up alike for the robber barons and the ethnic hordes is here
served with the same broad gesture. Nowadays this fake glass glitters
like diamonds. But, more particularly: a slaughter of the theatre, not
a nostalgic gloss on mass culture a la Carmines et al.

Sexually, a shocking desplay of vigorous hermaphroditic health and
moral decency (what the *National Review* might call anomie): confusion, stridency of pose, assertion of the deviant.

Director and cast are not concerned with the script. The dialogue is
mimed, which is all right (especially when the vocal mimicry is
accurately ambiguous, in which the cast occasionally perhaps disap-
points the director). You get the drama you go to the theatre for.
However: not only does the *sound* of language get a little lost, but
the plot-line is subdued since you cannot understand the words. Thus

---

* I wrote this in the winter 67/68.
** Rehearsing, in the summer of 1967, for a showing in a real theatre, the
Bowery Lane, the second script contributed by one of the actors in the group,
Charles Ludlam, *The Conquest of the Universe*, the director of the Playhouse of the
Ridiculous, John Vaccaro (also, with Bill Chamberlin, brother of Wynn, the pro-
ducer), fired Ludlam as well as some other core-members of the Playhouse from
the cast, claiming (at least a year later he did) that Ludlam interfered too much
with his directing. Charles went off to direct his plays himself at the Tambellinis'
Gate, with himself and most of those fired acting in them, on November 24th
1967 opening with a revival of his *Big Hotel* (first done, directed by Vaccaro, and
with Ludlam as »Cupid«, »Svengali«, »Drago Rubles«, »Aristotle« and »Norma
Desmond«, at 13 W. 17th St., February 2, 1967 ff.) and then opening January
1st 1968, i.e. New Year's eve at midnight, his own version of *Conquest*, under the
title *When Queens Collide*, – *Conquest* thus is the point at which what were to be
the two mainstreams of ridiculous theatre (Ludlam, Vaccaro) part.

the turning points of the plot also remain unaccented and in this an aesthetic decision has been made which might clash with the author's ideology. Natolia with Ebea's help for love of Cosroe kills Zabina who is also executed by Tamburlaine; Zabina's twin brother and lover Cosroe, combats Tamburlaine to free (then to avenge) Zabina. While other hints at a fable (e.g. Ebea's motives and kinship to Zabina and Natolia) are fake, this is a real plot – actually what's happening and why. Thus a private ridiculous substructure of public events is revealed by the author, but is buried with ridicule by cast and director. This *may* be good, though it is bound to disturb (after boring) the audience, reduced to spectators.

Tamburlaine (fascism, militarism, violence and stupidity) conquers the solar system without much opposition other than private, his opponents a huddle of queens. The burden of the spectacle is thus on Woronow, the superb actress who plays the overreacher. With hysteria, paranoia, she plays a bare core of sadist energy. Her Tamburlaine »comes in bullets,« distraught only by his lack of issue. Her costume in the previews was shoddier and better than later: it made her look ugly, a band of blue trouserettes distorted her magnificent (as I know from other productions) legs; they seemed desiccated, harsh. What makes me think she is a superb performer are her gestures: strangely articulated into demonstrative fragments. She speaks naturally in some American vernacular, her delivery cool, throwaway, violent. The raving maniac she portrays is of plausible efficacy, a bestrider of the world, animated by a frantic but steadily explosive spleen. Her acting is poetic rather than prosaic, portrays moods and temperament by unnatural demeanor (in contrast to the excellent representative vignettes of Beverly Grant's Mrs. Tamburlaine).

Otherwise, the cast consists of beautiful women and deviates, the intimation of whose cattily friendly concourse evokes the decadence of conquerable upper classes (pampered jades) if we want to look at it that way. (This is how they play-act. I know nothing of their private lives – e.g., if any of them is a »beautiful woman.« But, importantly, their acting style is such as to intimate private real sex lives. It is these artful intimation I am speaking of. *The Connection* gave rise to analogous confusions.) The play's style does not relate to science fiction (which is serious). It seems to me not unlike that of American cheap pornography (which is not serious, but vital and desperate). In the immediate, the rapid commotion of these strange and awkward and colorful figures makes a carnival spectacle of unusual entertainment, as at some dying country fair, the region's freakish squares foregathering, once ambitioning to be cleancut American kids, now placing their phony dollar bills on the rigged-up races.

How much credit is due Vaccaro as director, I am not sure. I get his past work confused with the Tavels! The spirit of reckless gaiety may even be largely his. Ludlam's script seems less terrible than the production, more inclined to fun and games, not as black as the production. The actors certainly lend themselves to this (Woronow more than lends herself), but I suspect much of the production's importance originates in a denigratory energy of Vaccaro's.

The Playhouse of the Ridiculous is pertinently a group. An admirable group. The *naivete* which makes Americans so disgusting from Hanoi to Paris and London has been transmuted here, in a native habitat, through camp, into reckless freedom, exhilarating. It is still innocence, but true: the filthy play of willfully childish persons. (I suppose that much of the director's effort – a participation – is not to distort this.)

Monstrous productions: *Vinyl, Indira Gandhi, Kitchenette, Juanita Castro* (I missed *Lady Godiva*). Filthy language to enliven weak puns, cuntlapping elbowing buggery, the characters crude grotesques driving toward the repetition of acts of cannibalism or murder disguised as sex acts: victims or victimizers. Inane plots, preposterous poses, cruel crudities – in short, a realistic theatre.

The verisimilitude of such theatre is endangered by technical perfection, by preoccupation with the finished product. For instance, Taylor Mead now acts too well (he's magnificent, the »best thing in the show,« as good a technician now, or almost, as Mostel or Lahr). The first preview was better than opening night. Perhaps ambition (fear) had slickened the choreography. Opening night, Mead was less acrobatic, Woronow milder, the music worked too well. A hint of disaster, I mean success.

Mary Woronow

The magic unicorn
that she would gladly ride
bringing to life the afternoon
slips through the margin of
her scary story she is a merest child
the world is fearful
and her imperious gesture

asking to her heart
some flower
is a dismissal.

A shadow
over
its cornflower eye
its cloudy ankles tufted
twinkle
away the beast is
vanished and was it there?

A child well lost in the woods.

John Vaccaro, 1968-1973: the gesture of hatred.

In the winter of 67/68, Vaccaro fired Ludlam and most of the old members of the Ridiculous Theatrical Company from the cast of Ludlam's *Conquest of the Universe,* launching Ludlam on his career as director. Ridicule by ridiculousness bifurcated into a mode of hatred and a mode of compassion.*

In the fall of '68, Vaccaro staged his grandiose, universally disliked *The Moke-Eater* (by Kenneth Bernard) upstairs at Max's Kansas City.**

Jack's car breaks down, he finds himself in this New England (Middle Western/Southern) village. He is the All-American boy, a salesman, and comes on big to the dense population of sinister mumbling half-wits, wanting his car fixed. Gradually, though trying to maintain a front, he comes to feel his life threatened by the mad monstrous growling mob. Alec (Sierra Bandit), local grass-roots con-man – the politician – leader of the people, thought totally screaming mad, because of his comparative sanity (intelligence) seems his only hope, seems to be protecting him (this is *Benito Cereno* with a twist). The freaks are all over him, pinching, scratching, biting. They want to give him a good time, they adore him – they also pretend to mistake him for someone named »Fwed« (they lisp) – everybody wants to have a good time, he must give a song and dance, he eats a geek's meal, is subjected to a fearful night of love with the schizoid village gypsy Maria (Elsine Sorrentino). Next morning everything is jake, he gets a good breakfast, the town mechanic (Claude Purvis) has fixed his car . . . he leaves. The locals, by now clearly a population of demonic ghouls, listen as the sound of his car grows fainter, then falters, peters out: the door of the local hostelry opens again, it is Jack again: he realizes he is still here, but this time it's the end, he will be eaten. The stage is dark, a film is projected on Jack's chest. We see hands in human entrails, an animal jewel in ruby, liver, crimson. The lights go on, the natives freeze, Jack is there with a raw liver, his own, dangling from his mouth.

The play is a compact scream of violent hatred. Vaccaro had his actors screaming from the word go. Sierra screamed at the top of

* There is also a female branch of ridiculous theatre: Rochelle Owens, Rosalind Drexler, Maria Irene Fornes.
** After a while he moved it to the Bleecker St. Cafe au Gogo, in the spring of 69 revived it at the young Abrams' Gotham Art Theatre on W. 43rd St.

her voice all the time except for brief fake sweetnesses, with the insincerity to the fore – screams and screams. The natives are totally antagonistic cannibals (faint suggestions that they are also New Blacks, Jack the White Man trying to con them into reasonability) – Vaccaro started his last run-through with the simple reminder »remember you hate him!« He threw away suspense, substituted an explosion – a drive toward climax.

The play is the sadist destruction of a person – of a rudimentary and obnoxious personality, the clean, making-out, smart-alecky, American businessman child-male: a sentimental education – the making of the square, inhuman victim. Vaccaro never allowed Bruce Pecheur to become likeable, made him substitute a lower-class vulgar accent for his middle-class one. He gets shattered, crushed, torn apart, but any time the pressure seems to let up a little, he's ready to take care of No.1, he's so fucking rubbery – a good breakfast, and he is almost back in form, ready to believe himself accepted. When he says »I don't bite,« he turns to the audience, bears his fangs, the cast freezes in a crouching huddle – he's lying. It is a feast of malice in action – hatred of anybody really – of somebody who insofar as he is alive withholds food – his own body – of what we hate most of all, this phony male, a deceived baby, blood-brother of all the viciously violent. The play starts with the pledge of allegiance by the townspeople: the American eagle, a harpy D.A.R., Rene Riccard in a horrid dream of feathers – later he plays Alec's pet crow getting drunk out of Jack's glass, also Harrington, gentleman cannibal in some graveyard, getting chummy with Jack who's made the mistake of going out for a leak – screeching O Say Can You See. Claude Purvis as the mechanic alternates between slick yes-sir humility and an animal more intelligent than the others. He and Sierra Bandit keep varying the degrees of hostility/madness/implacability/niceness: the gamut of impersonal personalness, conventional indications of relating that don't mean a thing and are always on the brink of jumping into quite another attitude. Bandit alternately caresses and slaps Jack while trying to make him appreciate all that the folks of Mount Pleasant are trying to do for him – he must, must, MUST appreciate it. Sorrentino's flat vulgar accents as slut, good-natured enough but of course without heart, golden or other, stand out as form of sanity from the muttered »Fweds« of the townspeople and from Alec's screams, but this is the kind of no-value, no-help commonness that Jack's initial come-on to the villagers had, the surface sanity of those integrated into insanity: humanity not revealing itself as bestiality, but at zero-level and in the final analysis terroristic enough, a show of absent emotion. She is cheerful – perpetually laughing. She switches abruptly back and forth between laughter/ indifference (»Want another pretzel, baby« – a little playful slap...), doing her job as whore (including wanting to be loved, wanting to be beautiful for you, dear), a frightened, take-me-with-you-out-of-all-this act, a paranoid fantasy of danger and glory (they are fucking on the bar, it is the Moke-Eater's hour, just before dawn). The American way of life: a breaking down of the individual by a rush of aggression of sweet concern and cannibal hostility.

Vaccaro drives his people so hard during rehearsals, when it comes to performance and he's no longer there to play for, they somewhat pale out. This way, and because the principals (Bandit, Pecheur) were somewhat scared of the total violence of the attack, performances were not quite up to the marvelous power *cum* wealth-of-subtlety of the last rehearsals: the power-screaming weakened and thus drowned out some of the subtlety (though nothing can make Sorrentino or Riccard falter). A major point, that it is the kindness of America that is the really horrifying thing about her, was lost. But still, the audience looked bewildered, disgusted, in fact sort of genuinely frightened.

February 1969. The New Theatre Workshop, an uptown, semi-swank, semi-grubby little place on East 54th Street. Three one-act plays by Kenneth Bernard, directed by John Vaccaro, presented in the »Monday Night Play Series«: *The Adjustment, The Lovers, The Monkeys of the Organ Grinder*. The last two have Crystal Field, a fine voluptuous, vulgar actress with somewhat sloppy timing in them. Though its theme is solid, – a man, any man, getting fed up with a woman, he just does not want to fuck her any more, moving from Brooklyn to the Bronx has nothing to do with it, – John makes Crystal play the woman, Eve, as desperately in need of a fuck, – *The Lovers* is too much of a gag. Grotesque theatre. The audience, old ladies, etc. – unmoved or indignant.

The Monkeys sends them out. It shows John's true spirit: madness. His very fine rhythm of action as such as his corny touches give the impression of an imitation of a play – commenting on »life.« An assembly (gradually) of vicious sex maniacs, giggling and laughing all the time, in the throes of an orgasm that never comes. A slasher of photos. A hermaphrodite (Frank Didley as Regina) invisible under a bedcover for quite a while making love-making sounds, – making bisexual love to himself. One sane person, the Photographer, finally arrives, but then turns out as insane as the rest. His camera pees at them. The show thus systematically counterposes normalcy and insane depravity and equates them: which way *this* equation works is ambiguous. John is telling the normal people they are stark raving mad, inside and on the surface. Surreptitiously he recommends insane depravity as a gay, healthy, normal mode of existence, as the only way to be.

Other than the just mentioned Kenneth Bernard's, Vaccaro's shows from the 68/69 Bernard *Moke Eater* to the spring-of-73 Bernard *Dr. Ma-Gico,* – revivals of *Lady Godiva* (with a marvellous performance by Lynn Reyner) and of *The Life of Juanita Castro, Cockstrong* and *Son of Cockstrong* by Murrin, Jackie Curtis' *Heaven Grand in Amber Orbit,* Bernard's *Night Club,** – were musicals. Like the shows before and after them, the moral parables of a fastidious imagination, black radiations, their mood was something special, a raging amphetamine mood. Showbusiness rock obliterated the feeble comebacks of desperate individuals drowning in frenetic populations of freaks, weirdos, cripples, perverts and degenerates, physically malformed, often with speech-defects, vicious, moronic and pathetic. There was little joy or humor in these grimly satisfying speed-driven attacks, lieutenanted with elegantly warped grace by inspired dragqueens. Vaccaro wasn't going to give THEM the satisfaction.

June 1969. *Cockstrong* at La Mama, directed by John Vaccaro. The text, by Tom Murrin, is feeble, but Vaccaro has arranged the music (humdrum rock) so you can't understand much anyhow. John is all over, handing out programs etc. The place is jammed. The projections, some on the side walls (e.g. a ghostly shadow of a motorcycle rider), some on the backdrop, broken up by the projecting enormous (6 ft. or so) prick and the two ball-flaps pendant and the keyhole underneath it, are excellent: emerging briefly, half-invisible. The play is about the poet Arthur (played by Francis Wm. Dudley), who is scared of fucking or not very virile or not much interested, – a poet. He pirouettes. His fiance Denise (played by Ruby Lynn Reyner),

---

* *Nightclub* opened at the admirable Stewart's La Mama on Sept. 17, 1970, from there moved to the New Loft Theatre. Ondine and Woronow played the hero-heroine Bubi. I didn't see this play which may have had more form and power than Vaccaro's others of this period. I got the impression Vaccaro thought of the New Loft Theatre production of this play as perhaps the best thing he has done.

from her entrance, scratching away at her crotch, pursues him desperately, Lynn splendidly ringing all the changes from whimper and whine to scream, a woman possessed by a craving, plagued by an itch. She ends up by strangulating him. Mike Abrams as the surgeon, with a heavy awkwardness, not unlikely in the part, performs a gruesome autopsy on him, but finds most everything more or less naturally natural, though a few organs are not so hot. He regains life, and in a barbaric court scene, indictment of a pointlessly tabooridden society, Claude Purvis (whose limitation is stupidity, but who has good control) as judge/medicine man/preacher condemns him to five years in prison for not playing the male part, plus a $5 fine for having underscored this by laying an egg. In a grand rock finale, the wall-projections for which are like a dance of death, the cast pairs off in trios screwing in all positions. The play ends up as the image of this bunch of sexy ghouls, – about a world of ugly sex-fiends besetting this mild, inoffensive, scared man – K. in Amerika. They are shamanistic demons. Their tongues loll, their hands are claws, their make-up is the one recurrently used by Vaccaro: colored geometric areas bounded in other colors over white paste masks, glitter above the eyes and on the lips. The accent is on ugliness, e.g. the roly-poly little girl with her bosoms coming out of her net-shirt and the flabby thighs, who is thrown into transports of moral approval, i.e., a sexual fit, rolling and rolling, all over the floor, during the judge's wild Afro-American sermon, or Reyner really playing up her scrawny thighs and pinched arse.

An odd reviewer read a praise of sex into this play. Of course, John is saying »that's how the world is,« and is a tough enough Italian so that that's that as far as he is concerned, but his horror and disgust at all this vicious filth, though glee at showing up the common people, – people, – acts as a kind of gaiety, is what the play clearly expresses. Sexuality verges on cannibalism, necrophilia, necrophagy, he is saying, and naturally does, for it is an unspiritual lust for bodies and an urge of aggressive domination. The women, as in the nunnery, a nest of whory vipers, in John's revival of *Lady Godiva*, are more particularly the vessels of impurity: but everybody is horrible. – If Ludlam's theatre is pot-poetry, the sublimity of vegetal narcotics, Vaccaro's is acid frenecy, fed by a claustrophobic hatred of the modern mob. There is much pity in Charles' derision. John has none.

Acting here becomes a matter of anti-aesthetic reductionism: concentrating the apparent type to a murderous id. Though hypocritically, Al Capp's black-clotted cartoons do the same thing, and by the same means, crudity and a combination of energy and vacuity. John's scenic fantasy is his own true underground comics, – the old-fashioned dirty kind with Popeye masturbating, Maggie and Jiggs doing 69, not the new counterculture kind, which goodnaturedly preaches liberation. In this play, the weak male excepted (Dudley abstains from putting a slobbering clown on stage, gives a portrait of a human [and male] man), Vaccaro forced his actors into abandoning themselves, they had to become abject, lashed them into projecting the demonic horror of the dead, galvanised them into a destructive orgy, in which their dementia takes on the color of a delirium of hatred.

Lynn Reyner, John's replacement for Sierra Bandit, who had replaced his previous heroine, Mary Woronow, unlike Bandit, has the required courage to be quite ugly, but though she has all the gusto needed, her aggression lacks a little in the substantiality that Woronow's domination had, there is no fury in her; though she is a virtuoso mime (Bandit mostly just had energy, could do only one thing, Woronow's gestures were great, but her face was immobile), her movements and expressions, never becoming obsessive tics, often during an evening's performance, and more and more often in the course of a run, soften into a pointless mugging in no way mad; like Bandit she has difficulty catching herself for sharply defined moments of real need, cunning etc. though she does them quite beautifully; and of course (like Woronow and Bandit) she does not have Elsine Sorrentino's marvelous power for character acting. I suspect Sorrentino has it over these three girls in this last respect by her lower-class origins: above the lower middle-class there is not too much real-life character-acting. John's relentless sadism goads his actors into splendid performances during final rehearsals, but as their fear of his reckless onslaughts wears off during a run, a fear of offending the audience takes over, and as the screaming energy he has charged them with runs off, they lose much of the modelling and many of the sharp effects that his drill has made dependent on that energy-discharge. They can not, out of themselves, go all the way. Thus also Jackie Curtis' act as mad Teutonic anthropologist, anthropologising a young blind brave (beautifully done by Purvis), amazing during rehearsals, faded.

Winter 71/72. *XXXXX*, words by William M. Hoffman, direction by John Vaccaro. It opened, after, according to John, only 9 days of rehearsal, at the WPA on the Bowery, but Vaccaro got into an argument, and took it around the corner into Ellen Stewart's La Mama, leaving the sets behind. Jesus freaking has been the thing since Altamount and the o.d.'s of Hendrix, Joplin and the Rolling Stones guitarist. With this play, John got on the bandwagon. It is short, only a little over an hour, reduces to 3 or 4 monologues and to two actions, Mary communing sexually with nature, and the agony of Jesus, which Hoffman in a trite twist on Paul presents as the crucifixion of the flesh on the cross of the law. You can't call it Christian, since everyone in it is arch-human, – if you consider its trinity divine, you might call it pantheist. Its gospel is sexist abandon to what's natural. God the Father, nude, sells it, Mary the Mother lives it, the Holy Ghost (mimicking fucking Mary) acts it out, Joseph deplores it, – the standard hippie variant of the anti-Calvinist consumerism of this country's middle-class since the 1920's. The writing is lousy, but there is at least one good idea, though reduced to a cliché by the writing: asked what she wants to name her son, Mary keeps coming up with adjectives describing her body-feelings as her pregnancy progresses. John directed this uplifting message as a faggot show.

Like most of Vaccaro's things since the *Moke-Eater*, but less frantically, it was a musical, an oratorio, – there was only a guitar and a little taped jazz, but most of the lines were sung. The make-up was, as in all of Vaccaro's plays, a suspension of the faces as in memories of the defunct: simple facial masks, broadly ringed mouths and eyes, strong reds and blacks, glitter. There were two casts, one an elevated embarrassing background of living male statuary, up there throughout the play, with not much to do except hardly to move, – they participate in an initial gloria, during which a spot moves from head to head, broadening from the focus of the head each time to include much of the figure, a gimmick that made them appear our own dead images. The other cast was out front, very active, dancing or moving in dance-style much of the time. The men were all extremely handsome, with striking physiognomies, especially the eyes, and beautiful bodies; the two actresses I saw do Mary on different evenings were more or less ugly.

The acting was unsure, people *remembered* to get into position, got *ready* to deliver their monologues, even the sympathy of the audience did not help them time their lines. There was a competition as to who could pose the best. The least competent were the best. Joe Pichette as confused, agonising Jesus, up on trial before God the Father, terrorised into incoherence by the Holy Ghost, was easily the most awkward. He didn't know what to sound like, had no confidence in the baby-words provided him by Hoffmann, didn't know how to build up, his timing was trite. But he was also the most interesting of the actors: by his speech. His style of delivery could perhaps be called super-cool, an absurdist dropping flat of all the lines in short segments, the mind talking to itself only, but scarcely even that: spinning off tokens, rather, each the eternally same response to a self-perpetuating situation, but all glib, and with no shame, – a new style, only lately, among the better actors (cf. e.g. Kilroy's film *Desperate Characters*), replacing the Actors Studio style of expressing your inability to express yourself: the despair remains inexpressed, expression is easy and represents the recognition that expressing yourself is out of the question. Pinchette seemed to be rejecting easier alternatives. Francine Middleton, the second of the two Marys, was very effective in her infinitely nuanced, coy delivery, – the pukey style of the professionals, in which, for instance, the three leading ladies recently castrated the great *The Screens* at the Brooklyn Academy of Music, the style of demanding from the audience the whorish counterfactual agreement that that's the way people talk when they are sincere, – or being themselves. The girl that did Mary before her didn't have half her skill, had to rely on letting Vaccaro freak her out into a mimicry of the screaming frenzy, that up to this play, which may be a turning point for him, he demanded of his actors. But her very disintegration managed to bypass Hoffman's white-collar earth mother, instead slipping us the powerful eroticism of the frigid woman that wants it oh so bad.

While most of the detail of the staging seemed to me just convention-al gimmickry, and the placements and displacements on the stage of no interest or impact (the middle of the stage often seems to me a hole in Vaccaro's work, and the trichotomy of his persistent theme, the devouring frigid female, the weak male, the female's slavering, sex-mad Lower Depths court, has yielded him no stage-organising principle), the use of the spot was humorous and intelligent, for instance where it picks out the less obvious, very beautiful body parts of a posing male (God), a bit of elevated faggotry, and the timing of the whole show, – it clicked into a whole, – was positively beautiful.

The Magic Show of Dr. Ma-Gico is clearly the after-duty work of a professor of foreign literatures, in fact again Kenneth Bernard, a fine, though thematically and in his developments excessivist prose-writer in a minor key. Dips into literature, Balzac, Hugo and others, provide eight (counting a poem by Verlaine and one by Poe and a quotation from the *Aeneid* as the fifth) quick evocations of the murderous cruelty of love in a fictionalised world governed by Sir James Frazer's magician-king, murderer of his predecessor, victim-to-be of his successor, servant of a cruel rather than fertile Diana. (1) murder of a king unable to implement power with knowledge – (2) execution and rape of an impecunious young lover – (3) murder by gang bang – (4) murder by castration in fellatio – (5) on the illusoriness of life, the inexorable passage of time, the cruelty of love and on the self-immolation of Dido abandoned by Aeneas – (6) murder by mistake (the murderer does not recognise his beloved) – (7) murder by coitus (the wife-killer is moon-struck by another) – (8) murder of a murderer. The play, in a very level style, is a moan silenced and twisted into a sneer smoothed out into a phony cool smile. Under Vaccaro's direction at the La Mama Repertory Theatre, where it had two runs of a few days each in March 1973, it turned into a threat. The tauric Diana, – Bernard's master-magician is male, Vaccaro's a she, played by Sierra Bandit, – assumed rule. It was another of the Vaccaro-Bernard horror-shows, but also Vaccaro's first well-made production in a long while, partly because the people he got to work with him all did pretty work, R. Weinstock on the music (nicely played by the »Magick Consortium« piano, cello, clarinet and tympani), Bernard Roth on the elegant costumes in black, white and red, E. C. Terrel II on the set. Vaccaro's art as director was much in evidence, he had, after a long series of rock freak and faggot shows, gotten himself together for some proper theatre. It was an exciting, satisfying show. Trumped-up emotion had superceded brutality.

The only actual actors were Bandit, carrying the whole show as a series of illusions commanded by her, – she was Dr. Ma-Gico, – and Elsine Sorrentino, as overly amorous queen fucked to death by her husband (Dr. Ma-Gico's 7th trick), and as the syphilitic crone who bites off her lover's prick (in the 4th episode: his young love Marie has laid love-making with the old hag on him as test of his love for her, but she is herself the hag, disguised). Apart from them, costuming, music, stage-sets, lighting made up the show, surrounding, in a pit, as it were, because of the steeply raked seating upstairs at La Mama, Vaccaro's usual huddle of misshapen, miserable freaks, with something like a cold 18th century splendor. We saw the world as contained inside a silvery magic box, shut on its victims, yet with entries for materialising threats, thus a space of danger. Openings, revolving silver doors in a silver backdrop,* – *hidden* doors or mirrors, – admitted the two configurations of danger, Dr. Ma-Gico's assistants, beauty (Esmeralda) and the beast (Quasimodo). In Bernard's text, Esmeralda and Quasimodo have no such roles as executors of evil, they are only among the victims. Creating these roles for them (without changing the text) Vaccaro lent theatrical life to an ontology of paranoia.

Since Dr. Ma-Gico is the narrator, and since what she tells happens instantly, we see her magic as the theatre's and thus as John Vaccaro's, – who shows off his power to us as that of a beautiful cruel woman.

Sierra Bandit is the dominatrix of the crew of freaks on the stage, tall and beautiful, cruel and inscrutable, the king and queen and a magician, i.e. an illusionist: the painted freaks are her court and people whom she holds in suspense and tortures and whose cruel vices she promotes. Since she is an illusionist, nothing is real, the victims do not really die, the happenings at court are scenes enacted from literature, and her power is an illusion of her subjects'. She treats us as her subjects also, with a vague mixture of threat and contempt, daring us to be insensible to her power: which she exerts over us in the form of the fascination of the show. Her manner and mode of speech were theatrical to the extreme: with the ideal artificiality (phoniness) that the participants in arranged masochist encounters aspire to, but find it so hard to achieve: the excess of phantasies removed from the ordinarily feasible, quite unreal. We might say that whereas in the *Moke-Eater* threat and cruelty were real, both those directed by the stage-demagogue at the stage-multitude, and those the play directed at the audience (not in danger of being devoured, but assaulted in its self-esteem), in this play they weren't, we are not tempted to identify with the freakish courtiers, they are too uncommon and too much mere figurants and the atmosphere of danger projected is metaphysical. The mock-threat projects Vaccaro's (and Artaud's) sense of a cruel universe, in which a delight in our suffering is abroad, and not only in our pain, but in our anticipation of pain and destruction, in the pain of that anticipation, a delight in our perpetual disequilibration, and which is full of forces to procure and raise that delight. The threat felt by Vaccaro (though perhaps not by Bernard) is as intangible as a name we cannot remember. It is

* Revolving panels of silver mylar.

of the essence of it that it may be only in our mind. When the *Moke-Eater* called us a fucking mob of cannibal cretins, in effect identifying our neighbour as the danger, this was a real threat not only because it pointed to something real as the threat, but because our neighbour is dangerous, as dangerous as we, but when *The Magic Show* delighted in imparting a sense of the dominion of impersonal malevolence, this was an unreal threat.

In Vaccaro's early 17th St. period and up to *Conquest*, when Tavel wrote for him and Ludlam got into acting with him, his grotesque shows made us privy to his filthy view of man like we were his chums, sharing his feelings: one kid showing his penis to another. People looked pretty much like swine. The stage-images were immensely awkward, – this awkwardness expressing the torturousness of the human animals. From the *Moke-Eater* up to *Dr. Ma-Gico*, the shows were sustained temper-tantrums, exhibitions of Vaccaro's rage (not outrage). We saw him in a fury of contempt at the iniquity of mankind, spitting his contempt at the race: but not only at it, but at us also. We were included. He was trying to be cruel to us, to frighten, even hurt us: a snarling rat. Though there was no formal address to the audience, the theatrical gesture was that of an attack on it, an insidious, but definitely invidious aggression. Though you couldn't prove it maybe, the ball was being thrown at your face, and hard. Mankind now was shown not only as a bunch of filth, but as a mob of vicious maniacs, – and there were dangerous leaders among it, not only equally insane, but more consciously cruel, and cunning. Vaccaro was talking about a threat to himself, and rebelling against it, shouting. The stage-image, one of a state of constant guerilla warfare within a population of feral predators, was now subjugated to the sound. You couldn't make out the words: the incoherence of rage, though the sound was not so much that of fury or insanity, as a roar of feverish pointless activity.

Dr. Ma-Gico was clearly designed as an elegant, even poetic entertainment. The view of humanity was pretty much as before, but the theatrical gesture was no longer that of an attempt to wound, we weren't being bullied, we were threatened. The spectacle by way of Sierra Bandit's delivery spoke of a threat outside the theatre. As circus magic often is given the form of sham-magic (without losing its delicious evocation of the possibility of magic, indeed strengthening it by discounting the tricks presented, as not *it*), this threat had the form of a mock-threat (as when bullies intimidate you into accepting their torture of you as just fun, or like the sarcasm of banter in which insult has become the form of intercourse and must not be taken seriously). Thus the (of course ridiculous) threat of the previous period, that the performance or its director presented a present if unclear danger, was ironically avoided, but in addition, the world's actual threat to us all was proclaimed of a sinister sort: *directed* at instilling fear in us: by systematic but – deliberately – patently *insincere* evidencings of good will. The danger is real: your lot is suffering. But the air is playful: you are being mocked; you can never be sure there is a design. The world is cruel.

Whether cruel in its allures or suave (and cruel only by its positive refusal to let your dread lie), whether in the form of rage or of phony dalliance, Vaccaro's has been a theatre of cruelty: in the sense of Artaud of making itself a funnel for the cruelty intrinsic to life, – though without Artaud's anyway not so sincere obeisance to life.

Though people do (more often say) mean or vicious things, though most children in their fights and friendships exercise broad streaks of cruelty, though meanness and viciousness is a prevalent form of self-assertion and entertainment in the criminal class, and though social repression, the state, like crime, tends to take the form of mean and vicious procedures, institutions that not only kill and hurt, but do so cruelly, – hierarchic bureaucracy like and even more than competition by no means only affording opportunity for cruelty, thus attracting sadists, but requiring it, viz. that power be made *felt* and that the will of others be *broken*, – it is rare to find a mean or vicious or cruel person. Cruelty tends to be merely an arms in the power struggle, defensive in personal life, aggressive in the exercise of rule and in the war of all against all of the criminal class, a way of staying on top of things, of not getting swamped, expression of a fear and insecurity so great that cunning is brought into the business of survival and that the infliction of pain becomes pleasurable, – qua relief from fear, – but not exercise of spontaneous malevolence. Competition, the state and criminal life are evil, and personal relationships are wars, but I have never met an evil person.

Now John either disagrees or views the distinction as otiose. He portrays mankind as a swarm of demons evil by instinct. He may of course be right, but one thing that suggests his misanthropy is just a personal hang-up of his is, that in most of his plays (*not* the *Moke-Eater*) there is a hero, a weak little man, who is not a raging little devil, and that, qua hero, this figure figures as The Individual, so that the point becomes only: the others are monsters – a point that is an apology for a projection of paranoid viciousness: to which one may respond.

Misanthropy is one thing, a vision of Satan's reign another. John's theatre conveys this vision by a recurrent figure which in the immediate only expresses a puerile potentially homosexual hang-up: the cold, haughty, mad and cruel lady who exercises a kind of reign, – the evil queen. This is a traditional figure, e.g. the fairy-tale stepmother, Lewis Carroll's duchess, – and $1/2$, the other side, of some fertility goddesses, the death of autumn, bad seasons. The point is, she reigns. – *As the stage is by nature a metaphor for the world* (becoming less only by the special will or lack of courage of author and director), stage-sovereignty not otherwise specified naturally works as theological metaphor. John's earlier plays brought this home to us through our empathy with the suffering hero, *Dr. Ma-Gico* makes it almost explicit. John's plays show the reign of a cruelly evil providence over the affairs of men (and of women!), a providence that John makes beautiful, charming and capricious, and whose power over us he derives from our impotent desire to possess her.* A child's lovehate of its mother that bears fruit in an aberrant puerile fantasy that the prom queen is a cruel goddess, if it takes hold of a man as his hair grows, and magnifies and hardens into his life-stance, when put on the stage, by inversion yields an isomorphous image of universal cruel power. The feeling that the others are out to get you and delight in torturing you in this perspective becomes secondary to an awareness of a cruel and pointless fate, not yours alone.

»OPEN AUDITIONS for YMCA (A New Musical Workshop) by Ragni-Rado-Margoshes Directed by John Vaccaro. LOOKING FOR: People with combined athletic and singing abilities. ATHLETES (gymnasts, body builders, etc.) ACTOR-SINGERS DANCERS (male and female, ages 16-45) INTERVIEWS: March 8, 9, 10, 11, 12 10 AM-1 PM and 2 PM-6 PM 47 Great Jones Street (3rd Street between Bowery and Lafayette) (No previous theatrical experience necessary)« (Advertisement, Village Voice, March 8, 1976).

»travelled up to Director John Vaccaro's Riverside Drive digs. John had invited the cast of YMCA the (*Hair*) authors) Jim Rado and Geri Ragni $60.000 workshop musical which had just completed a two

---

* Kenneth Bernard's plays in part recommended themselves to Vaccaro because of a recurrent figure in them, the demonic master of ceremonies, – e.g. Alec in *The Moke-Eater* or Bubi in *Night-Club*, a play Vaccaro put on at La Mama on Sept. 17, 1970 ff., Ondine and Mary Woronow playing Bubi.

month rehearsal period and a two performance backers' audition. John had directed the production, which is probably the most expensive musical for and by children.« (The gossip columnist Weiner in the Soho Weekly News, July 8 1976).

»(Interviewer.) What happened to it? (Vaccaro.) Rado and Ragni are rewriting.« (Soho Weekly News, September 23, 1976).

For three four-day July week ends of 1977, Bernard's *The Sixty Minute Queer Show* (presented by La Mama and something called Theater Strategy) showed in the 10 p.m. slot at La Mama. Directed by Vaccaro, it had 6 courtesy-of-actor's equity (among them Renos Mandis) actors, 4 others (among them John Byron Thomas) and – an old Vaccaro performer – Marie-Antoinette Rogers in it, and Vaccaro came on, from the audience space, as director in his own image. There was no story continuity, but within a frame provided by an opening and two closing scenes showing performers on exhibition, the figure of a weak but vicious ruler reappears 5 times over (the last time as lion tamer), and all 8 scenes of the play were on the theme of EXPOSURE and HUMILIATION. Friday nights, Ludlam's *Hamlet* (*Stageblood*) on the son unwilling to take on the father's role, Saturday nights, his rendition of Wagner's anti-bourgeois epos (*Der Ring Gott Farblonjet*) were running right across the street.

In scene 1, an opener, a night club chanteuse endlessly is getting into her act in front of the audience, alternately sweetly wooing them in avowals of her ineptness and breaking out in snarling hatred of them, finally booed off the stage by the cast. In scene 2, the king sodomises the shepherd's daughter and bedmate to death with Wonderbread; in scene 3 attends, scared to death, bound and gagged, a lethal scene of rural home life in which the faggot (Thomas) son refuses to milk the cows, announces his artistic destiny, he will become a hairdresser; in scene 4 comes on his would-be-adulterous queen and faints as she charges on him with dildo and sword: the hot Turkish queen has employed the services of a captive Don Juan (Mandis) whose amatory expertise has elevated his art beyond the grossness of mere intercourse; in scene 5 in a game devised by the queen, on trial for his victimisation of the shepherd's daughter, not dead but hugely fat, the king shifts back and forth between assured tyrancy and incipient victimisation; in scene 6 as lion tamer, while his mistress, the aerial artist (a puppet), pushes her luck again and again, forces his snarling captive, a lean and hungry female, to suck him off: his mistress falls and he is stabbed. He remains on the vacated stage, dead in his light blue infant's plastic bathing pool, his heart blood a steadily spurting fountain of water in the air, a powerful ridiculous image. Scenes 7 and 8 close the show. In scene 7, Mandis gave a suave synopsis of Racine's *Andromaque,* bloody story of love and death, of the murder of a king and the survival of a queen, becoming, in frenetic French, sweating, in bits and pieces, victim, in desperate madness in Latin ending up in Virgil instead, cursing the dead king, who was himself slayer of another King's son and of that son's royal father, – a gripping performance of the performer's humiliation by his trade. In scene 8, Thomas did a knife-edge street-queen, infinitely vulnerable, in his jive beat telling a story of put-downs and put-downs.

Vaccaro had lost none of his zest. His misanthropy has outlasted Ludlam's more qualified bent, his Italian apostasy more radical than the Irish one and his black temper better preservative of comic sense than philosophic intelligence. Dealing death, Vaccaro has maintained his energy.

He has, however, lost his bite. The professional actors' performance was pleasant, exhilarating even, but the viciousness seemed a joke. One sensed, not a mellowing, but an enfeeblement. Bernard's script* may be one of his best things yet, – a harsh, cool poem, its airiness supporting perfectly its heavy essences, a round of rage, aggression, murder. It prescribes 8 scenes (Vaccaro dropped the last three), framed and punctuated by 9 appearances of drag queens (of which Vaccaro kept only the 1st, 8th and 10th). The scenes present the norm, an idiotic, sadistic humanity, their story the again and again delayed imminent then achieved slitting (at the queen's instigation) of the weakly vicious (heterosexual) king's throat. Its theme is not humiliation but VICTIMISATION. The interludes present THE DRAG QUEEN, artist-hero of Genet's novels, the anti-man, in hatred dedicated to his own beauty, beautiful and/or ridiculous. The last performance was weakened by the huge good temper and confraternity of cast and audience, – in celebration, perhaps, of a march that day:

---

* »I thought you might find it interesting to see some fundamental differences bet. prod. (which I was very unsatisfied with) and script, e.g. my drag queen blocking bet. each episode, much colder scenes as Drag Queen # 3 (p. 13), which John found too offensive. Don't think John understood too well my *shaping*; first time we've had *extensive* differences: my play is a lot *less nice* and *less mild* than *his* production.« (Kenneth Bernard, letter, 7/13/77.)

HOMOSEXUALS- MARCH FOR EQUAL RIGHTS

Thousands Parade in New York and Other Cities Across U.S.

Waving placards and chanting rallying cries, a vast sea of homosexual men and women marched up Fifth Avenue under bobbing banners of liberation yesterday in what many called the largest homosexual rights demonstration ever held in New York City.

The sponsors attributed much of their success to spreading resentment caused by the efforts of Anita Bryant, the singer,

Paraders Jam Fifth Avenue
In New York, where tens of thousands joined the line of march from Greenwich Village to Central Park, the paraders jammed Fifth Avenue from curb to curb, chanting and shouting slogans for equal rights. The police did not interfere with the march – which was staged without a parade permit – and the afternoon was peaceful, if boisterous.

Some Parents Participate
About a dozen men and women carried signs proclaiming they were proud to be the parents of homosexuals.

»I am a proud gay parent,« read one sign held aloft by Richard and Marsha Ashworth of Bronxville. »I am proud of my son – I don't care whether he is gay or straight.«

A flat-bed trailer carried lesbian mothers and their children.

The line of marchers stretched for 27 blocks up Fifth Avenue. Many of the protesters said they had come from the metropolitan area and New England regions. Many embraced each other as they marched, and hundreds wore buttons bearing Lambda, the Greek letter, which has become a symbol of the homosexual-rights movement.

The march began at Christopher Street and Seventh Avenue in Greenwich Village, a short distance from the site of the old Stonewall Inn. Many homosexuals have viewed the site as a symbol of resistance to oppression since 1969, when a riot broke out as the police moved in to raid and close the tavern.

As the march continued uptown, loud boos erupted as the throngs passed St. Patrick's Cathedral at 50th Street, apparently expressing opposition to the Roman Catholic offical position on homosexuality.

(N.Y. Times, June 27, 1977.)

Charles Ludlam, 1967-77. The gesture of compassion.

It was midnight. I had stepped out of a bar in the theater district, and as I paused in the doorway a spectacular woman passed by ... not a woman, I should say rather a cloud of hair, an aura, a whirl of feathers, velvet, sequins and lace. She was holding the arm of a short, gallant, scholarly-looking man, was flicking her boa back and forth, saying in a husky voice, »I think tonight I'll take my curtain call stark naked.«

I watched them as they went down the street. Her head was erect and motionless, but she swayed her hips and flung out her arms in elaborate gestures. Needless to say, this woman was a man, a man who by no means wanted to be mistaken for a woman, and who yet wanted us to realize that he would be delighted to be mistaken for a woman. What strange sanity there was in this! And what obvious obsession! There occurred to me, abruptly, one of those insights one has long possessed, namely, that I was observing, at that very moment, an authentic, if limited, work of art. It seemed, moreover, that this authentic work of art was about to participate in a second work of art, apparently a play. They turned into a doorway at the end of the block. I hastened after them. A placard proclaimed in outlandish letters that *Whores of the Apostles* would commence at twelve, starring Cynthia Gateleg, Mary Ann Moxie, Lamarr, Moonmaiden, Beetle, and among others an actor who had chosen to call himself Duc de Guermantes.

The little lobby was crowded. There was an air of excitement, of connivance, actually. The curtain was forty minutes late. People chatted. At last the lights were dimmed. The strains of *The Star Spangled Banner* burst forth, mixed with a radio announcer's voice, and heart-rending animal cries, as of cattle in a slaughterhouse. The curtain opened. But it would be a mistake to try to describe this play to you. My very memory of it is false to its clutter and grandiosity. Nor is there any way to convey to you the chaste effect of these actors' extreme licentiousness, or the childlike modesty of their headlong plunge into vulgarity. The first setting was of a charnel house. Some six or eight persons appeared in chains amidst skulls and bones, the victims, all, of Maldonado the Second. As for Maldonado the First, his skeleton was prominently, in fact blasphemously, displayed nailed to a cross, grinning evilly, distinguishable from all skeletons one has ever seen by a gigantic, segmented penile bone, erect. The dialogue was bombastic, elevated, decorated with lines from Elizabethan plays, from comic strips and films, homosexual bars, politicians' speeches. The spectacular woman I had seen on the street, her femininity reduced now to an enormous wig, did indeed take her curtain call stark naked, reciting a speech beginning with the words »Devour me!«

And what was it all about, all this wildness and grotesque carnality? Why, it was about the same thing as that little performance I had seen in the street, the performance of the man dressed as a woman, for in fact the

choreography of his gestures belonged neither to the masculine world nor the feminine, but to the world of the imagination. More specifically, to the imagination captured by yearning. Their play-acting was like the make-believe of children, who with a few gestures and rags of costumes, skate as it were over sunlit ice, a ground of infinite possibility; with this difference, of course: that the grown-up actors had chosen a ground of the impossible, one would say the *eternal impossible.* Their blasphemy, their outrageous egotism, their sense of magic may have seemed demonic, but in fact they were priestly figures, they were acting out for us the wilderness of lust and crime against which we experience our social cohesion. In the biblical sense, they enacted the scapegoat. Their method, too, for all its wildness, was a spiritual method: be true to impulse and delight, be true to yearning. It leads to catastrophe, of course, but that was already behind them, for these were not ordinary people. Or put it another way: the catastrophe, already, is behind us all. It is the death of the heart to deny it. And since there is no other ground to dance upon, why, dance upon it!
Yes, I trusted them. I trusted their delight.

My friend George Dennison inserts (American Review 16, February 1973, p. 65-68) this anecdote into the lucubrations of the unfortunate *author of Caryatids,* one of two counterinstancings that this author makes to his own preceding observation that

there are actors who want to liberate themselves, and liberate their audiences – yet they begin with the premise that they *are* actors, or even artists, and they persist in this premise, quite ignoring the fact that serious liberation of the self cannot accept such foregone conclusions. And how pathetic it is, really, to imagine that salvation can be achieved symbolically! (George Dennison, *interview with the author of Caryatids,* ib., p. 63.)

He, Ludlam himself, has compiled all but one of his plays, handing them, typed up by Black-Eyed Susan, scene by scene up to or beyond opening, to the members of his (Ridiculous Theatrical) Company, produced them and staged them, – rehearsed in some actor's living loft, – with himself in a leading role. They have played weekends, often at midnight, in a succession of 8 or 10 shoddy, run-down, small (60-100 seats) houses in Soho, on the lower East Side, around 42nd Street west, generally for half-empty houses, with much of the audience admitted on comps, a way of paying the cast. Up to *Bluebeard,* and some state and foundation grants notwithstanding, no member of the company other than Charles has made even starvation wages, though since *Bluebeard* they have. Charles has kept the company together, – for it has had a continuous core, – by a balance of terror and seduction, and by making it possible for them, appearing in good things, very much to their liking, to become very good. He is an infinitely tricky, guilt-ridden and treacherous, vicious, weak and powerful, charming and lovable man.

The theatre of this GREAT AMERICAN THEATRE GENIUS, after its primitive budding (November 1967 – June 1968), flowered classically (March 1968 – February 1970), for two years (March 1970 – summer of 1972) flourished in vernal loveliness, and held on, its fruit perfect but dry, for a fall of a little over two years (November 1972 – February 1975).

The pubescent Ludlam, actor, deciding in his mid-twenties to direct as anyone might,* irrupted spitefully midnights into the funky play of *Big Hotel* and *When Queens Collide*: transvestite frolic, horrible fun, street-corner rebellion, all guilty innocence. *Big Hotel* (Nov. 67-June 68) is pulled from the movie of almost the same name and is about stars, – the transcendental seediness of glamor and vice versa.** Jack Smith was Mr. X, so slow he was out of this world, Mario Montez the Cobra Woman, Charles, Norma Desmond etc.: the performers seemed to be having a good time, but there was perhaps a marginal feeling they were watching you, – one was waiting for some somber motivations to come out in the open. Instead (*Queens*, New Year's Eve 67-June 68), the play-acting turned into a high-spirited extravaganza: those doing it seemed to be stepping out, and, as they placed themselves, to be standing severally alone (though not separated from . . .) in a high place, in danger of death, and visible. The subject was kings, – the grotesquery of power: Christopher Marlowe in interplanetary space. These plays were endless and had the structure of a firewall collapsing a la Cocteau. They were irresponsible and irresistible.

* Ludlam claims (personal communication, 1968) to have had an acting group in high school responsible for the world premiere of O'Casey's *Figure in the Night*. At Hofstra College, where he got a B. A. in drama, he directed Lorca's *Blood Wedding* (1964), and Elena Garro's *A Solid House* (1965). His first serious directing job (in 1966) was his *Four Pah* (he acted prince Piotr Lopukin), based on Ripley's *Believe It or Not*, done once, at The Bridge, at 4 in the morning (*Lady Godiva* was playing at the 17th Street theatre at the time), at the end of a long program, including a showing of the film *Life, Death and Assumption of Lupe Velez* (Mario Montez as Lupe Velez, Ludlam as a lesbian who seduces Lupe), and a burning of the American flag by Jose Rodriguez Ortero, for which Ortero was indicted. In 68, *Four Pah* stood out to Charles as the kind of thing he really wanted to do, his work with the Play-House as ›the long way around‹ to it, Charles' ideal in 68 being acting having no expressive function relative to psychological character, but acting out – ecstatically – personal and symbolic meanings in contrived disguises, – *Four Pah* made the actors incredibly anxious, he said.
** Cf. Jack Smith, *The Perfect Filmic Appositeness of Maria Montez*, Film Culture, No. winter 1962-1963.

Sofar it was all perfectly preposterous, not at all meant to deceive, totally inept, but all bravura and the performers most glamorous in their imagination, and these five years later I still see the many double images (e. g. Jack Mallory as the gambling man), each over-lapping with itself, held up by Charles like signals along some fast track.

Still in the flush of his first imperfection broadcasting untellable riches, Charles immediately without hesitation entered his Classic period, putting on *Whores of Babylon* (by Bill Vehr) and then *Turds in Hell* (based on an idea of Bill's),* grandiose Christian moralities, personal pictures of homosexual misery in the grand format of existential maps. The party-going camouflage of naive fun shed, no longer a living-out on stage, their opulent disorder, aristocratic crudity, unostentatious shamelessness was the adequate form of a content in ideal beauty, which is why I use the word »classic« in spite of these plays being Romantic outcries of panic anxiety and disgust. The poetic despair of an awful misogyny is passionate *in* their images and their just disorder.

Whores was a gloriously cut-up collage of comic-strip cartoons, – Superboy, Mano, the Emerald Empress (Charles)... Everybody's coming in at odd angles and being located out of place created the effect of a volume of 4 1/2 dimensions: all the little scenes enactments at the same time and in the same space, each one a naive lustre-image like those that candy-tobacco stores formerly sold to children for a penny each. It never seemed to work in rehearsal, and at first turned out a little draggy in places (the queens carrying on out front as the 3 Delilahs), but the stage had become one of the little glass paper-weights with a Christmas or so scene inside that if you turn upside down and back snow falls inside; the inside of the paper tube of a small kaleidoscope resolving the furnishings into diamantine and elegant rearrangements; and a lit-up revolving gigantic ferris-wheel high-turning above the fair, the individual wagons, from each of which you know the rotating scene is different, coming near and shooting away and up. When Charles took it up again late in the following season as a *shadow* play, it didn't seem much of anything either when rehearsed, Charles just decided to open and for the open-ing night Leandro Katz rigged up the lights jellied, and the play, on some screens Ken Jacobs had given, turned out incredibly beautiful

---

* *Whores*, March 22 – early June 1968 at the Tambelini's Gate, 2nd Ave. nr. 10th St. and March – end of May 1969 at the Masque on W. 42nd St. – *Turds*, Nov. 1968 at the Gate, Dec. 1968 – May 1969 at the Masque.

poetry, the colored shadows, – 5 colors as fine as in *Rashomon, Red Desert, Julieta of the Spirits*, – superimposed but not at all quite (the lights coming from different sources), purple and violet, green and yellow (Leandro playing the lights), jumping sometimes, so that the gestures had the most elegantly discreet finesse and poignancy. We all, when not on, stood in the back of the audience watching the Chinese shadows moving, silent music, coming into and going out of existence in the very flatness of image: someone else's dream that, imagine! you have been privileged to see: and when a few of the performers from time to time broke through the self-contained surface, stepped out front and did a scene, it was a gathering of small boys out on the street at night after supper, unsupervised, enchantedly playing something partaking of the nature of ceremony, perhaps standing around a little fire they are entertaining, their faces lit up to the view of a pedestrian pausing in a cross street. The universal unity of the planetary worlds had been rendered visible. The play said that love is murderous, but in the main it turned on women, penis cutters that they are. It followed the regular program of dirty movies in one of the M theatres at midnight on a dead stretch of 42nd Street. Stray drunks would ask if there were girls. *Turds* in a dazzle of naive gigantic illuminations tumbled out the vast panopticon of our earth and hell, a casino run by mother, the stakes of which are shit, her pandering cathouse. The foundering of Charon's ferry (Cleopatra's barge) in a storm on Lethe during a yachting party given by the Duchess de Guermantes, – Proust is Charles' psychologist, – dissolved into an endless, hypnotic underwater ballet out of *The Tempest,* and this into a burlesque of naufrage, the gourmet cannibalism of the shipwrecked. Orgone-baby, »pinhead, sex-maniac,« an infant boy who is a dirty old man (played by Arthur Kraft, – casting that Charles has recently compared to that of Divine's mother, Babs, in *Pink Flamingos*), stumbles through in search of the mother that abandoned him (Jeannie Phillips). He catches up with her on the cannibal isle, and as he is cooking her, stirring the soup, she in the long tirades of *Phaedre,* act. iii, sc. 4 admits her guilty love of him, so much like Theseus his father, when Theseus came, young, to Crete. In *Turds*, the globular cosmos had become unrolled, it stretches, an undulating expanse, ingrained time, on which events of figuration transpire at diverse locations, little flickering flames on a plain, but each a real person living out a whole life (in the forever repeated gestures of his obsession) little wooden mechanical dolls under a vast sky-atmosphere of soundless laughter.

None of these plays sofar had any plot, though they all had super-abundance of it. Instead they were based on incredibly complicated blood relationships between all the characters, implicit, but unknown to them, or known only to some of them and then only secretly. Charles would explain them differently each time, but it was all one family, beset by the danger, nay certainty and even impossibility of incest.

The summer and fall of 1969 were a time of crisis. There were no paying customers to speak of at the Masque in May, the plays had not been reviewed, the receipts went for an exorbitant rent and for ads, people had no jobs or were disgusted with them, Charles did not know where to play and felt his group falling apart, but above all, the serenity of frenzy achieved challenged him to rise beyond expression to statement or even demonstration. By having expressed his Weltschmerz, he had come up with a Weltanschauung, which feels like having nothing to say. A brief revival in June of *Queens*, and a first run of the new play, *The Grand Tarot*, in the fall, quite unfinished when it opened, at a friend's loft and at the Millenium film studio, were mad improvisations, falling apart technically, the bloody explosions of the power of a divided mind in desperation. They were no way gay. Nor were they funny, though they were hilarious. The center of intensity of this *Queens* was a 20-minute long rock and roll (everybody had to play some instrument) ritual birth, an entertainment at the banquet at which the king is to be murdered: Charles as a witch doctor-midwife in the style of the Chinese Opera successively tearing Alice's (Mario Montez as Tamberlaine's wife) 9 bastard planetary babies out of her, throwing each away. At the end of the play everybody has been assassinated. The orgy scene was a more complete compendium of perversions then ever. Charles' Hamlet/Cosroe was some of the finest acting he has ever done. The scene had changed completely. Performers and performed had become nude – but so much, that their skins were the engravings of their nerve-endings, a burning *cloak*, in which they broiled. This torture they feigned to ignore in their languorously busy gesticulations. Hilarious scenes: of secret identities, conspiracies, brutal surprisings and revenges, poisonings: all the secrets, – all the secrets riding the grotesque performer – swelling toward revealment. But when the pustule of this ridiculous pretense – form of the action – breaks before us, it is in the presentation of birth-agony, – and the new life is murdered on the spot. This was Ludlam's wish that the horrors of life might cease uttered, the grand gesture called for: or was it an intuition of his own still birth? I still see the limp dolls he with unimprovable unconcern spills into the corners. No secret was revealed. Instead everyone was silenced. And this cancer of the occult now spread. Something that might conceivably be construed as Ludlam's own operation of reconcealment and repression – quite possibly of nothing much really – or of something already in plain view – was with the ironic cunning of the mad given the public form of a theatre of secrecy. The astrological *Grand Tarot* was a grandiose wreck of a play, – of grandiose ambition. Conceived and rehearsed in a smog of marijuana, it was for a few performances as utterly grotesque as Harun al Raschid's court seen in a small brilliantly festering sore. A great writer, Frederick Castle, contributed lists of words that were never used: each of the major arcanae, avatars of the naibis in 1393 recommended for children, was to have its own language with which to converse with those others that stellar fortune – the cards being thrown at the beginning of each performance – would constellate it with. The scenes and their sequence would thus differ each evening: an insuperable problem as it turned out for costume-changes; and too ambitious an anarchism for this devoted band of thespians. The figures have all themselves turned into walking riddles spelling out ineffable compulsion in indecipherable but meaningful hieroglyphs: encountering untraceable obstacles, they manifest the reign of concealed power. The stage has become very quiet, almost chuckling, and when, once again, there is issue in rebirth, it is accepted with the lyrical serenity of a confession finally consented to after unspeakable tortures. – It may be that this endorsement of life, so adult in appearance, was the moment of Ludlam's failure of nerve: was he not up there crucified? From now on we are confronted by the opaquely glittering surface of high artistry. The hand that opened to reveal its lifelines reclenches.

Charles at this juncture found himself with an asset. His actors had become really good and they were for the most part with him and into *theatre*: Lola Pasholinski, a blonde venus (by Rubens, not by Botticelli), actress of instantaneous resource, sure nuance, great control; Black-Eyed Susan, a touchingly awkward vamp, an intense, powerfully evocative actress; John Brockmeyer, a gentle and sinister cadaverous hulk, a mysterious comedian of astounding comic skill; Bill Vehr, angelic charmer of indefinable youth, an actor of such easy, sustained smoothness and response in presence, that the high precision of his always exact statement becomes almost invisible;

Lohr Wilson, a handsome gnome, capable of investing his performances with an intensely touching sweetness; Jack Mallory, a raw-voiced derelict, on his way to becoming a forceful grotesque character actor. (There had been some defections: Jeannie Phillips, a handsomely forceful Negro woman, her characters naive and disconcerting comic hashish dreams; Gary Tucker, a figure of strong boyish grace, actor of agile charm; Mario Montez, Jack Smith's film star, a gravely sweet man, unique interpreter of his own poetic image; Jose Arrango, an image of the Gothic imagination, evoking suffering with the precision of a dancer.) – On stage, having absorbed their personality into a figure they have made, they appear not real and even strange, but each in himself quite right. Personally, they are courteous, quiet people: by and large, like Charles, of lower-class Catholic origin. – They are not respectable. – The Welfare Department of the City of New York, subsidiser of one-eighth of its population, had graciously consented to the part of Maecenas.

Shifting their diet from pot to brown rice, Charles in the winter of '69 opted for entertainment. The point was to be just funny. What was funny was evident: the ridiculous obscenity of the human race. It needed not be insisted on: a high theatricality in the French tradition, – which would spin off beauty, – would presume it. By this *grand* ambition, Ludlam became a worker, foregoing a liberty and writing off some significances: for form and laughs; and preparing to sink a now matured, grandly sad misanthropy and grudging adoration of life, henceforth to be dimly perceptible as implication of *plot*, below a surface of wrought images. In fact, he stepped out of the Bigtime. His rebellion was over, he dropped out of the rebellion.*
He was now without THE FUROR OF THE FURY OF ADOLESCENCE. And he did not manage, as have other playwrights before him, a transition into classical sobriety.

The skill, intelligence and control of the actors polished the first of Charles' formalist or decadent works, inspired by the Laughton film of the Wells novel, *Bluebeard* (March – Dec. 1970), to such high precision it appeared a splendidly comic exhibition of brilliant stunts, as for instance, the good doctor's i.e. Mad Scientist's – Albert Einstein, Wilhelm Reich, John Neumann, Wernher von Braun, Henry Kissinger, – (Ludlam), – businesslike, studiedly passionate seduction

---

* which, as far as grandiose art in the form of people imitating people is concerned, was continued by John Waters and his group, who by then had made *Mondo Trasho* and were getting into *Multiple Maniacs*.

of his intended victim's matronly high-minded but cooperative cha-
perone (Lola) and cohabitation with her on a relatively small couch
and all over the floor. Horror and pity being so thoroughly muted,
being powerfully insinuated, surfaced only as aftereffects. The
Faustian hero pursues the creation of a third gender (concretely: the
destruction of the female sex) by surgical means: the cosmic principle
of duality in fact precluding success, he botches every job. The successful achievement by the intrepid energy of genius of an unachievable purpose is solidly articulated by three (3) acts, viz.: exposition
of how things are on the secluded isle, and inception, yet once more,
of evil purpose; setting into motion of the necessary means: monstrous
result. The lovely hysterical victim of this Victorian tale (Black-
Eyed Susan) ends up nude with a chicken-claw-and-sponge sex that
she agitates faintly by a visible string. Sexuality is our fate, but we
can't get no satisfaction. The spectacle has changed to pure laughter,
– the content has become torture itself, the central fact. A satin
cocoon of excellent ribaldry so smoothly encloses a black widow
spider you can hardly see the insect move, it does not seem real. The
images, frank and strongly colored, to a closed eye reveal little grey
shadow workmen, moving in the structure of bi-polar procreativity
with delicate impotence, pale fingers of a feeble hand, vainly trying
to fuck up the works, tugging, adjusting. It's all under cover.

After *Bluebeard* had provided two successful, i.e. favorably reviewed
though not remunerative seasons in 1970, – this big dirty town with
exquisite sensitivity will stay away from where its arse is not kissed,
– Charles (in February 1971) reverted to his last frightened reach
for the stars, the *Grand Tarot*, soberly trying to retool it into an
Egyptian follies. At first more the pale Magician's, Osiris' (Brockmeyer) search for his eternally virgin beloved and sister Isis (Black-
Eyed Susan) (she later appears as Greta Garbo in a Lewis Carroll
courtroom scene, refusing to make a statement), the play turned into
the sacrificial apotheosis of the Fool (Ludlam), whom Death (or
Seth, – Bill Vehr) has taught to want nothing and the profession of
being kicked in the arse, essence of all employment, and who is also
Horus searching for his father Osiris. His father repeatedly does not
know him, denying him gently with a kick in the arse, and in a
penultimate passion spectacle au grand decor (Charles' crimson loin
cloth), the son now Jesus, is prepared for immolation. Charles
dropped a last act he had rehearsed, a Day of Judgment, one of the
English Medieval chronicle plays, based on the lovely Matthew XXV

31-46. Instead, the Empress (Lola), according to the Marseille Tarot la puissance passive du Monde matiere, force qui se renouvelle, ends the play by giving birth to an earth globe while singing a hymn to spring. – Though ending up crammed with joke-book riddles, its two jostling stories brutally manhandled by the enlarged part of a Sphinx for Charles' lover, its paleness, – the occult as matter of memory, – was seductive, and the genius and skill, and even more the astrological affinities of director and cast compelled the secret loyalty of the Powers, who infused disconcerting poetry. Everybody was lost and just as in ordinary life everybody was human, star and deity at the same time, and did not know which they were. The sexes can't make it, death vanquishes the son but not the father, all is vanity, life goes on.

Ludlam took *Bluebeard* and the *Grand Tarot* on a starvation tour of Europe, and in September 1971 opened his next play, *Eunuchs of the Forbidden City* (issue of the abandonment of a microbiotic comedy on tong warfare; and based on a trashy life of China's last empress by Pearl S. Buck) in a Berlin cabaret: a starring vehicle for Black-Eyed Susan, a gilded trap in which to expose her weakness. But avoiding the silliness of creating a character and the artistic humiliation of coming on as a star, Susan, by detail work and tight control, underplaying, reduced the female to a sustained expense of will, and rendered a stunning abstract of the super career woman, growing from delicate ambition, sniffing opportunity, to harsh purpose beset by peril, to incarnation of mad power. Though apart from her and the of course generally fine (rather than powerful) acting, the play took on the appearance of a thought- and direction-less procession of mildly funny scenes, scented with sadness, Ludlam's paraplegic logic crept in, overcoming the impotence the play bewails, loosely gathering up its precarious pieces into a surface-image of rule as cancer, enveloping an obscure vision of life. – The empress in a cruel scene wrests from her dying husband the succession for her son, saves her son's life by the sacrifice of her sister's child's life, survives her obstreperous son by giving him the pox, grabs sole rule by poisoning her gluttonous childless sister with monosodium-gluta-mate, but finally in an exercise of the essential female virtue of vanity allows her pregnant daughter-in-law's clever stratagem for survival to succeed. She feeds on the tits of pregnant women, but in the end reveals herself Kuai-non, Goddess of Mercy, protectress of children. Her city, forbidden to men, is the apiarian universe of the uterine power of woman perpetuating Life, the empire of the cold and imperious womb served by a nauseous swarming of devirilised castrates, the Virgin Mother's world of cuntless cruelty. The stage of the court magnifies rejected impotence and self-loathing into contempt of humanity, unshaded by charity, a Catholic disgust by its mercilessness surpassing the acting-style's exposure of all our gravities as a senseless joke. (It is for the sake of this exposure that children love this theatre.) But a marginal hymn to life garlands this medallion of man the monkey, scratching an itch of envy, distracted only by opportunity for vicious games from chasing the spasm in his crotch.

Corn (Nov. 72-Jan. 73) achieved Ludlam's descent into professionalism and ostentatious harmlessness; His plays from now until the end were minor demonstrations of mastery in the genre of burlesque comedy, funny, intelligent, in good taste, excellently acted, with a faint glitter of philosophy. The success of *Bluebeard* generated, up to the unsuccessful 1975 *Stageblood*, the support of the important critics (N. Y. Times, Women's Wear Daily, Village Voice), an uptown middle class audience (the American middle class consists of office employees and ›professional people‹), both queer and straight, and steady financial support from the foundations and government. In the winter 73/74, he took a 3 year lease on the Grove Press Evergreen Theatre, a small, clean place in a quiet part of the Village, at something like 1300 dollars a month. *Corn* was *great* fun, but, whereas up to the *Grand Tarot* the pleasure of reincurred intoxication was ever undiminished, nobody would have wanted to see it more than 2 or 3 times, for there was no evil in it, none of those sloppy crevices through which Ludlam once seduced you into the fissures in your soul in which incipient truths lurk, unguarded by definition. Wrapped into the twang of insipid Country-Western (as *Eunuchs* had been packaged in B'way sets and costumes), whose idolatry of simple folk its stage-image inverts into the total caricature of Lower Slobovia and Tobacco Road, it was a crafty exercise of entertainment, a knot of plot, a deft concatenation of the millenial burlesques of low comedy: all surface, and to my mind not (as Robert Wilson ventured) profound surface. It transported *Romeo and Juliet* into the hill-country where Paw Hatfield (Ludlam) and his two boys feud with Maw McCoy (Brockmeyer) and her two girls, everybody getting married in the end, a Pyrrhic victory over artfully ill and hating parents. There is a brilliant poetic invention, a scene in the language of flowers with translators, and the play is a small masterpiece of comedy, in two scenes (a doctor's diagnosis, a moonshine jug drinking contest) rising to the level of the early film comedy shorts, i.e.

the absolute level.* With nothing on the tiny stage, the acting, take-offs on the media, was everything. It was vigorous, nuanced, anciently traditional, refined to the perfection of crudity, Vehr with the discreet elegance of lassitude did a night club comedian's act on a city slicker, sleaze throughout, Ludlam clowned out his comic-strip character with the (slightly tired) routine of a burlesque comedian touched by Buster Keaton, Brockmeyer did a female impersonation, by its rough and subtle naturalism of type-portrayal transcending the genre into stunning low-comedy character-acting, Black-Eyed Susan did her part as a grotesque, a clinical study of a hill-country degenerate, her stunted body malformed in a feed-bag dress, with tics, twisted, compressed lips, squinting eyes mimicking timidity, pretense

* Lola-Lola (Lola), the star with a golden heart – country-western singer, – local girl that made good, – is returning, accompanied by her agent, Dude Greaseman (Bill Vehr), to the place of her birth, Hicksville, to check if her roots are real, and to stage a mammoth jamboree. Here the immemorial feud between the Hatfields and the McCoys is being continued by Maw McCoy (John Brockmeyer) and her two daughters, the brazen hussy Melanie (George Osterman) and the shy deaf-mute Rachel (Black-Eyed Susan), and Paw Hatfield (Ludlam) and his two sons, Ruben and Moe, women against men, the younger generation somewhat unwilling participants, in fact Ruben loves Melanie (love scene: »stop, don't – stop, don't – stop, don't – stop – don't stop«) and Moe loves Rachel (they declare their love to one another in the language of the flowers, Lola-Lola and Greaseman acting as intermediaries, since Moe doesn't know the language.) Nothing will do as site for the jamboree but the joined cornfields of the Hatfields and the McCoys, now separated by a wire fence, so Lola-Lola undertakes the seemingly impossible enterprise of getting the owners into a joint venture, deciding, after initial rejections (the rejection by Paw Hatfield ends a moonshine jug drinking contest between her and him, won by her,) that to get her site she will have to settle the feud. The lukewarm feuding spirits of their children have made Maw and Paw take recourse to illness, sentimental blackmail; equally disgusted by the doctor's opposite diagnoses, – (Lola-Lola, still drunk, disguised as Doctor Skinner, with Greaseman as nurse Parker, who has, unlike the doctor, had the benefits of a college education, and who smokes the cigar from which Greaseman the agent is inseparable, diagnoses Maw as very ill – her right arm is sucking the life out of her left, her right eye is taking all the vitamins out of her left eye, the arm has to be amputated, the eye removed – and Paw is in perfect health), – they call in Aunt Priscilla, the very Christian faith healer (Jack Mallory); Aunt Priscilla partly cures their hating spirits by diets of corn, giving Paw Hatfield, Rachel McCoy (disguised as Shaker) as nurse, and Maw McCoy, Ruben Hatfield (likewise disguised as Shaker): a spanking from their children finally (?) cures them; everybody gets married, including Paw and Maw, though in the meantime they have taken to their nurses, a joyous square dance is followed by the jamboree, Lola-Lola as finale belting out a song in which she rejects Greaseman's marriage proposal. Rachel has been cured of her muteness, her first screeched words exhort her new husband Ruben to get to work. Lola-Lola is told by Aunt Priscilla that she is the love child of a Hatfield and a McCoy. Ruben turns out to be a McCoy, Rachel a Hatfield.

grown into disease. Lola Pashalinski, her face by make-up vast and vastly insipid, a wholesome homeliness transfiguring into colorations so superb it was simply glamorous, composes the star of another time and another medium (popular song) as seen through the shifting screens of still two other media (film, musical comedy) out of a dazzlingly intelligent run of exact pastiches: an incredibly empty warm smile of the mouth, flashed on and off, or rather »placed« and combined with a head-stance of appeal, studiedly abrupt transitions from down-to-earth practicality, even downright shrewdness to high sentiment, poetic outlook, innocent nostalgia . . . . a living searchlight on the vileness of commercial entertainment commuting it into art. A great performance.

But beyond its reference to the media (baser and more vicious now than ever), which it plunders, reviles and out of which it composes a high art of performance, the play was nothing. Honorable by the intransigent contrast of its sheer fun to the corruptly ideological (and morbid) fun of the media, it totally refused (unlike Ludlam's earlier shows) to use the medias' symbolism to engage us in the realities of our existence.

The central theme of the Greta Garbo/Robert Taylor *Camille* is the redeeming power of pure love: a fallen woman, wooed by a lover bearing her a pure love, is redeemed into transcendent nobility by her pure love for him. The acting, directing and photography show their love to be not only pure, but irrational and absolute, interminable except by death, its fitting issue, an absolute separation precluding carnal consummation. One is surprised to realise that this outlandish concept of love, at first sight only a convenient fictional device for serving persons of the female sex, is indeed classical romantic love, the love of Tristan for Iseult, etc. One instantly, automatically, with the superficiality of alienation, has shoved away this ideological bit – just another component of the movie's evident trashiness, mendaciousness, something not to be taken seriously. It is astonishing to realise that there is no indication that while Mlle. Gautier may have been frigid as haetera, she comes with Armand Duval, or has any kind of vivifying physical response: no friskiness, no teasing, no giddy gaiety, no rosy blush momentarily enhancing the spreading flush of consumption, no tendency to cling or touch, – and no silly cockiness on his part. The story is spiritual and that is the essence of it. When Taylor for the penultimate time redeclares his love for Garbo, the close-ups of her face signify that what matters is that it is her face, that unique person's, and that his love is for the person within, above, transcending the flesh, a love for this individual as such, who has irredeemably captured one's total capacity of devotion for persons of the opposite sex, and even capacity for being interested in them: sexual attraction being at most a minor component of this fixation, – though of course a previous scene has suggested that in view of the coarser and more violent male nature, male love of woman does have this side of physical passion. The beauty of Garbo's face, – a little peaked, a little dry and hard, – stands as a spiritual sign of her absolute value for her lover. The evil lover, the Baron de Varville, goes for her beauty and for the charm of her healthy sanity, frivolous gaiety and generous kindheartedness: but true love is beyond such tenderness of infatuation with externals.

Inspired by the fact that it worked on the screen, Charles Ludlam adapted the play to himself as its star and ran it in the spring of 1973 at Mrs. O'Hare's 13th Street Theatre between 5th and 6th Avenues. The way he did Marguerite, – out of sympathy, – cleaned the story of its moralisms, but, with only a slight shift of emphasis, kept it a paean to pure love: though in the form of low comedy. His magnificent acting achieved this implausible result by alternating rapidly between drag-queen impersonation and a milking of the part's sentimental potentials. He did the former when Marguerite quipped, showed her common sense, or acted the haughty cocotte with her butter-and-eggs man, de Varville, the latter when she related to Duval pere ou fils.

The shift is from the transcendental absolutivity of pure love, its mystique, to its tenderness and sacrificial nobility, its psychology. The naturally loving but much misused creature responds to a man's true love, but after a brief moment of happiness, she, – motivated by her boundless love for him, – gives him up, and resumes a frivolous and unhappy life of degradation, and one that is bound to give t.b the upper hand over her: for the sake of his family's respectability, of his career, and of the happy marriage of his pure young sister. She goes to her death within the year. Ludlam's sentiment conveyed the tragedy, nobility (moral beauty), and above all, the grandeur of her love. His irony absolved us (and him) of some of the shame of sentimentality, allowed us to be moved. His intelligence focussed our tenderness on nobility of sentiment.

The drag-queen act is fun for the numerous queers and faggots in Ludlam's audience. He half-pretended he was a drag-queen, which he isn't, and he did a drag-queen: drawing humor from being in reality a man; by incessant movements of his body under his clothes, nervous petty gestures of the hands drawing attention to it, glances checking up on whether it was getting the attention, turns of his hipbone polishing it against the stream of our attention, stances that put the length of the front of his body on exhibition, identified himself as, qua woman, sex-object (thus identifying woman as sex-object par excellence); affected the bitchy lassitudes and elegancies of a superior sex-object, an object of worship and desire; expressed the enjoyment of this power. An element of caricature implied the drag-queen's envy (and resentment, even hatred) of the sexual power of women over men, his acknowledgement of their preeminence in exercising this power, and in misusing it elegantly, – hinted that he was himself subject to it, not entirely insensible to their sex appeal.

The erotic, civilised lust, is being or having a sex-object, and becomes pornography only in art treating its conflict with civic respect and dignity as degradation. His act combining life and art, the drag-queen obtains and (to those that find him attractive as a man) gives the erotic pleasure of sexual objecthood, tainting it with the contempt for women implicit in his caricature's point that their sexual objecthood is degrading. Ludlam, in doing Gautier, a high-class whore, as drag-queen, only dallied with this contempt: imitating star actresses of the theatre, unhappy artists lording it over their philistine audiences, he parodied not Woman, but the aggressive status-mannerisms of hardness and disdain of some upper-class ladies and their middle-class imitatresses. He made no effort to make up for beauty: he looked old and ugly in the part: there is no question of his transvesticism's making the point made by George Osterman's Nichette, namely that I – or a man – can be as pretty and alluring as any woman. It was not a way for him of appropriating female sex appeal. Nor did he get any sexual kicks out of it, unless it be a masochist kick from being degraded by garments and mannerisms madly inappropriate for any sexual role he could conceivably manage. Ludlam's transvesticism was a sadly humorous invocation of the erotic: it was about the uses of power. Since female power, a compelling aura of the body in space, a waiting stillness, a contained revelation, coldness in heat, is the cerebro-glandular product of a marriage between womb and psyche, men find it easy to parody, but hard to simulate. Homosexuals in particular, who have anaesthetised themselves against it, can hardly even distinguish its presence (which they or at least the drag-queens among them tend to identify with the limited appeal of sexual object-hood) from its uses, – put-downs, invitation, – in bargaining and blackmail,

– or from the gestures conveying sexual objecthood. Ludlam as drag-queen pretty much confined himself to these uses and gestures, which, divorced from that manifest power, did not have much reality or interest, even when imitated (parodied) with Ludlam's excellent artistry.

But the vamping and the bitchery in this play only served as frame for sentiment, as ironic setting for sentimentality. They were interspersed with innumerable, rapid, isolated but classically pure pastiches of sentimental film poses, – the large pleading eyes glancing obliquely, the bent head, the hesitant voice, the pose of gaiety, piteous vanity, childlike anticipation, infinite longing, wounded pride, desolation of rejection, – largely dating back to before Ludlam's birth, the classic repertory of gentle pathos, of sentimental stances, gestures, intonations and facial expressions, that the movies of the first half of this century had taken over from 19th century theatre, a repertory, by the way, not much utilised by Garbo, who acts in a truly realistic manner. The vagina's appetite makes the heart noble: these poses were softly beautiful formal distillates of truly noble sentiments. Ludlam's unadulterated and precise rendition of them moves us to respect, admiration, sympathy and pity. We see Gautier as a pathetic creature, but a noble heart. We become sentimental.

Sentimentality is a predisposition to uncircumspect, though conventionally prescribed, feelings of tenderness of a mild and approving, though possibly compassionate sort, more indulged in for their own sake, i.e. with a degree of hypocrisy, because they feel agreeable and reflect credit on oneself, than stimulus to generous action. Gautier's love for Armand might be considered sentimental in that Ludlam neither portrayed it as grand passion nor evoked the classic mystique of love, but acted it as response to love. But the play was not about the nature of her love, left out of his portrayal, but about her self sacrifice. Neither Ludlam nor his Gautier were sentimental. They were hardheaded, but given to strong feelings, – his Gautier to strong feelings of tenderness, on which she acted strongly, – and this play might be considered a forceful action of his, stimulated by a strong tenderness for the figure of a fellow outcast, fucked over all around, by the Duvals no less than by her paying customers. But the play and the way Ludlam does Gautier are sentimental in the sense of being designed to appeal to sentimentality. He advertised it as »*Camille*, a tearjerker.« He chose not to do it in the grand style of violent passion. He suppressed the dialectic of sex and sentiment. The dirty joke that has made Norman Mailer famous is told at a mildly riotous dinner party, at which Lola Pashalinski (playing Prudence Duvernoy) displays red panties, and there is a brief and hilariously overcharged, – essentially pathetic, – s and m scene between Gautier and de Varville at the piano, but there was no dirty stuff in the play, and the only intrusion of sex was an instant access of hot lechery of Gautier's the moment before she died, – the mini-affirmation of life which Ludlam usually builds into the tragic endings of his plays. Only the drag-queenery was erotic, – abstract recognition of woman's sex appeal as sex-object, concrete only as a painfully weak and distorted male sex-appeal of limited appeal.

Remarkably, the sentimental appeal of Ludlam's clean and pure sentimental poses, – not camped up, neither exaggerated nor twisted, nor played in quotational style, – was not destroyed either by their being recognisable derivatives from films shown at night on TV, and from old films at that, that is, in a style of expression gone out of style in art and in life, given up together with the ideal of woman as fulfilled by her sacrifice of herself to man and procreation, nor by their isolation in an ornate setting of stridently ambiguous poses of enviously competitive, ridiculing adoration of woman as powerful sex-object. This artificiality and this setting of his sentimental style did not destroy its power to move us by making it itself ironic, but affected us as an irony directed at the conventionality and hypocrisy associated with sentimentality, i.e., purified it. They left the play a tribute to tender love and loving generosity, by their ridicule distancing it from the passé sacrificial ideal of woman, twin of the pornographic version of the image of her as sex-object, conventional and hypocritical ideal to which an unalloyedly sentimental treatment of the corny story would have been a tribute. Instead we saw a person victimised by bourgeois hypocritical convention. The frosted window of sentimentality was opened onto a landscape of noble sentiment.

Ludlam's achievement as person and actor seemed so remarkable to me that I have neglected everything else. He wrote the play for himself, so he didn't give anybody else much of a part: which made the others' strong vignettes the more remarkable. Brockmeyer beautifully sketched de Varville as the baron Charles. Lola Pashalinski and Black-Eyed Susan, casting vanity to the winds, made up for and played ugly bitches, – Susan in the unsettling hysterical style she first developed in Corn. Bill Vehr out of almost nothing gave to Armand Duval an appealing and quiet presence invisibly holding the play together. Callejo's pretty sets in foreshortened perspective gave to the tiny stage a claustrophobic spaciousness. My wife, Mary

Brecht's costumes, beautiful and ridiculous, with exquisite sensitivity supported the individual characters. Acting, sets and costuming combined into a disturbing image of the tenderly noble heroine's passage through a world which, though peopled, by and large, by gentle friends (even de Varville comes across with a final New Year's gift sent from afar), is a callous and dangerous world, glittering coldly.

Ludlam's artistic career seems to have ended with *Camille*, – at least that's how it looks as of this writing (in 1977). His imagination having failed him some years previously, the burden of supporting his heart had been on his intelligence and now his intelligence failed him. He could no longer make his brain work for his art. He found himself without the energy for thought. I would say that what happened was that he found he NO LONGER HAD ANYTHING TO HIDE, – and thus found himself deprived of the GLEE OF HIDING: and found that it had been this glee that had pumped energy into his intelligence. His work had consisted in hiding, – not in revealing: I would say that was how it had felt to him. But somehow the secret had slipped away, – not revealed, exactly, just disappeared. Perhaps there hadn't been any. Nothing seemed sacrilegious anymore, – or even shameful.*

The (February-March) 1974 offering was *Hot Ice*, done at the company's own house, the Evergreen, and modelled on the last 20 years' TV and comic strip serialisations of the big city's police department's fight on crime, with some reference to 1930s Warner Bros. gangster movies: specifically, Cagney's *White Heat*. The title blinked in neon outside. Ticket prices ranged from 4 to 6 1/2 dollars, the program came in On Stage, publication of the Special Program Department of American Theatre Press, Inc., sets and costumes (there were no sets to speak of, the somewhat dull, comic book science

* In 1977, New York, despite last minute vicious insinuations, elected a bachelor mayor living in Greenwich Village, who in the 3rd week of his administration ordered the fire and police departments not to keep homosexuals out, and appointed as Cultural Affairs Commissioner (budget, 24 million) the star of Warhol's first movie (Soho Weekly News, Jan. 19, 1978: the film was of Geldzahler brushing his teeth), narrator of Ludlam's garter-and-stocking movie *Up in Svetlana's Room*, – first shown during Miss Stalin's passage through New York, and projected against the backdrop during the hell orgy scene in one of the productions of *Big Hotel*, – performer (with Vaccaro and Claude Purvis) in Ludlam's unfinished high porno sex-and-violence film *Gooseflesh* (Vaccaro: »he looked like Queen Elizabeth ... like a plain old whore really ... that's what Charles wanted us to be ...«), living with Christopher Scott (performer in *Big Hotel*, *Eunuchs*), patron of Edward Avedisian (who did the sets for *Hot Ice* and *Caprice*), and of Tom Schmidt.

fiction costumes had been gotten up by the cast) were credited to one
Edward Avedisian, ›one of our leading young artists,‹ and were reported to have set Ludlam back 5 grand worth of foundation money,
the cast had been expanded to include various inept members of the
Manhattan queer set, attendance, helped by a good proportion of
uptowners, was good, the reviews were almost all raves. Tomkins
reports 84 performances.

The forces of life, represented by the C.S., the Cryogenic Society,
a gang of maniacal criminals headed by the epileptic Max Mortimer
(John Brockmeyer), son of Piggy Mortimer (Robert Beers), currently
on ice in the vaults, periodically, to his son's discomfiture, thawed
out by his widow Irmtraut ›Moms‹ Mortimer (Lola Pashalinski), the
power behind her son, are battling the briskly efficient forces of death
represented by the E.P.F., the Euthanasia Police Force, captained
by glamorous Tank Irish (Richard Curry), whom we see on the
department's regular TV public service program promoting death:
a bunch of guys, – good boys, – such as rough and ready Lt.
Sczutcareski (Jack Mallory) and Buck Armstrong (Ludlam), the
department's clean-cut trouble-shooting hero. The highly sexed, a
little crude and suburban, widow Mrs. Romona Malone (Black-Eyed
Susan) comes to the E.P.F. (in the opening scene, Tank takes her
complaint in a joke-book-jokes interview) with a plea for help. Her
marriage contract with her late husband, in effect annulling ›till
death do us part‹, has obliged her to conserve him posthumously:
the C.S.'s inflating storage charges threaten her with the loss of a
diamond necklace, surrendered to them as security for her payments.
She wants it back. Buck, – the kindling romance between them will
have to be put off till the emergency has been met, – inducts her
into the force (she has to do some slimming down exercises to get into
the uniform), – and obtains her heroic consent to being used as decoy
(which since she has to simulate death quickly eliminated her from
the play): he is going to take her to be frozen. A 9-inch radio-
transmitter secreted in her vagina (Ms. Malone: ›I can handle it!‹)
will lead them to the secret storage vaults. While Buck, posing in an
Afro wig as an Ordinary Joe, – Puerto Rican refrigerator repair-
man, – consigns Ramona over to Max, Max has an epileptic fit. Buck
becomes pals with him by taking his absent mother's place in admin-
istering aid. (When Max has a fit, he turns into an erection, needs
to have his neck massaged till the spit dribbles white from his
mouth.) The C.S. happen to be having trouble with their refrigeration. Max invites his new friend to the crypt to see what he can do

about it. Piggy, apparently chairman emeritus of the C.S., is letting Max' vulgar girl, – moll, – a common tart, Bunny Beswick, wear the jewels. Moms, jealous, has a fight with Bunny. The E.P.F. are waiting back at the station. The boys are drinking beer, playing cards, talking about pissing:

Lt. Sczutcaretski takes a piss into a butt can upstage. Buck is now in the crypt with Max, Bunny, Moms (who is horrified at his admission) and the bandage-swathed, supposedly defunct Ms. Malone. Trying to delay the injection of the freezing fluid, he induces Max, quite enamored of him, – Buck has fixed the refrigeration system, – to expound to him his professional ideals. In a lovely tete-a-tete Max explains to him that his dream is not so much human immortality, as, more modestly, survival for the length of a Platonic year (= 9940 solar years), unit phase of cyclically repeating history, thus providing mankind the indispensible basis for rational action, knowledge of its fate. The E.P.F., having in a dramatic scene wirelessly traced Ramona's transport to the vaults (which turn out to be located in The Tombs), in the nick of time burst in on them on their red unicycles. The general confusion is confounded by Piggy's appearance, thawed, he lurches off the service elevator, a bundled-up, snow-covered mummy, Captain Irish with the aid of a magnifying glass establishes that he has turned into a mere vegetable. Ms. Malone recognises him as her late husband. Moms makes a plea for him: he knows so much, they should all learn from him. The captain and Buck, disgusted by his abnormality, shoot him even as he starts spouting learning. A debonair narrator in black leather pants (Bill Vehr) having previously distinguished two branches of modern theatre, the Ridiculous Company now, enacting them both, offers alternate endings. In one, the E.P.F. and the C.S. in a shoot-out kill one another off, in the other, the American Medical Society Inc., a conglomerate, takes over both. After Buck, he-man, stuns her, smashing a bottle over her red E.P.F. helmet, he carries Ramona (who has retrieved her jewels from Bunny), off, his woman.

A lady from the audience protesting, on behalf of her mother, an elderly lady played by a female impersonator, against what she sees as a callow endorsement of euthanasia, at one point interrupts the performance and is allowed on stage. Having induced her mother to join her up there and having introduced her, she makes her point by describing how her mother recovered from a state of near-total invalidity to an active life of mentally defective teaching of children. (Everyone stops acting the play during this audience-participation and acts out various attitudes, – irritation, boredom, interest, – toward it. After the lady and her mother have been induced to regain their seats, everyone acts out having trouble getting back into the play and Ludlam, acting the director, has to coax them, – suggests they try the Stanislavsky method.) During the intermission, the mother demonstrates her recovery by conducting a bingo game, the prize being the poster for the show, autographed by the members of the company. At the end of the play, the protestress regains the stage for an apology, she now thinks that both sides of the question have been fairly presented. The narrator squashes cream pies in her and her mother's faces. The play, its dialogue mostly quips and gags, was fairly funny, – faintly subversive, but in a *way* so it could almost still play in the blue-collar suburbs. These infinitely contemptous off-spring of the hard hats don't see life so differently from their parents.*

As in the earlier plays (no longer in the next play, *Stageblood*, the mode of which is anticipated by the acting during the arranged interruption and in Ludlam's Ordinary Joe and when Brockmeyer explains his philosophy), the individual is resolved into a few essential relationships, notably that to parents and the sexual ones, – not psychic modes, not character, but a bent in a milieu and a situation, – these relationships structuring a role-playing role modeled on media-representations: the caricature-role a transparent robe over those naked universal relationships. As in soap opera. But whereas hatred animates the role-eulogising cynics who write the soap-operas, Ludlam's contempt is compassionate.

Ludlam's, Black-Eyed Susan's and Brockmeyer's acting was superb. Lola curiously had not arrived at settling on a role (she spoke of the character of Mr. Christopher in *The House on 92nd Street*), remained somewhat weakly suspended between a Jewish mother, a bull-dyke and Ma Barkley or the Outlaw's Outlaw Mom. In various ways these 4 performers move their bodies as the stems of flowers grow, slipping them into supportive stances for their faces, on which the play takes place in a succession of slide-projections, their expressions: Ludlam making more use of his blue eyes, Susan and John of their mouths. The verbal wit attaches to these colorful faces like tag-lines. Mallory, his part as small as ever, densely projects all the unwieldiness of his personal integration. He is the only one of the old crew that has not become proficient. He was the only *interesting* performer in

---

* The same is true of Waters' movies: apparently the cops etc. don't bother them too much when they shoot on location.

this show. – Osterman, best of the new people, did a younger urban variant – drop-out rather than high-school – of Brockmeyer's tough bitch in *Corn,* with more brio than power, no detail rewarding or inviting attention, let alone inspection. Beers and Currie were as lifeless and shallow as in *Corn,* playing thin roles thinly and without bite, Enright, female cop, ragged rubber tits prominent, just did a transvestite bit. His make-up was nice, – borrowed from Divine. The new girl in the company (she didn't last), Susan Kapilow, younger than Black-Eyed Susan, with a magnificent pair of breasts, high even under her red chest band, enthusiastically playing the South American Lady with the Poodle who mistakes the cryogenic establishment for a pets' beauty parlor, did the normal off-off-B'way imitation of B'way. With all these people there, the stage got a little crowded.

There was no great part. Nor a set of cameo parts as in *Corn* or even *Camille*: somehow the energy for bravura precision hadn't been there. Beyond the fun and the routine brilliancy of the acting, the company's poignant fatigue exemplified the play's tragic theme of mortality.*

*Stageblood,*** a not altogether ridiculous because somewhat sincere *Hamlet,* dedicated to the insincerity of the actor and to the love homosexual sons bear their ridiculous fathers, a brilliantly tightly scripted and directed (it lasts only a little over an hour) slight witty improvisation, acted with fantastic eptness, – its composition and rehearsals were said each to have taken only about 3 weeks, everyone

* Ludlam blamed the play's not so hot performance on Walter Kerr. He dropped it, did – during the summer of 74 – *Camille* instead.

** »Stage Blood* ran for three months. But I got a feeling of disappointment from the audience. They'd come expecting something else – expecting a product, something they were used to from me. Nobody was in drag in *Stage Blood,* although the Hamlet character, you feel, turns out in the end to be homosexual. I love the play. It wasn't really finished when we opened, wasn't really together. Nobody really got the idea that it's a play about an actor who is reluctant to play Hamlet. I've done a lot of work on it in the meanwhile, and I can't wait to try it again. Such amazing things happened when I was writing it! There's a speech that I do in my dressing room, that I took from Joyce's *Ulysses* and changed around – about the relation between a father and son. »The son unborn mars his mother's beauty: born, he brings pain, divides affection, increases care. He is a male: his growth his father's decline, his youth his father's envy, his friend his father's enemy.« And at that moment the ghost of my father appears to me. I'm nude – I'm changing from my street clothes, which are all black leather, into the black Hamlet costume – and my father appears and touches my hand in that gesture of Michelangelo's God in the Sistine Chapel, and he delivers a speech from Kyd's »Spanish Tragedy.« It's the same speech that Joyce was parodying in »Ulysses.« He says, »My son! and what's a son?/A thing begot within a pair of minutes, there about/ ... Methinks a young

97

(the cast was pared down to the 6 regulars) had their roles down right off, Charles hardly had to direct them, – opened (at the Evergreen) Dec 8th '74 and folded February 9th '75. Though not *exactly* an excellent play, well digested in the scenes, set down with as much modesty as cunning, nor as wholesome as sweet, it didn't please the million, was caviar to the general: Ludlam blamed the deficient attendance on an unpleasantly tight-arsed review by Julius Novick in the NYT of Jan. 12th; but I think the reason the play flopped, apart from Ludlam's lassitude in the fashioning of it and his exaggerated reliance on his public's familiarity with *Hamlet*, – it is for Charles *the* play, – he identifies with Hamlet, – was that Charles and the company in a break with their tradition in their own queer way acceding to Hamlet's request not to split the ear of the groundlings, lay off the overdone and the come tardy off, but to hold mirror up to nature, in *Stageblood* took a turn toward realism (of settings and characterisations), thus disappointing their public, come to see players that, neither having the accent of Christians nor the gait of Christian, pagan, nor man, would so strut and bellow that one might think some of nature's journeymen had made men and not made them well, they imitate humanity so abominably, i.e. come to see the old company. The straights missed the grotesquery and outrage, the gays the camp's reassurance that being queer is gay and is not merely the same old painful and sad human condition of bondage, so the word of mouth was poor.

Stageblood is a clever inversion of *Hamlet* inasmuch as while in *Hamlet* the play is staged in the service of real life, to scorn the image of virtue, – Hecuba's instant Senecan clamor, fit to make milch the burning eyes of heaven, commanded to reflect on Gertrude's wicked speed, and *The Murder of Gonzago* rigged to probe the recent shenanigans at court, – in *Stageblood* life is staged in the service of the play. Since the inversion serves to express Ludlam's Wildean ideal of life, that it serve art, his satire had to fail him in a play about players.

A lovely double set by Bobjack Callejo of a bare, constructivist *Hamlet*-stage and a miserable cluttered dressing room with photos

bacon,/Or a fine little smooth horse colt,/Should move a man as much as doth a son;/For one of these, in very little time,/Will grow to some good use; whereas a son . . .« And suddenly, when I was writing this, I remembered my own father saying, »Children! I should have raised pigs, I'd be better off!« The real murderer of the father was me – killing my father in fantasy, working through and finally forgiving him. It was a milestone for me.« (Charles Ludlam, quoted by Calvin Tomkins, *Profiles/Ridiculous*, The New Yorker, Nov. 15 1976.)

tacked behind the mirror, open toilet, mounted on a rented turntable was turned by hand by Gibbs the stage-manager. The costumes, rented B'way cast-offs, were appropriately theatre-tacky.

The company arrive chatting, camp on the deserted stage. Carleton Stone (Jack Mallory with a grey Vandyke, in his first big part since he was promoted to be Bluebeard's housekeeper) has brought his theatre company to Mudville (U.S.A.): they are to open that evening, with *Hamlet*. Stone (to play the part of the Ghost) has fired their Ophelia, but a local girl, stage-struck Elsie Fey (Black-Eyed Susan), entering through the audience in her raincoat presents herself, (with beautifully stilted awkwardness, but intermittently in a poetic rendition of the part, reputed not much to Ludlam's liking) auditions as the mad Ophelia, gets the job. She strikes up an arse-sucking friendship with Mrs. Carleton (Lola Pashalinski, under the stage name of Helga Vain playing Gertrude) and takes to the gentle, somewhat glibly easy, blandly open, a little sad and cynical Carleton Stone Jr. (Charles Ludlam) who, the company's (blond-wigged) Hamlet, is to run through their scenes with her. Carleton Stone Jr., a homosexual, in the course of the play develops an affair, – at one point, for the benefit of his novice lover by him termed ›an experimental relationship,‹ – with the more neuter than straight, serious and somewhat tempestuous Jenkins (John D. Brockmeyer), the playwrighting stage-manager of the Carleton Stone Company. Jenkins is anxious to have his first enormously long modern play played by the company. Stone Sr., Stone Jr. and Jenkins have different conceptions of theatre, Stone Sr. calling for grandeur, the high emotional tone, Stone Jr. inclining more like Hamlet to elegance and moderation, – Jenkins is a modern. Mrs. Stone, we find, is having a fiery love affair with the somewhat vulgar and pushy Edmund Dundreary (Bill Vehr, the Claudius in their *Hamlet*), a practical joker. Their love-making, he is gently whipped by her while eating her, is the only thing shocking remaining in this play.

The plot develops backstage during the evening's performance of *Hamlet*, of which we now and then hear a declamation or see parts of a scene, either full out or from the wings. Stone Sr., bloodied head in the toilet bowl, is discovered dead in the dressing room. Helga and Dundreary immediately commence scheming to have Dundreary rather than Stone Jr. be the new manager. Stone Jr., distraught, incidentally trying to fend off the usurpation, is the only one anxious to discover the culprit, suspects his mother, her lover more. (Everybody suspects everybody in turn, when questioned freely admits to the murder.) The practical joker plays his practical jokes (an excellent comic effect contributed by Bill Vehr.) A certain Gilbert Fey (Mallory), an older, somewhat phony-seeming gent, not unlike Polonius in his shiftiness and indignant moralising, claiming to be Stone Sr.'s brother and to have brought up Elsie Fey, whom he discloses to be Stone Sr.'s abandoned daughter, shows up, demanding of Stone Jr. that he prevent Elsie from embarking on the immoral career of an actress. He says he knows who killed the old man. They strike a bargain: in exchange for Mr. Fey's telling him who did it, the young man will, by a feigned brutal callousness disabusing her simultaneously of his love for her and of the romance of theatre-life, get Elsie to quit the company, abandoning her ambitions. The young man, at one point almost mad with grief, indignant at the others' lack of concern for the defunct, keeps his side of the bargain (though Elsie unexpectedly turns out attracted, even aroused by his brutality, to her a sign of his passion), and after various other scenes, including a rather tender though by no means sentimental one between mother and son (he is as little shocked by her affair with Dundreary as she by his homosexuality), and various impersonations of the Ghost, – sometimes there is more than one, no one knows who is filling in for Stone Sr., – Mr. Fey does too, revealing himself to be the murderer, viz. Stone Sr. in disguise. He had faked his death in order to enable his son to identify with his part, precondition for a valid performance according to his, Stone Sr.'s though not according to his son's conception of the precepts of the profession. Elsie in a bathing suit, turns out to be his young mistress. Dundreary is demoted for his scheming. Jenkins gets his script accepted. Everyone is happily paired off. The father triumphs.

The play is superficially in the forms of 19th century provincial melodramas and of the 20th century movie representations of those that performed them. Insofar as it borrowed popular-culture forms and mocked them, it was in the tradition of the company. But, and probably not only because of Ludlam's veneration for the great play he persiflages and his feeling for the truth and poignancy of the psychology of its family-schema, or just because his inversion of it, making the court the mirror of the theatre, made it a play about a theatre company, i.e. about his and the company's own way of life, but also because in New York in 1974/5 something prompted the innovative theatre that had developed during the 10 years preceding in the direction of the conventional, the company instead of ridicule, in its characterisations attempted a sympathetic realism.

Neither Ludlam nor Brockmeyer played a faggot or a gay, nor even a queer. Ludlam played somebody who is queer, quite simply, gently, masculinely and Brockmeyer a quite normally male-acting feminine person who may become a closet queen or just an inhibited straight. This was the first time either played a homosexual. Their portrayals were delicate and true to life: Jenkins' self-contained feminine sensibility under a Calvinistically stern exterior, shyness masked by aggressiveness; Stone Jr., a tortured, embarrassed young man, genuinely open and friendly, though a little theatrical, affectionately under the domination of his father, attracted to and repelled by his big-breasted, powerful mother. I was immediately struck by the finesse of Brockmeyer's interpretation and execution. His performance got a little less fine, a little cruder in the course of the run, – possibly because, with the whole company, the play not doing too well, and the venture into the life-like being frightening, he kept trying harder to play it for laughs. Charles' performance at first impressed me as glibly trashy and brash both by an excessive boyishness and by its audience-directedness and its humble exposure of the person of the actor to the audience (i.e. to the audience of *Stageblood*). He often goes into his parts unprepared, in a half-improvising manner and his performance may actually have improved during the run. But mainly I think it was that I simply didn't realise he was trying out a realistic style of acting he hadn't attempted since he escaped the tutelage of the Hofstra College Drama Department, – and along this line was giving a portrait of an actor who's an actor off-stage also, – plus was complicating this by a partial caricature of a certain variant of conventionally realistic acting, often indulged in by older, tired and somewhat vain actors of the pre-method Stanislavsky school, defined by its pandering camaraderie with the audience. I now think of it as having been good and courageous acting. Vehr played in his usual excellently subdued style which allowed him realistically to intimate the callousness, meanness, superficiality and crudity of Dundreary by mere nuance. Pashalinski with less exaggeration and with more transitions than in her wont style gave a rather naturalistic portrayal of a tired, hard-bitten, ripe woman and professional hack-actress in love. Mallory, whose part of old ham invited caricature the most, abstained from it: the occasional hollowness of his lines was plausibly in character, and similarly for Black-Eyed Susan, whose acting oddly enough, perhaps because her part was not strictly that of a person *in* the theatre and was at the same time most purely a cliché, stayed closest to the company's old style of acting.

After the show closed, they thought of reviving *Eunuchs*, – there was the theatre rent to be paid every month, – and started rehearsing it, but gave up the idea and put on *Bluebeard* instead for an 8 week run, opening after a week of previews, April 18. It received good notices and was as good as ever: its acting style as when it was done previously. Its high points were perhaps a little over-elaborate and rigid. In March or so, foundation subsidies started coming in again. Ludlam intended to work up the next play, *Fashionbound*, at a workshop they had contracted, one of a group of avant garde theatres calling itself The Bunch, to give at a theatre festival in Connecticut. They lost the Evergreen Theatre to the Bahai Church, their last performance there Nov. 20, 1975, a one-night gala, $25.– a seat, consisting of scenes from 11 plays they'd done, plus one from the forthcoming *Caprice**.

Ludlam had started his (Professor Bedlam's) Saturday afternoon *Punch and Judy* shows (›Kids $1. Adults $2‹) some time before *Stageblood* opened and kept them going through and after the run of the play. They were quite witty, noways nasty audience participation shows. He provoked the kids and managed to be really funny

* *Caprice* ran to empty houses first at Schechner's Performance Garage, then at the Provincetown Playhouse, Feb. 10-April 30, 1976. It was followed by a 3-hour Wagner-parody, *Der Ring Gott Farblonjet*, which opened April 14, 1977 and soon, supplemented by an equally once-a-week revival of *Stageblood*, was restricted to one showing a week: they were getting the Truck and Warehouse Theatre for free and the point of the showings was to qualify for grants the next year. The plays closed at the end of July 77. For the *Ring*, Charles had expanded the company incredibly (to about 17 performers), – rehearsal time was paid for! – $85.00 a week, after deductions, maybe more for the many stars. The grant money was flowing on a Wagnerian scale. It was the first play of his Charles wasn't in, tho after a while he took on 3 small parts. Both shows were pathetically unfunny, – naked personal disasters, the products, it seemed, of a brain afflicted by paresis. *Caprice* had the designer Poiret (played by Charles) for its subject: I could not say what its theme was, certainly not the power of a homosexual man over women, certainly not the ridiculousness of fashion. To make a hero of Poiret, Charles had to make him a victim: but this yielded no sense. Charles' *Ring* made nothing of Wagner's denigration of the commercial way of life (the curse on gold, the loss of love): partly perhaps because Charles' feelings about money and commerce are quite positive, partly perhaps because his feelings about love are quite ambiguous. In between, in 76, Charles worked as a script writer for Adele Holzer, a dealer in plays, cars and other commodities whose returns on a $50.000.–, investment in *Hair* were reported to have been $2,000.000.–, and who has since pleaded not guilty to 137 counts of grand larceny, falsification of business records and violation of stage security laws. The Paul Taylor Dance Company's *Aphrodisiamania (A Macaronic Imbroglio After the Commedia Dell'Arte)*, scenario by Ludlam, opened at the Brooklyn Academy in November 77. I didn't see it. Dec. 77 – Feb. 78, Ludlam with Black-

talking back to their back talk. Judy talks a little like Bette Davis, Punch hates the baby and is *really* a bastard: Ludlam makes it his job to engage the audience's sympathy for him.

Black-Eyed Susan in the winter of 74/75 thought she'd like to extend her acting in the direction of doing characters in the round and that acting classes at the Actors Studio might help her. After *Stageblood* closed, Brockmeyer started rehearsing her and a friend of theirs in the *Woyzeck* murder scene by the lake. She auditioned, – 5 minutes, including the time for setting up, – but was not accepted.

Bill Vehr on Groundhog Day, – also James Joyce's birthday, – began a serial weekly reading after *Stageblood* performances of *Finnegan's Wake*. Most of the company, some sexoid street people, Stuart Sherman, – an audience of perhaps 2 dozen, – showed up for ch. 1, section 1. Vehr came out with a nice clean copy of the book in his hand, smoking a joint which he passed around. He had Gibbs take out a smoky-yellow projector that was in our eyes, sat down on a crate center-stage with 4 jellied lights bracketed on him. His presentation of himself was in impeccably good taste, he is elegant. There were almost no slips in his reading, no gestures of apology for those there were. With not untoward youthfulness, the audience chuckled at terms conceivably having sexual de- or co-notations. Bill read the text marvelously, as a straightforward, old-fashioned (perhaps 19th century) literate tale, – emotional, even sentimental, of some savagery. As he read it, with a warm flourish, with few gestures, the tale and its catalogues made good sense, the over-lay words (a childishly mechanical way to improve on language, get away from the embarrassment of plain fiction or account) presenting a super-tale, weave in many a tale, the large body of Finnegan-Gulliver overarching the Europe-Minor, marginally Celtic, stubbornly marginally Celtic, settling down in 566 A. D., and in 1132 A. D. still, little darling Annie dancing in the upper right-hand corner or the lower left-hand corner, all the little people bustling about fleshily and the greenery

Eyed Susan and a dummy, Walter Ego, in sundry Village night clubs (Reno Sweeney's, a weekend and a week, The Bottom Line, The Village Gate, –3 weeks) did a superb ventriloquist's act/play, a one hour comedy horror routine in the 1940s radio show style: the sleazy, nervously sincere entertainer (and earnestly devoted husband) becomes obsessed with the fresh, sexy little dummy, and, liberated from its domination by his wife's dismembering it, turns into it, insane. This stuff goes back to the beginnings, – the psychotic shaman-trickster's impersonation, awkward, ingratiating, feeble and powerful. Like his ancestor, Ludlam held his awful earthbound audience: caught it. A night club comedy routine is the purest form of the performing artist's workaday confrontation with death.

of wood leafy all around and over. It's curiously easy, as soon as and as long as one concentrates, to catch the splintering crystal showers of meaning. Bill stuck to a straight, simple, word-exact-pronouncing reading of tale as tale: no leers, no avant-guardism, no significant expressions or emphases: perfect great artistry: simple acknowledgement of the greatness of great language, Joyce's or Shakespeare's.

Charles afterwards said, ›makes one want to write.‹ The kinship (his to Joyce) is there in their child's elevation or their childlike elevation, ironical, above Culture (Literature). And his earlier things, like all of Joyce's in their Catholic death-minded savage despair of guilt, gave an immigrant's equivalents of Joyce's warm music gathering up Old Europe into a Breughel dance/Irish wake of a peasantry's milling about, dirty, smelly, farting, sexy, dirty-minded, warm, quick, in color.

Ludlam's genius as an actor is in the totally energetic facetry, each facet, cracked or murky, radiant, of his portrayal of social conduct as a face of single asocial purpose: the many human masks of the monkey. The insincerities succeed one another with incredible rapidity, each totally true to ludicrous nature. That the rapidity of succession of complete gestures of hypocritic concern is incredible means (1) growth, transition, continuity of the character are intercepted, and (2) no putting on of any mask of covenance is observable. Thus on the one hand we are prevented from assuming a sane natural man in his various outward turns, on the other, we cannot discount these grimaces as mere artifice. Hypocrisy thus is presented as the nature of social expression itself, intercourse as insincerity. It is the ability of the actor scared into his wits that provides this frightful comment: less ability would not. We see him mastering his insanity, for instance (in *Bluebeard*): so rapidly that the sanity required for doing so is clearly insane.

Ludlam's actors must shed the reticence of irony, abandon the poetic refuge of indefinable style, bear up under the vanity of their wish to be beautiful, etc.

Not only by point-by-point, to-the-point directions, but by setting up the requirements in the parts relative to one another, Ludlam demands of his actors that they strongly define each expression of the moment as a stance, unashamedly facing the final simplicity, idiotically poor, of all definition; and then that they *do* it.*

* The American movies from the 20s to the 40s, clean of the pretension to a spirituality intimated by an appearance of complexity, taught this art. To begin

The audience is to *get* what the expression *means*: this can only happen on the instance. The actor has to be frozen into it on the spot, body, voice and face impregnated with this single gesture. He has to have his mind made up what he is is going to do: specifically, at this point, next ... Clear perceptions of what he is doing will tell him what he is going to show (express): not vice versa.

He conceives an appearance. He can then proceed to work with it. Being, for him, to begin with an external image held up for an audience, it is intrinsically exaggerated: it is to stand up. For a moment he has to fill it altogether, if he hangs back, loath to lose himself, it slackens and is gone, never was there. But he enters it like it was a colored diagram in space and time, i.e., can leave it instantly. His work is primarily bringing up the definition, getting it into focus for an audience; then enlarging it. When the actor gets good, not only can he do this materializing with a continuum of personal elegance, some care for his person, with a degree of playful pleasure and fucking-around quoting from the history of theatre and screen: but he can start ragging up the edges and superimposing images on one another. It's a strange art. One strange thing about it is that even the audience it works for, a poetic audience, the child not yet finally suffocated, is apt not to realize what is happening to them: they see and keep seeing a bunch of clownish performers, some more awkward, some very skillful, while all the time these really colorful pictures are building up and moving, but as though somewhere else, detached from those performers, to whom nevertheless they are grateful. This capacity for conjuring up detached fantastic images seems to distinguish the theatre from the movies: the challenge posed by the actor in person seems so to outrage our imagination that it can perform this feat: whereas the actor's photo on the screen slips right into it, ready made for it, prefabricated day dream. Ludlam uses the *freedom* of this power. ✦

The expressions are chosen like colors in a make-up kit. They have been used many times, in front of the film camera, on the stage. They are conventional – have become explicitly conventional – designations (as in some manners of Asiatic theatre). Of course there is an

with, the actor knew he had to impress a camera! and retakes and cutting cleaned out fusking tentativeness. It was not enough to be interesting. The cheapest American brands are still the best, they have a little flavor left. Those stars showed the truth: the lies we live. Cf. Jack Smith, *The Perfect Filmic Appositeness of Maria Montez*, Film Culture, No. Winter '62-3, on the grandeur of these clear-cut phantasy-images, all aspiring emotion.

art to this. Not only must you not fumble in putting one of them on or taking it off, must know how your hand goes with what intonation, how your body might turn with that look so that none of you is a blank at any time, but you have choices, the text being *all* sub-text, so you have to use your head to figure out what's going on between you and the other actor at this point.

Ludlam's work, because of its beauty, artistry, humanism, comprehension and its comic and theatrical excellence is the finest form of ridiculous theatre. It stands by itself.

This is a poem I wrote for Charles' *Whores*:

Ludlam's Projection

SHADOWS cast
by a small portion of the sun's limb,
from opposite sides,
alternately. On the other hand, the earth
is the shadow-casting body,
and the moon is the screen, and
we observe things according to our first point of view:
here
the picture has ceased to be one of the sun,
it is now a picture of the window. But if the wall
could be placed 100 yards off
the picture would be one of the sun.
. . .
The apparent rapidity of motion of this phantom
may exceed in any ratio
that of the spectator
– enabling us to see how
velocities,
apparently of impossible magnitude, may be accounted for
by the mere running along of the condition of visibility
among a group of objects
no one of which is moving at an extravagent rate.

Ronald Tavel 1967-1973.
Cleverness: the disgusting use of language.

In 1965, Tavel was the Warhol dramatist in residence. He did the
scenarios for what were, except for *Harlot* and *Drunk*, Warhol's first
sound movies: *Screen Test Number One, Screen Test Number Two,
Life of Juanita Castro, Vinyl, Suicide, Horse, Bitch, Kitchen.* His
Warhol scripts, directed by John Vaccaro 1965-7, also became the
first plays of the Playhouse of the Ridiculous.* When in 1967 Vaccaro, because the language, Tavel's preoccupation, got in his way,
decided not to use a play Tavel wrote for the theatre, – *Gorilla
Queen*, copyright 1966, a fart-sniffing jungle-extravaganza, in March
1967 staged at the Judson Church by Kornfeld, – its smart repartee
is a fine example of Tavel's neo-Joycean enterprise of decomposing
speech into obscenity, thereby to show that the mind is filthy (rather
than lewd, say), – this broke the liaison, and Ronald's brother Harvey
staged one of those Warhol scenarios, *Vinyl,* based on Anthony
Burgess' *Clockwork Orange,* and written for Gerald Malanga, who
starred in the film, – at the tiny Cafe Cino (November 1967).
Vinyl was a sadist spectacle that worked: it excited. A moral play.
It moved quickly to r and r: two simultaneous happenings very
skillfully arranged in an altogether small space perhaps 10' by 12', to
one side a continuous highly formalised mime of torture, to the other
the action, including a dance. The actors were in black, there was
an impression of plastic, the play had the quality of ballet, its action
was fated, routine. Except for Mary Woronow, the actors were
neither here nor there, hardly actors at all. Their awkwardness and
that of their lines was almost redeemed by seeming almost a formal
aspect of this equation of a culturally deprived subculture with the
culture. An analysis, a qualified endorsement of the Hell's Angels
scene. Woronow, in a uncalculatedly childish manner, acted out the
ice-cold sadist (»Doc,« representing science, social science, welfare
therapy), the fiend is enjoying himself, – cerebral sadism, e.g. de
Sade's tends to childish fantasy.
The protagonist, »Victor,« is a child of nature, the cool head of a

* We presumably owe Tavel the information in the program blurbs of his '69 *Boy
on a Straight-Back Chair* (copyright 1966, based on a Life magazine article, directed for the American Place Theatre by John Hancock) and his '73 *Secrets* (cf. infra)
that he »founded and named the Theatre of the Ridiculous movement« in the
summer of '65.

gang of j.d.'s (junior delinquents), a vigorously terroristic hood and sodomiser, dancer, music lover – he's »beautiful.« Provoked by an ugly pig in his gang, »Scum,« losing the fight (he fights clean, the other dirty), delivered over to the police, arrested and convicted on a charge of music loving, he is restructured into a good boy, i.e., a masochistic and impotent victim, by therapy consisting in Doc's torturing him sadistically while showing him T. V. newsreels of riots, fires, etc. The cop and Doc are themselves members of the gang. The background mime of torture coincidentally with the main action transforms its book-loving victim, »Pub,« into a hood.

Script, directing, acting oppose good to bad sadism: the anarchist Victor's expression of vital energy and sexual spontaneity, the infliction of pain as condiment and reaffirmation of a masterly imposition of individuality is contrasted to the gang members' ugly, purely vicious, dumb sadism, substitute for sex, infliction of pain for the sake of enjoying the helplessness of others, affirmation of power. The essence of Society, the play's protagonist, is this latter, negative because negational, joyless sadism, its essential objective emasculation. The monologues, somewhat submerged by the defiant power of the superb staging, express these ideas by Burgess' jejeune philosophy of free will.

The power and direct appeal of the play was sadist or sado-masochist, which is not the case with Genet's works. Since this appeal is not specific to the positive species of sadism distinguished, the play was ambiguous in the manner of the vitalist ideologies of Nietzsche and Italian fascism. Like Victor we were shown images of torture: but for our delectation.

March 1968. Ronald Tavel's *Shower*,* and together with his *Cleobis and Bito* (directed by Ron Pratt), at the Extension on East 7th Street, a tiny ephemeral club. Harvey Tavel directed it. He's obviously a talented director: it was a quick, chic show.

In the first one or two previews, Ondine took the lead part, »Mark Stark.« Coolly modest as actor, not so much *shoulder* as Cosroe in *Conquest*, good delivery, he gave the image of a cool son of a bitch, – and of a person as totally evasive as really only nobody could be.

---

* *Shower* was originally done with The Life of *Juanita Castro*, by Vaccaro at the Dakota Gallery in the spring or summer of 1965, and after 6 successful performances taken to St. Mark's Playhouse, where Vaccaro says it flopped. He also says (1968) that he thought both plays atrocious, scenarios rather than plays, that he staged them as underground movies: the projector breaking, going too fast, too slow, people are left in the dark ... and did *Shower* as spoof on James Bond movies with »Brechtian interludes.«

No faggotry. Harvey Tavel who replaced him was too nervous to act. Marti Whitehead as »Terrine the terrible tart of terracotta« did a female counterpiece to Ondine's Mark, also with real elegance, though not quite as strong a personality. The show owed much of its attractiveness to her mostly wearing only panties. Though some might have thought her breasts not firm enough, her arse too broad and a little flat, her waist not narrow enough, and her sides a touch too fleshed, her most pleasant wifely body with her witty face made a show in itself. Ray Edwards was quite funny as »Dick from the Delicatessen,« and everybody really quite quick, funny, – drawling disdainful, threatening, inviting, – smart in the sense of »are you trying to get smart with me?« – wiseguys. The surface-tough, rasping sound of New York was counterpointed by the slapstick burlesque showing up everybody as Shlemiel: a Jewish concept.

It's a love story with a happy ending. The Tart has with undying hatred been looking for the guy that took her cherry and then dropped her. She discovers that Mark, a pick-up, is him. He swears he has been looking for her all this time, – to return her cherry. As he searches for it in his pocket, she swoons, and when she comes to, she knows she still loves him, he's the only one. A love song ends the show. Hatred = love, love = hatred. – The play is a spy melodrama. Everybody while making everybody is spying: extracting confessions, imparting bits of information. The secret is who is spy MX-35? The information always is about the play, – who is playing what part.

The dialogue was an exercise in the pseudo-wit of smutty puns, the author's attempt to elevate the speech of the boroughs into art, an art that would provide a kind of entertainment. This art, though like Oscar Wilde's an art of speech, is literary rather than theatrical in that, a play on language, it focusses the audience on language rather than character, and does not create tension or advance action. The puns hinge on meaning, a not too clever double entendre, but Tavel is stuck on sound, addicted to alliteration.

The object of ridicule is the womanising tough-guy. His women here are tarts or bull dykes. Everybody except Mark (who has Terrine in a shower) is making it with the giant »Miss Termite,« a tough dyke contemptuous of men. The play *uses* Whitehead's body as Warhol uses females, not like burlesque used to do: there is an element of humiliation in her half-exposure. I.e.: the men are the ridiculous fools ridiculed, the women are strong personalities, but the women are put down as females.

There are two showers on stage and the characters keep taking showers. There is no symbolic or other significance in this.

Some plays* of Tavel's were produced during the late 60s, he revived some during the early 70s. *Boy on a Straight-Back Chair,* which opened at St. Clement's Episcopal Church in February 1969, but dated back to 1966, saga of an electrocuted All-American-boy-murderer of girls, adored by the local ladies (he had what it takes) wasn't trash.

Tavel's *Secrets of the Citizens Correction Committee,* presented at the same place in October 1973 showed that wit is not just a matter of nerve. Unwilling to exploit his compassionate insight into the teenage rebel's truant mind, – cf. in this play f. inst. the kid's reiteration that something, whatever he did, was boring, – Tavel persevered in directions he has closed to himself, humor and poetry. Really aspiring to grace of image (e.g. the final oratory of »The Kid,« figure of a rational psychopath, variant of the leads in *Vinyl* and *Boy,* well played by Ben Morris Kushner, a student at the High School of the Performing Arts, who last year made his »professional debut« (program) in Tavel's *Bigfoot*), he settles for the awkward clichés of dreamy poesy. His word-substitutions (in the official speechifying of »Mrs. Fugelman,« principal of a public school for disturbed kids, avatar of »Doc« in *Vinyl,* e.g. »degeneration« for »generation« in »the next generation«) are always »clever,« never clever. They are his own malapropisms. One senses the constraint of a lack of intelligence on his imagination; and the *will* to be clever and poetic. Like Harry Koutoukas, he is vulgar. The pointlessly harsh images or turns of speech are thrown in as though sops to who might think him goopy, assertions of a right to displease (he will be loved even so). His moving compassion for the young in the grips of sadist parental and state authority, not the less beautiful for its pederast tinge (the young to him are boys, parental and state authority are personified in the mother, the female principal, the female psychoanalyst, and their authority is bent on demasculation), is marred by his liberal pose. The play is no cry of rebellion. Tavel *deplores.* In fact he means to perpetrate on the English language the outrages his junior heroes, our graffitists, muggers, gratuitous arsonists, commit on persons and property, identifying with them in the

---

* Gino Rizzo, in one of two eulogies in the Village Voice of March '69 with some brilliance making much out of nothing, calls these plays, – *The Life of Lady Godiva, Gorilla Queen, Arenas of Lutetia,* – »camp epics,« a »sudden explosion of a mock-heroic genre« and »put-ons.«

theatre, without taking their risks on the streets. He must thus not *allow* himself to be funny, poetic or intelligent. To defile, he must stay vulgar. This ambition is not without nobility. The vulgar, witless stance is rebellious.

The Kid tells of bombings, visits to the movies, of getting his mother arrested for his crimes. The principal lectures evilly, whips the boy's genitalia (»Whips courtesy of the PLEASURE CHEST, 152 7th Ave. South«) to »decentralise« him, masturbates while he tells her of his mother's nightly sexual usage of him. This main largely spoken, action alternates with mimed minor actions, a series of visits to the movies of »The Stud,« during which the stud establishes his sadist dominance over the girl, arguments among the obsequious teachers, queen Elisabeth's receiving the homage of a crowd, while members of her guard faint away, penis in the air. This interspersed minor action has no plot-relation to the other, relates to it by their shared identification of authority with sadist oppression for the sake of sexual exploitation. The play thus falls apart into talk displaying Tavel's writing and adventitious illustrations of his anarchist contention. Its other technical fault is that the representative of authority is a caricature (which the director forgot to carry to the extreme of hysteria), while the victimised youth is real-life.

Tavel's *(How Jacqueline Kennedy became) Queen of Greece*, presented in November '73 by Theatre Genesis at St. Mark's in-the-Bouwerie Church, was another display of Tavel's wit. One out of 30 quips got near being either a bon mot or an epigram. The desperate urgency to act mordantly witty, to cut, and thus to rise above the dirty streets, negligently, on wings of elegance slightly soiled by a species of street toughness, coarseness, together with a grotesquely assured assumption that everybody or everybody worthwhile, i.e. getting into the news, is queer, defines the role of being a queen. When the defensiveness of an author's assumption of the role inhibits his intelligence and insight the resulting theatre is saddening and yet obnoxious. The unpleasantness of faggot theatre (R. Tavel, H. Koutoukas, Harvey Fierstein ...) is not that it is nasty (in this play the tough Ms. Onassis is the object of the bitchery), but that it is a plea for pity advanced on the grounds of one's being pitiful. It is *intended* to be a series of failures. The author's (or actor's) display of himself as pitiful, – e.g. lacking in wit, or being grungy, – is to express his sense of failure. Neither homosexuality nor its voluntary display as one's identity constrain to obnoxious pitifulness or pitiful obnoxiousness: there is gay theatre, cf. infra the Hot Peaches.

Centola, the Hot Peaches.
Dialectic of the ambition to be beautiful.

Gay theatre to charm the gay nation (though everyone is welcome)
with the phantasy of glamor reflects the nations's anarchy and
sadness in a mirror of gaiety cleansed and polished by Gay Liberation: The Cockettes and the Angels of Light, San Francisco troupes
that visited New York in, I believe, 1972, utterly charming, but of
course, being from out of the Big City, utterly empty-headed, – the
Hot Peaches.
The first Hot Peaches show I saw was their 9th, *The Magic Hype*, a
musical comedy done November 1973 in a loft at the lower edge of
the garment district. Touching Minette, queen of Brooklyn, recently
busted in a Supermarket for selling slugs serviceable as subway
tokens, is their musical advisor. Mascot of Ludlam's company, he
now flies as guardian angel on their wall, or as fairy queen, scattering a golden dust. Mario Montez is wardrobe assistant. Music and
costumes are fabulous. There is a piano and tape off records, everybody sings, everybody has a song, – old-time *swinging* music, as those
bastard black to white cabaret blues of the 20s. The gowns, 7th
Avenue specials and slinky originals, everyone changing costumes
often, make of the stage a compact garden of exotic flowers, each
unique, but what's stunning is that camp (camp as play, the style of
this group and the point of this show: not camp as mask) isn't
everything: the initial costumes of the 3 innocents that the play is
about, »Flame,« »La La« and »Harlow,« as they set out on the stations of their crucifixion* are gay and handsome child-hippie
outfits, their subdued colors faintly conveying the tragedy of clown-
ing, and their clothing changes progressively.
The play's language is a very light, elegant street language all its
own, metaphorical before it is anything else, though (never coarse or
lewd) and heartfelt, absolutely real in the beat of its declamatory
flow: nobody is posing. The sisters may be right or wrong, but they

---

* Their vocal leader Flame, when »Randy Whorewall,« playing the Herod to their
Christ, doesn't want their own phantasies for his commercials: »Some thanks. You
work your way up through the palm parades and last suppers, giving them your
body and blood and they try to nail you before they even offer you an
easter egg for your efforts.« Perhaps Catholic boys often see themselves as the
crucified son of man. Numerous allusions show that Centola wrote it with this
parallel in mind. At one point Harlow claims that she »fell for, lost and found
Flame again,« as »Mary Magdalene in Ophelia drag.«

are talking to *one another*, and to the point, spelling out their complaints, giving their advice. Obviously such sincerity and insight can not be sustained in real life, at any rate not so compactly and elegantly. Centola's script really dances.

The hero of the play, »Flame,« remotely a Christ figure, played by Ian McKay and representing Jackie Curtis, is a speed-freak. We see him shooting up with a large crude red and tinselled wooden hypodermic syringe in the shape of a cross, when he is making up for his appearances as star in »Randy Whorewall's« (played by Robert Arr and representing Andy Warhol) commercials. The magic hype he is shooting up on, face to face with his own image that he is *making up*, is illusion, the illusion that *it's the illusion that counts*, the illusion that he is that image, a star. Randy Whorewall, the play's antagonist, is the exploiter of this illusion.

Warhol around 1965* discovered the addictive ingredient in stars. He found that not only are stars among the industrial commodities whose use-value is a product of consumer phantasy, a phantasy that publicity can addict to a given brand of product, – stars can be made, – but that what addicts the consumer is the quality of stardom itself. The capacity to sustain an image (talent) or to project it (personality), denotation of a sexual or social *virtue* by the image, long on the West Coast considered essential, were dispensable! He set out to isolate this ingredient, succeeded, proceeded to market it under the brand name »Superstar,« – Warhol's Superstar. Superstar is star of extraordinary purity: there is nothing in it but glamor,* a compound of vanity and arrogance, made from masochist self-contempt by a simple process of illusio-inversion. The commercial advantages of this product originated in its area of manufacture: the raw materials, any self-despising person, were cheap, and the industrial process simple: to make the trash just *know* he or she is a fabulous person envied to adoration. You didn't have to teach them

* Ondine, one of Warhol's Superstars and a talented actor, is quoted in S. Koch's *Andy Warhol's World*, as saying of the period late '65, early '66: »At that point in my life, in everybody's life, that was the culmination of the Sixties. What a year. Oh, it was splendid. Everything was gold, everything was gold. Every color was gold. It was just fabulous. It was complete freedom. Any time I went to the Factory, it was the right time. Any time I went home, it was right. Everybody was together; it was the end of an era. That was the end of the amphetamine scene; it was the last time amphetamine really was good. And we used it. We really played it.«

* Glamour ..., sb. Also (obs.) *glamer*. 1720. (Corrupt f. grammar. Orig. Sc.; introduced by Scott.) 1. Magic, enchantment, spell. 2. A magical or fictitious beauty attaching to any person or object; a delusive or alluring charm.

anything. If the customers would take them for a star, they would be a star: if they were a star, the customers would take them for a star; if the customers would take them for a star the customers would be fascinated by them. Exposure would turn the trick. Here again Warhol's true genius for abstraction paid off: he invented a camera-technique that was nothing but exposure, and simply, having made himself the first superstar, utilised the superstar's public sycophancy to himself as advertising for the superstar, gave them exposure by association (at Max's Kansas City, an arrangement of mutual benefit to himself and the restaurateur). An aspect of his industry that paradoxically turned out a further advantage, a managerial one, was that, while Superstar was fully as potent as the adulterated brands, – stars with an image that stood for something, – it wasn't as addictive. The public loved the individualised images of being worthless, – no fucking good, – but instantly tired of the individualisations. Warhol continually had to work up new people. But this carried with it the benefit of the company's not having to contend with the exorbitant demands of fixed stars. Rather they had to be junked almost instantly. Centola, representing labor, the raw material of the industrial process, calls this tragic.

Warhol's earlier shooting stars, tragic beauties* and non-beauties with a college background,** were fag-hags, female impersonator impersonatresses. Later they tended to be trade. He switched from classy to tacky trash, – real people, street people, with whom Centola's sympathy lies more especially. But Centola's concern is for all the kids crowding into the discotheques decided to make their beauty known, showing off their little tits or their chests, acting out, by their disdain and phantastic *apparel*, some strange being they don't quite themselves know what is, except that it is them because they have created it, and the point of which for them is (1) that it is strange so that they escape definition, (2) that it is trash, defying everybody's demand for sexual and social virtue. »Take your phantasy and make it real,« – the youth rebellion's counter culture.

Gay theatre, entertaining parade of female impersonators liberated from their coon-status in burlesque shows for straight salesmen, stages the party-parade by which drag-queens realise their phantasies. On the rock-scene, not a fashion show, but theatrical forum of the white teen-age rebellion, phantasy is realised more grimly (because the kids haven't left home and because their competition with one another

* Cf. appendix I.
** Cf. appendix II.

is not fraternal), but less sadly because, though sexual definition is among the imposed definitions they are rebelling against,* they are for the most part making it with the other sex rather than failing to grow up by making it with their own, – which doesn't make Jackie Curtis less their spokesman. After all, what original point can a 14-year-old or even a 16-year-old make by posing as a man or a woman?

Since everybody is beautiful, being a beautiful person of your own making is not an illusion even when it is a matter of dress. But since this is no mere masquerade, it is apt to become illusion through the narcissism of identifying with one's image. Having (1) created a beautiful appearance in terms of which you wish to be accepted, you (2) separate it from yourself by thinking of it as how you appear to the intrigued and admiring others, make of it an image external to yourself, and (3), the lethal step, now re-identify with it, not as appearance of your real self, but as thing real in itself, real in the others' charmed awareness, – becoming that thing, a corpse in glad rags.

This transformation of a realised phantasy into an illusory identity happens to stars. Warhol manufactured his superstars by doing it for them. It may be no illusion that one is a star, incandescent in glory, for there are thousands of little stars. The illusion is that *one* is that star. For one has vanished and is nothing, – or if not nothing at least not real, for one acts out the phantasy of others. Telling drag-queens not to fall prey to the illusion that they are women, Centola is telling us all not to *lose* ourselves in our realised phantasies. His show warns against acting the star only because it makes a zombie of the person, and attacks Warhol only as representative of the institution promoting illusion, – commerce.

Seated at a dressing table, Flame is making up as a beautiful woman, trying on wigs etc. He is facing us, there is no glass in the big mirror, it's just a frame, distorted into a triangle and dressed in gold, – he is using a shaving mirror on the dressing table, inside the frame. He is humming to himself, the piano is playing. But he is not very satisfied with the results. A divided plastic curtain bunches to both sides of him, the stage is open, the same not too clean concrete floor our chairs are on continues under him a short way into its depth, various advertising signs are visible in the dark there.

* Whence Jagger, Bowie, Alice Cooper, the New York Dolls, symbols neither of bi- nor of homosexuality, but of prancing maleness refusing definition. – Cf. appendix III.

After we have been allowed to watch this extremely relaxed scene, – informality marks the show, – for quite a while, the front drop, a crazy quilt curtain, is drawn, but reopens almost immediately to reveal »Silva,« a tall thin queen with an elfish beautiful triangular face, dressed in a childish imitation of a golden priest's robe, standing in front of the now drawn plastic curtain. In a spaced-out voice he announces that it is time. Taking a small basket off a table, he tells us he is about to hatch 3 easter eggs he has just laid. Flame, La La and Harlow, making chick sounds, become visible, billowing out the plastic curtain from behind, we see them emerging from the cocoon. Silva tells us they will travel to earth to become superstars. Curtain.

»Talukas Harrymore,« »queen of the theatre,« representing Harry Koutoukas, a pretty, puckish boy, appears in front of the curtain, delivers a prologue as though telling a fairy tale. It is about a poor little rhinestone (there are no stars, only diamonds and rhinestones), who goes to the big city: commercials have convinced him he can become a star by using the right deodorant. The theatre draws him, a perfect showcase for his brilliance, but he doesn't want to act, that's work, he wants to shine. He is discovered by someone that can make MONEY off him, making him believe he is a diamond, that he can shine like a real star, Lana, Clark, Bette. Knowing you can't push rhinestones as diamonds for very long, the man dumps him. He tries to make it on his own, puts on a play for himself to star in. But even if it's a hit, it fails, because the little rhinestone refuses to do the work of polishing on himself that would really make him glow. – This is the fable of the play.

The next scene is in The Streets. Flame o.d. 'd that morning, Harlow tried to gas himself. They discover La La, who likes to drink, lying there without her bottle, having been mugged and beaten up. La La is a sweet- and plain-looking boy. His character in the play is that he is timid and clumsy, couldn't possibly sing or dance. Harlow, petite and pretty though big-nosed, is a self-centered fool, a transvestite acting the lady. He is powerfully able to fool himself. Their clothes are scruffy, Harlow is not yet in drag. They are in the pits, but there's got to be a way out. They will ask Bella Della Bossum, who's made it out of the pits. They take turns singing this scene's song, *The Pitts*, La La acting the one that can't sing:

When life is funky, starting to stink,
One thing can save you, diamonds or mink,

It's time to call it quits.

THE PITTS !

Look all around you, what do you see,
Your name is not on that movie marquee
And life just ain't a series of hits.

THE PITTS!

. . .

Look at them out there, watching our song,
Come on let's tell them, what can go wrong?

Although it's rough to bear,
You all know why you're here,
Cause you're all out there . . . stuck in the PITTS.

The next scene is just Bella (Wilhelmina Ross, perhaps representing
Mario Montez), a tall, sweet, glamorous Negro drag queen in pink
taffeta, interrupting the shooting of a movie to talk to her old
friends. Vamping it beautifully, – each practiced gesture carefully
underplayed and dropped, a mere friendly quote, no representation
of it within an established convention, – she gives them her advice:

»Dahrlings, there is only one way to make it out of the pitts. Take your
phantasy and make it real. Be whatever you feel inside and don't let
nobody stop you, because as long as you play their roles, they'll only
push you deeper into the hole . . . Become a superstar, honey. Turn it out
and make them feel real. But you got to be careful, cause one wrong move
and they'll nail you.«

She sings her song, *Call Me Drag Queen* (to the tune of the *Beal
St. Blues*):

»I was down, messed around, clocked and read to the dirt.
So misused, and abused, honey, how it hurt.

I tried to hide, what I felt in my soul,
But now I feel, I must be real, I'll play my own role.

. . .

Call me Drag Queen,
Cause it's my claim to fame,
I'm not a woman, I'm not a man,
It's my own game.

. . .«

After suggesting they try out for a show down in the Village, open to all, she proceeds with the filming. Posing:

»Hi, I'm Bella Della Bossum, the drag queen superstar you've all been hearing about and I'm here to tell you about Camay. I use Camay and it makes me beautiful. If you want to be beautiful too, and a superstar, like me, use Camay.«

Now dressed as clowns, they arrive at a Happy Hippies Rehearsal. The Happy Hippies (the Hot Peaches' image of the Angels of Light), »Brother George,« »Wacky« (played by Marie d'Antoni, the only girl in the show, luscious) and »Bruce,« in fairy costumes, are cavorting in a ridiculous show of childlike innocence, singing snatches of *Bye Bye Blackbirds*, etc., – »illusions and dreams forever and ever,« »reality is irrelevant, like a dirty stinky elephant« Harlow gives a marvelous speech imagining she's Marilyn Monroe, and the three sing *Fabulous Freaks* for the HHs:

> »They let their inner light glow
> Put on a walking side show
> So when you see them you know
> They are fabulous freaks.
>
> They just let their yin and yang hang out
> Proud to tell the world what they're about
>
> . . .
>
> They
>
> . . .
>
> Said Dylan was unsteady
> Thought Jesus was too heady
> But they just weren't ready
> For fabulous freaks.«

Unlike the creatures in the HH's show, they are »REAL freaks ... freaks of life.« The HH are stuck up, stars, find the trio tiresomely real (»it's the illusion that counts«), tell them to get out, – why don't they try Randy Whorewall?
Whorewall (tall, gaunt, arty spectacles, enormous head of hair, coolly supra-normal), – in Centola's script it says »demonic looking, schized out,« – is scouting for em. Alone on stage, he gives a speech:

»Look, these are the hard, cold facts. My backers want money. Millions. And there are only two ways to get it. With the best or with the worst, and we can't afford the best. So I want you to go get out there and sweep em up out of the streets, pick em up out of the gutters, fish em out of the sewers...I want the lowest of the low, the cheapest of the cheap, the tackiest of the tacky. I want real people.

Real people with real illusions. Don't bring me in good looks, personality or talent. In short, I'm looking for pure, unmitigated, unadulterated, polyunsaturated tacky trash...I'll explore their slimy souls. I'll explode them on the silver screen. I'll exploit them to the tits to raise that money. In short, I'll make them SUPERSTARS.«

They arrive, dressed in tacky 20s evening dresses, at Whorewall's studio where a Campbell bean commercial is being prepared. »Silicone Sally« (Marie d'Antoni – representing Brigitte Polk?), in silver lamé, is massaging Bella, »Beba« (representing Viva, played by Lance Norebo, the performer that plays Silva also) is »preoccupied with herself,« seated on a dresser, Talukus Harrymore (here George Morissey?) is pacing, reading. Randy has been telling his girls he is going to glorify »American trash. Real American trash«: the girls are trashy enough, but not real enough:

»This is a Campbell baked bean commercial we're shooting at it's got to be real. I need real trash. I got to glorify that trash into a fabulous illusion so those motley little housewives from Maine to Missouri will think its fabulous. When I get finished with them, I'll have them thinking that trash is glorious. That tackiness is the only way to stardom.«

Silicone Sally has got the message:

»for sure, ...I am truly a trashy personage. That's how I became a superstar. I am funky, tacky trash personified. They don't call me Silicone Sally superstar sex symbol select for nada. Move over and check this out.«

She belts out *Tacky Trash* (to the tune of *Charleston is Back*):

> »We're the worst
> But we're elite, when we're in heat, we rake in cash.
> We were the first
> To be rehearsed, to be worst, taught to be trash.
>
> . . .
>
> Get tacky, trashy,
> Do your thing
> But make it sting
> Get trashy, tacky
> Make them gasp and make them sigh
> Drop them when you get them high
> And soon you too will be tacky trash.

Check out my brand new tits, they're silicone and plastic
(fan) – tastic.
I can swing them clear from here to Maine
I'm a superstar
Since my tits are what they are.
All in the name of tacky, trashy fame.

> Degenerate spastic
> Christmas trees of plastic
> Decadence phantastic
> Aren't we all that you desire
> Dying in pollution
> This is your solution
> Decay – – – to-day
> That's the price you pay.

Watch this here pervert's act, he wallows in filth
Beats it
Eats it,
He can gross you out and mess your mind
He makes life obscene
Divine as he screams and creams
And puts the blame on tacky, trashy fame.«

The scene's rivalry about who's the tackiest-trashiest parallels *Pink Flamingos'* rivalry for who's the filthiest, referred to by the last verse. Bella ruins Silicone Sally's act by telling her she is to meet her mother at the Plaza for lunch. This doesn't sound very trashy to La La: »These aren't real street people, are they, Bella? I feel uncomfortable around class.« Bella agrees with Flame that it is both very tacky and very trashy, but doesn't think it's very real. Harlow has fallen for the hype. She is willing to give up a little realness for lunch at the Plaza. She sucks up to Randy: »It's the illusion that counts. Even Randy says so.« Beba, in the meantime, calling for more and harder, is being beaten up by Talukus.

After an intermission that was sometimes omitted, we find Flame waiting for Beba while making up for a Wizard of Avis commercial. Beba arrives with the syringe (the stuff is »guaranteed to make you a movie monster«), wants to know who Flame *is* in the commercial: Dorothy, Judy Gee or himself (»Little Rock«). Flame finds it hard to decide, the illusion of who he is supposed to be has got him so fucked up he doesn't even know anymore how to drink a cup of coffee. Beba, frighteningly shifting back to the role of the archangel Silva, gives her 30 seconds to decide who she wants to be before putting the hype on her (shooting her up). Flame can't decide:

»Dorothy's the audience's trip. It's the pits cause she never eats, sleeps or screws. Complete phantasy. And Judy Garland, STAR. That's Randy's trip. All work and no play. It's the pits too. Then there's always me, the little kid from Little Rock. Sometimes I think I'd just like to go back.«

She/he sings the touching *Going Back*. Viva shoots her up in the middle of her indecision.

When we see him and the two others again, at Randy's for a Diet Rite commercial, they have finally decided they are stars, superstars. They have dressed up according to their hearts' imagination, Flame in butch drag, he's James Dean, Harlow is Marilyn Monroe in a white dream creation, La La, looking perhaps like Martha Raye, is in mad drag. Though La La is scared and embarrassed, they are flying high, feel like all the real (movie) stars at once. Warhol will have none of it:

»So, you think you can make your illusions real. Well get this. You're my phantasy. Nothing changes. Now let's start. WE'RE LOSING MONEY . . . Stars? You are not stars. You're trash . . . garbage . . . money.«

They rebel. Flame is going to shoot the commercial himself, around Harlow. He's busily baring Bella's fine brown thighs, doing like a camera man, framing her cunt. But when Whorewall who, disgusted, has exited, »wants to see him,« he goes.

Whorewall has the next scene. »He's dumping em«

»They are magicians, magical and they have made millions, but they've got to go. The speed's eating out their brains. They really believe in this super-star hype. What am I going to tell them? We wanted tacky trash and you gave it to us. Now you're just burnt out, crazed. You're so off the wall we won't be able to control you at all. Then we won't make a dime off you. You got to go.«

He reads off a list of accusations:

»coming up from the pits, . . . being a drag queen . . ., blasphemy . . . of MGM, Paramount and the Happy Hippies . . . going through hell and shooting speed . . . real illusions and illusive reality . . . falling for the magic type . . . treason and revivalism . . . being real and that hard . . . Max' Kansas Citism . . . and finally . . . returning to pitism . . .«

They are out but Flame has decided to put on their own show, *Hollow Happiness* (take-off on Jackie Curtis' *Vain Victory*). It is a success. It' revolutionary: there are no stars, super or other, stardom is a vain victory, unfulfilling, an illusion. A person can't really *become* a star. Stardom does not bring happiness! Flame tells off Randy, who has condescended to come to the show.

»this is MY reality Randy, without phantasy or illusion, with the pure insanity and truth and life, so up yours Betty Furness.«

Harlow has really come to believe she's a woman and a star:

»Sorry I am late, but, a woman must have certain privileges. And besides, I'm the star of this show and don't need you. I don't need anybody.«

Flame in a beautiful speech tells him he won't find happiness as a woman either, it's not a stable role anymore, and then, freaking out looking for his speed, breaks up the show within the show, works his way through the others' layers of names, starts addressing them by their real names, which are not their baptismal names either, begs them to shed their illusory identities and »go back.« The success of *Hollow Happiness* has provided only a hollow happiness. The show breaks up into a splendid momentary mess. Curtain.

After an interlude in front of the curtain, in which Talukus Harrymore concludes his fairy tale narration of the plot by conceding us a view of what has happened to the three seekers of glory 5 years later, we find Flame, who has achieved the glory of having become a living legend, in butch drag a street hustler, and Harlow, small and slender in a splendid evening gown probably the same though she gives herself airs, while La La, the totally untalented lovable lush, as much a kid and as clumsy as ever in an opulent white gown with a vast trailing train, on Whorewall's arm entering the night club to which Flame and Harlow have not been admitted, has indeed become a superstar, but pours out his woes to his two old friends: it's still the pits at the top, her jewels are rhinestones and he is not allowed to drink. Silva, the spirit from heaven (in this play the »egg factory«) comes to gather up Harlow, apparently leaving La La (»successfully scrambled superstar«) and Flame (»cracked egg«) on earth. Flame starts to remove his make-up. After we see Silva reporting on the whole operation to higher authority, we see Flame, by himself, but »not alone,« in front of his mirror again, shooting up (in the tongue now), »remembering«: the others come on, singing bits of their songs a capella, Whorewall coming out last:

»Whorewall: Degenerate spastic, christmas trees of plastic, decadence phantastic, (to audience) Aren't we all that you desire? (group joins in whisper which builds). Dying in pollution, this is our solution, decay, to-day, that's the price you pay. You pay.
Flame: A star.
All: You pay.
Flame: A star.

All:You pay.
Flame:A star, etc.«

Centola (seated in his cellar Tea Room on 23rd St., he's been writing something) says they do not consider themselves actors, but entertainers. They are not just modest, but right. They perform in the manner of musical comedy. In musical comedy, the character is known and need merely be indicted, and the indication is by the presentation of a fixed vocabulary of gestures with which the audience is familiar from a long tradition of like theatre, so that the character indicated is itself a theatre figure. There is a presumption that this theatre figure is an entertaining concretion of real-life types, but this presumption, though a vital justification, plays a minor role in the theatrical experience. No character is created. The quality of the performance, to which the audience is attentive in a primary way, is a function of the timing, of definition (sharpness, clarity of delivery), and of the surprise of permutations and variations of the terms of the vocabulary, – qualities of the performance of music. Musical comedy is itself musical. This is why it breaks out into songs, – not vice versa.

The comedy and the individual performers project good nature. The comedy and the individual performances are presented as due to this good nature and as expression of it. A dour or self-contained performance is out of place in musical comedy. The theatre figures presented concrete real life types in a good natured way. The good naturedness of the presentational gesture and of the comment on life includes good humor. A playful air and a spirit of fun are to prevail. The performance is entertainment because it is arranged to make the audience join in the good humor and the good naturedness. This intention is likewise part of the presentational gesture, – an invitation. This invitation is itself apt to put the (proper) audience in a good mood and to assuage its ill nature. Being catered to and being told it is catered to, it will more readily forgive qualitative lapses of the performance. None of this excludes satire, didacticism or tragic pathos, though it does exclude offensive satire (agreement on issues is presumed), disputatious or antagonistic professions of heterodoxy, authoritative teaching, and a tragic stance. *The Magic Hype* presents a tragic view of life and its heroes are pathetic. But though it suggests despair is the proper attitude, it does not make sadness incumbent on anyone. It teaches phantastic realism and the unhappiness of illusion as facts of an experience in life that makes of audience and performers a fellowship. Its satire on the phantasies we may realise is compassionate. What makes it superior to the conservatively liberal musicals manufactured for the uptown business community – charming rather than disgusting, – is that it isn't shitty. What enables it to be free, truthful and so generous in its compassion as to approach nobility, – instead of being shitty, – is that, not being addressed to appropriators, it shits on property. Its concern is with the dialectic of seeking to be beautiful.

Centola also says that they are non-actors, because, like children playing house in a sand box, they are not ›remembering,‹ but are acting out their phantasies, phantasies very far from reality and very close to it. This refers to the fact that the figures indicated by their performances, though focussed reflections of a half century's worth of screen stars, so preoccupy them in their daily lives, that these appearances are second nature to them. Their imaginations, though bound to the phantastic, and bound in a very personal (rebellious) way, are as bound as those of the teenagers slipping into the roles of their parents.

P.S. When I next saw the Hot Peaches, in June 75, at the Theatre for the New City, the show was no good. Centola had written and directed it, but of the group of a year and a half earlier, only Marie d'Antoni (doing Mary Pickford and Athena done by Pickford, and also author of the show's music and lyrics), Cynthia Stardust, his 73 business manager, doing Marilyn Monroe and Helen of Troy, and Ian McKay, the 73 Theatre Manager, doing James Dean and Achilles, remained. The show was called *The Sensual Savages,* was about a competition for stars between MGM and 20th Century Fox put in the form of the Trojan War. Everybody was some famous star or other, the drag queens' make-ups were excellent, the prologue well done by Sister Tui as Louella Parsons/Homer, d'Antoni sings well, there was a dazzling opening (strobe lights over white and silver stars), . . .: the whole thing was heavy, awkward, terribly boring, no fun, a dead moth, making it very clear that the Hot Peaches had been a group-effort, altogether dependent on the grace of a fragile group spirit, perhaps on a passing street mood.

Centola, the Hot Peaches.
Appendix I: Warhol's *Nude Restaurant*

This is a movie shown in a movie house. This being the case, its primary effect is that of a departure from the genre, non-conformity with the genre's conventions. You watch a movie being made (the camera is rolling) and/or/but you are practically told: »We are not making a movie.« This negative reference is not characteristic of underground movies generally: they come on as new movies, defying Hollywood. It is a dadaist provocation of the audience, frustrating its urge for an audio-visual fix.

Next, there is a pretense that somebody modern, who wouldn't dream of living without a movie camera around any more than without tape recorders, etc., in the course of everyday living, routinely and without special purpose, though playfully, makes these movies, shoots what he and his friends happen to be doing, almost as a part of doing it (it's his »thing«) – that this movie was part of the footage, he having been somehow induced to release it. Just as he likes to fool around with his camera, give a bit of structure to the day, his friends like to kind of play games, not impersonations exactly, but posing in adopted attitudes. Naturally this lends itself to being photographed. Naturally a person who doesn't like not to make movies would hang out with such people. One senses that these people have one party after another. They and he play these games all the time. It's what they are apt to be doing at any time any day. It's what they do.

There are such people of course, always have been, a real leisure class, though a demimonde. To that extent the pretense is plausible (and the movie decadent). This sort of life – life as a party – in fact tends to polarize into posing and observation, so that the introduction of cameras and sound recording equipment does not really change it, is just a way of being more modern about it.

This pretense is consistent with that primary effect. Something like it is, in fact, called for to create it. If they are not making a movie, what are they doing? But the pretense goes a little beyond that dadaist effect. It carries the suggestion that we all ought to be filming ourselves: formally acknowledge and externalize our social self-awareness – be self-consciously self-conscious, and not one by one but in groups – make our own movies of ourselves, instead of going to watch movies made by others of others about ourselves. Socialize the movie industry! Appropriate the means of communication! Under the aspect of this suggestion, that pretense is a deceit rather than a deception.

But the pretense is phony for, notwithstanding it, a movie has been made. Essentially: a woman's plaint that she has found male heterosexuality to be sadism, delivered against a background of rough trade, in an enforced competitive duet with the fey *non sequiturs* of a middle-aged homosexual boy effortlessly contributing the role of uninterested listener. Viva divagates over her life (sexual »experiences« and »relationships,« her dad pimping), a clanging monotone out of a pure-contoured face over which few expressions pass. The face is posed over two small round breasts, emblems of feminity. There is a body, the camera does not dwell on it, a dry-skinned structure. Soft breasts, a harsh voice, a beautiful face. The large eyes move for the camera. She seems a nice person, a classic bitch's blind. We don't see her arse: this is not pornography – though a bathtub sequence with a laughing, limp-dicked male and a nibbling kissing scene stir the crotch.

Ingrid, a »pig,« appears briefly.

Apart from their genitals, which they carry in a black bag, the actors are in the nude. They look censored.

They do not act, the camera does not film, the cutter did not make a movie out of the footage. So the action – whether the bitchery between Taylor Mead and Viva, the funny idea of a bit of bar life in a nudist bar without a liquor license, or Viva's story – is not a line but spongy tissue, and the movie is neither shallow nor profound but flat: in the surface on which it is projected, and in the nature of the photography, which nature it proclaims is its reality. The actors don't move much – they sit (Viva stands, she serves) and pose. The camera switches from one face or other bit of epiderm to another, making you aware of its whir and swivel. The film presents itself as film, not as film of something. The action is that of the camera, not that of the actors (let alone of characters portrayed or impersonated).

The theme of female demand and dissatisfaction is thus made to compete for your attention with the enterprise of making a movie about such (though not with any »camera work,« »treatment of a theme,« »personality of a director«) a movie, not even this movie. Obviously, of course, and however, Warhol was not about to shoot just anything: most likely he was out to get Viva. She seems to be under the illusion of being »some kind of a star.« You couldn't say she was anything but the star. She's also being a good sport.

She is not a good storyteller. A queer etiquette obliges people to be blasé, non-serious. Non-seriousness is not the same as unseriousness. In a quiet way these people are serious about themselves, which is why they cannot permit themselves to be serious, but which is incompatible with unseriousness. Thus, for instance, levity is out. Mead, an excellent comedian, is studiedly unfunny in word and gesture, humor being the poignancy of concern. Viva's stories are interminable. She is terribly boring. Of course, the on and on from time to time adds up to being funny, but I would suspect it would be underestimating this gang to think that it was a governing purpose of theirs to be funny. They are really quite serious, though not about anything. And then, the telling of a good story in a non-film would be incongruous.

Mead's dialogue with the war resister is a draw: the resister comes on slow but steady; the camera lovingly on his acne'd face, he delivers his challenge to Mead's moral position, Mead swerves, sideswipes it. One is free to admire the young fellow's integrity or Mead's commitment to himself (»personal rights«): the general public will be spared disgust with both by not going to see the movie. All in all, perhaps, Vietnam is brought up in this decadent frolic as apology for its cult of boredom.

To an admirer of Jean-Luc Godard, perhaps thinking of a scene in *Masculin/Feminin*, that dialogue seemed every bit as good as things in Godard. But such qualitative comparison seems to me to insinuate a nonexisting identity of genre. Godard's camera operates on fictions (symbolic representations); Warhol's records staged events. There is an inner relation between the active handling of Godard's camera, creative interpretation of acted action directed by him, and a symbolic reference to a larger social reality; another one between the simple foci of Warhol's camera on the poses of his poised creatures and the absence of reference. The resemblance of genres is delusive. The cavalier way Godard treats his story with his cameras and sound recording equipment implements that story's tragic play on life; whereas Warhol's informal recording of his naturally histrionic (narcissist and exhibitionist) friends, the off-hand capture of glacial poses, expresses his and his friends' common strenuous unconcern with (I quote on their behalf) »the society.« Of course, Warhol's address to the audience is finally direct, whereas Godard's is the traditionally oblique one *a travers* the art object. Mead and the resister are really fighting for their lives – and right before you. The contained desperation that Warhol exhibits is his own.

At the 10 P.M. performance on West 44th Street only a few men, looking like business men, attended, watching the self-consciously unconcerned naked figures, listening to the desperately harsh, »bright« voice delivering the monologue.*

---

* Babette Mangolt later appropriated Warhol's camera for shooting a masterpiece by Cantal Ackerman in which Warhol's tragic male asexuality is inverted into a tragic feminist existentialism, and the cinematographic nihilism of his waste of film on the trivial into a technique of camera passivity adequate to recording the waste of life on chores. – Queer art extends from the tropics of Jack Smith to Warhol's arctic.

Centola, the Hot Peaches.
Appendix II: The New York Dolls.*

Chairs, tables. The place is crowded with timid, unflashy youngsters.
Many are in couples. No indications they are to any extent queer.
A high school crowd really, – though most are probably around 20.
From the outer boroughs? David, 3 guitars, drums. The sets last
about an hour each. Dancers crowd onto the 3 by 7 ft. or so strip of
open space between the audience and the bandstand, – David and his
mike.

David sings, occasionally plays the mouth harp. The amplified
guitars are monotonously strummed in their lower register. No slides
or whines to speak of. Probably the kids haven't gotten past those
few chords as yet. The main fact, overpowering, is: they are tre-
mendously loud, – a steady stream in absolutely that one beat of
the organ sound that hifi gives to electric guitars.

Their pants are tight. their hair is long. David wears a knobbled red
garter around his left black pants leg and glittery clothes. One
beautiful boy, his long black hair in a nice hairdo, seconds some of
David's lines in his clearer but inaudible voice: he looks David in
the eyes and gets his mouth real close to David's. Another, pretty
spots of rouge in his cheeks, wishing David a happy birthday, gets
something like a faggoty whine into it. But the Dolls are just that –
real dolls: nice, pretty, gentle, friendly, clean youngsters, nothing
more (except that David is intelligent and a good performer for a
public), nothing else. There is no sexual ambiguity here, no faggotry,
no decadence, nothing sick**. A high school band. Of course, they

* The group had their breakthrough at the Mercer Arts Center in the Village in
the spring of 72, disbanded, after not making it in the country or on AM radio, in
the spring of 1975. It was an afterbirth, – rock was dead when they started, – and
a local act, – their 2 Mercury records sold 100,000 and 55,000 copies. Their last
put-on, at the Little Hippodrome, early in 75, was that they were a Maoist group.
The Mercury A and R man, Paul Nelson, wrote their obituary in a May 75 issue
of the Village Voice, an excellent article, a real appreciation.
** Starting perhaps with Mick Jagger, a variety of rock stars in contrast to the
Beatles' merely faintly dope-hued decencies have turned their personal messages
(manifestos of adolescent non-conformity) into splendid theatrical performances in
which likely as not they appear as megalomaniac magician kings of sex, neither
homo nor hetero, but perverse, encompassing and undefined, and/or very cruel, the
callous torturers of teenage girls: but often enough victims. These powerful record

are on the line between nothing and a name, so their put-ons are a little tentative.

The lyrics are inaudible as always in rock, i.e. you can't make out any statement hardly, just words and an occasional phrase when the band is momentarily letting up a little. A friend said it was partly that the p.a. system was bad, but had to acknowledge that the idea was that you knew the words from the record: they were »understood.« Another friend, who is also a friend of David's and admires the lyrics especially, said he understood them as sung, having heard them so often, and that David wanted them to be understood only gradually, – on repeated listening?

I think nobody makes out the statements by listening to a live performance. This may be the paradox defining these performances. They present themselves as emotionally charged verbal addresses, to the young audience in and on their own terms, of an individual's felt statement of their feelings. This individual is not only expressing him- or herself to them, but is speaking for them. They are being expressed: even when the communication is a ballad, it is a statement about life. Thus the very point to be made is, they know what is being said. Care applied to intelligibility would destroy this point. They want to hear it said, they don't need to hear what is being said. Ostensibly, at least, nobody is being told what to do.

The non-verbal noise i.e. instrumental music provides the appropriate setting and mood not only for what is communicated, but for the act and event of communication: the communal excitement of the communal occurrence.

The sound of this music is not funky, nor hard, tough, or even just wild. There is no scepticism, sadism, irony or rebellion in it. I hesitate to call it gentle or loving, but it expresses gentleness and lovingness. The sound affirms. Teen-age soul? teen-age white soul? It affirms individual quest for romance and the righteousness of this stance, not just the right to this quest, but the righteousness of a devotion to it. The words one may snatch convey the same claim: to the right to an uncommitted tentativeness (beautifully strong in Johansen's hand-gestures) in evading, by a total preoccupation with intimately person-

---

company puppets are the queer cousins of the queer histrions here described, as truly queer as they. Their working class affiliations and that in private by and large they are nice boys, thrilled by oral sex, throws light on queer theatre. That their oppositionist and even rebellious stances takes the form of a put-on, and has only a temporary and primarily stylistic effect on their peer audience is not against them, for their shows are not phony, and what are the effects of art anyhow?

al problems and with »one another,« the peers, the other young, especially those of the opposite sex, the demands made by the institutions (family, school, corporations, police). The loudness or voluminousness and the pressure of the sound convey not wildness, but the forcefulness of this claim, due to its intrinsic validity and to the urgency of expressing its foregone rightness. United in the sound,* audience and band assert themselves. The setting of a steady, machine-made roar − electronically, i.e. magically brought about, − yet originating with the gyrating or still instrumental performers, by their lack of skill so like their listeners, − a roar so preemptive, that after you leave, the extraordinary quietness of a snow landscape pervades the night streets merely *outside*, − needs to be simple and powerful to fulfill this function of (shakily) emphatic assertion, assured but not insured.

The mood of the sound (in the context of the event, at any rate) conveys two other aspects of the statement. It is to be uncerebral and unemphatic, neither whine nor scream, − not »we want to be left alone« but »we are on our own,« − a natural utterance from the body, from a body come into its own, in a spirit (note »spirit«) of autonomous enterprise. And the statement pertains to the body, namely to placement in sexual space. Not that there is anything flagrantly or pointedly sexy or erotic about the sound, the auditors' shuffling dancing on the crowded floor, or about the beautiful, modestly spaced-out pants, vests, medallions, buckles, silken shirts in which the slim − to haggardness − boys are dressed. No sexual relations are being thrown up, but spiritual relations in an inescapably, naturally sexual space. The first point is not to be phony, the second is to be cool (whence the word »sincere« is out of place), the third, to be beautiful: the band, the performance, the event were all three.

Both because there is no question here of enunciating principles, disporting oneself in the arena of contention, but of affirming attitude, and because that attitude is to be one of the beautiful person in the flesh, − beautifully dressed because beautiful, − with if not toward his like, the mood is physical. It is the aura of bodies

* Communion between auditors and Dolls seemed to me less than perfect, and not only insofar as the inspired and commanding artistic personality of the giving individual, David Johansen in this case, naturally would as such have to have a place in the event, an individuation of necessity fissuring the communion, but in that the crowd at moments showed a slight embarrassment at the margin of chicness of the place (Max's Kansas City, upstairs) and occasion or because of their reasons for being there and enjoying themselves.

immersed in a volume of sound, in its vibration, the sound going through them besides being around them. So the sound has to be big, the words drowned out. You can hear the voice, and it's the main thing, – it's there almost continuously, the inchoate drone is there to flesh it out, – and there is no doubt a stand is being taken, the tone of affirmation rings the pulsations about, but the particular points (and the singer, David, is careful about his enunciation) are sacrificed in the bonfire. The paradox is perhaps also that of individual and group, perhaps that of idol-leader and community (congregation), but perhaps chiefly that of word and speaking, the speaking being the thing: but in any of these forms it is not the event's inconsistency, but its life.

Ridiculous Ballet

Ekathrina Sobechanskaya dancing ›with‹ The Original Trockadero Gloxinia Ballet Company gave 4 concerts, April 3-6, 1975, at the La Mama Annex. I missed all but the last and regret I wasn't able to see the program (the same each time) over again, for it contained a number of beautiful, touching, powerful dances, arrangements, poses, ... that I should have liked to describe.

By self-aware pride and justice of taste,* Larry Ree (Sobechanskaya), whom I had occasionally seen dance in Charles Ludlam's plays, has imposed a peculiar place on the work of this all-male company (founded by him in, I believe, 1972): between camp (but it's definitely *not* camp, much less irony or persiflage), the funny and fun (but it's neither, rather is tenderly humorous and even witty) and pathos (but it's poignant rather than pathetic): perhaps a unique place. In his own dances he not only occupies this place of dignity with power and precision, but makes daring use of it: his dances are perhaps minor masterpieces.

Recurrently, watching him or one of the 2 or 3 others in the company capable of a clear presentation of themselves as dancers pirouette, glide or twirl, one's imagination is induced to a sublimating complementation of the actual image by a shadowy, faintly colored, larger image surrounding the actual one: of that same gyrational deployment of body executed to ideal technical perfection: a phantasm not only as pleasing as the high-point images (school products, products of drudgery, torture and tradition) furnished by established ballet, but superior to them by immateriality and ideality, providing the exhilaration of the play of one's imagination (though not of gravity seen played with), and actually complimenting the heavy, dense, delimited stage-image of which it is the aura: as the enhancing radiance of human suffering by certain crude 15th century black-and-white woodcuts does not redeem the dumbness of these but witnesses to their humane power. In which context I should mention that neither Ree nor those 2 or 3 others, nor Richard Bruce (more heavy-fleshed than any of the others who all seem heavy, – they are almost all

---

* He was always a man heroically resisting interpretation, no matter it was so easy. I saw him off Christopher Street looking like someone having in mind doing something, one could not tell what. When he danced, I used to be so embarrassed I almost wept. I thought it was cruel to use him. I thought everyone was always laughing. He was laughable. Yet his face would always be bland.

very tall, – but with the heaviness of bone, he enacts the role, complementary to Ree's star-role, of the Madame of these dancers) struggled against their limitations (nor attempted to sell them to the spectators as humorous): they have found them and are using them. E.g. Ree makes brilliant use, – for dance, – of his isolated technical achievement of being able to move on the points of his feet (his right foot often curving dangerously under his weight). Bruce, who hardly dances at all, or doesn't, with the brilliant modesty of a craftsman effectively uses a vocabulary of late 19th century ballet-gestures, without pretending to or attempting mastery of it, for expressing emotions and not for theatrical effect, but within the medium of dance: his heavy gestures work perfectly. I mentioned the strange phenomenon of complimentary sublimation: it is due to the combination of Ree's and the company's workmanlike and artistic acceptance of their personal limitations with the will to do art and with talent.

Ree's own achievement as a solo dancer and, in the *Scenes of the Willis* (remindful of *Swan Lake*, programmed as work in progress), in the traditional role of a ballerina using a male partner for physical support, repeatedly goes beyond this invocation of grace. Using lighting (colored, dim) and costume (scintillating with glitter, say), he does dancing that is powerful and moving as seen: more or less in place, with his body and arms, e.g. rapid snake-like movements, angularly sinuous, and, in one dance, with a Cunninghamian head movement, a stage-trick.

Using that male dancer (costumed as male and dancing in the traditional male style), a capable, skilled, trained and, I would think, quite good dancer in this show is a beautiful, successful act of daring: his high leaps, coordination of arm with leg movements, precise stops do not show up the others and do not even figure as reference, but rank as ornament, – dance otherwise gone into. And incidentally: just as I did not see this dancer as professional among amateurs, I did not see him as dancer in the tradition's male manner within a general representation of dance in its female manner. Though the minor members of the company (not the 4 or 5 I have referred to) by way of horse-play engage in some fairly charming female impersonation (the traditional facial and gestural mimicry) and though all the dancers perform with imitations of the gestures of ballerinas in classic (and sometimes, e.g. in *Fanfare for Diana*, modern) ballet, and by wigs, make-up, costumes present ballerinas, this is not a transvestite show. You see men impersonating not women but ballerinas;

you see impersonation not as affair of the heart but as mimicry; and you see this mimicry not as done or presented for its own sake, nor as theatre, but as subsidiary element of dance, – of dance maintaining the asexuality of classical and immediately post-classical artdance. Yet, as sometimes the art of some of these performers momentarily magically creates illusions of ideal perfection, occasionally the figures' neutral ambiguity of gender gives rise to an intuition of a transcendence of gender, – not that any of the dancers ever seem to be or become women (at most, momentarily, they seem just like women), but at moments an obliteration of difference intimates the ideal identity of opposites.

Anthony Bassae (stage name: Tamara Karpova) founded his ballet, Les Ballets Trockadero de Monte Carlo, in a secession from Larry Ree's ballet. Thanks to exposure in the N.Y. Times and New York Magazine, their ›4th season‹, a 5-day run of 4 different programs and one evening of repeats, at the small Vandam Theatre west of Soho, opening March 8th 75, was sold out. Genteel faggots and uptown culture fiends, all no longer young, tittered and guffawed during the early part of the program at their faux pas.

The company's style and repertory are classical, their decor and costumes tasteful and better. The dancing seems pretty bad, – they can't balance and are too busy doing the gestures to even begin to individuate them, – though some of the dancers have moments of adequacy. The comic stuff they do, not bad, is negligible. There are few moments of visible grace, no poetic mystery nor mysterious poetry.

The only positive way of looking at their shows is that an expressive theatrical style, – gestures, postures, movements and placements on stage, – has been derived from and substituted for the dancing style of classical ballet: providing not so much beautiful tableaux as moments of emotional poignancy, relating to romantic love. Though it might work grandly for some individual, this is a negligible contribution to theatre art, notably because it isn't serious: it's not intended as such. Anthony Bassae, small and quite ugly, with a bulldog face, is a touching heroine, with some of the power of naive and tender Romantic aspiration of Mario Montez. Like him, he seems Puerto Rican.

The terror of their performances comes from the performers' willingness to expose and exploit their failures, their individual failures, the failure of their individual ambitions to become classic dancers.

For surely this was their ambition, – they must have put in *some* work, considerable work even, – but they lacked devotion, energy, stamina, or perhaps opportunity, or talent. Now they are selling their being no good as a joke. They are not gracefully built. It is as sad that someone should desire to become a dancer of classical ballet as that someone should desire to become a singer of classical opera, and in the former case, classical ballet being a dated exploitation of women's bodies for the representation of an anti-feminine ideal of womanhood, and thus by its form and content offering opportunities for fulfillment only to female performers, especially sad if that someone is a man. But this does not make the failure of the ambition less shocking. The staging of personal failure, regardless of however much the ambition failed in was a person's original failure, has a grand power to move: which makes the BTMC's shows effective if unpleasant theatre, raw tragedy. Of course, they have invited us neither to despise them for their self-contempt, nor to pity them, but under the transparent pretext of wanting us to join them in some lighthearted foolery, with them to have a little innocent fun at the expense of the loveable sillinesses of classic ballet, – to have us admire the courage of their self-flagellation while put off-balance by a reminder of our own failures and lack of beauty.

Ambition in all its dimensions, the hunger to be great (sustained by the cunning, ruthlessness and purity of egomania and by an utterly naive willingness to forego ego in monomaniacal self-alienation), the desire to be good at something (be it only at Platonic seduction), the craving for admiration, stymies itself. Nothing can be done without it, but its pressure interferes with the achieving of anything, Insofar as the wistful ridicule directed at the suspect adored graces of classical ballet by the angularity and discontinuity of movement in these shows works out as a making light of ambition and thus lightens the load of ambition on us who watch, the shows liberate and thus are art. They don't, however, achieve this effect to any appreciable degree. The group's selling out to the comic effect of their awkwardness, – prostituting their failures, – sucking the arses of the lovers of ballet, – freezes them in the posture of a failed ambition unrelinquished.

Ridiculous movies - John Waters, 1968-75.
The joys of transgression, the morality of filth.

Having graduated from a Baltimore parochial school and been expelled from the N.Y.U. film school, John Waters, born around 1947, in 1965 and/or 66 made *Roman Candles** and *Eat Your Make-up,*** which I haven't seen, and, in 1968 or 1969, *Mondo Trasho.****
Mondo Trasho is on the subject of feet and follows the schema of *Justine, ou les Malfortunes de la Vertu.* – This inexpressive, tough-looking, pretty young made-up chick (Mink Stole) in hot pants, seamed stockings, thonged shoes, emerges from her house, lenghtily walks down the street, for a long time waits for the bus, reading a dirty book, rides it a long ways out to a park, walks a long way through the park, finds a secluded bench, settles, gets some muck out of her bag and proceeds to feed the bugs crawling in the dirt as though they were cute birds. She has been trailed through the park by what is evidently a dirty rapist, long-haired, crawling through the underbrush, crouching furtively as he loops through the open spaces. He slithers on all fours around the end of the bench and starts kissing her feet. Having at the first sight of him, unstartled, her face as sullen as ever, retreated to the other end of the bench, she returns to where he is on the ground. Her legs are crossed. A ridiculous girl with a pram walks by, mimicking outrage. The Chick gets up and walks away into the woods, followed by the rapist. He in a clearing takes off his jacket, spreads it on the ground for her, a true cavalier, she sits down, reclines. Her legs remain crossed during the following. He proceeds to make love to her feet, taking all the time in the world to take off her shoes, and seeming to lick them more than her stockinged feet. She is on her back, heaving in erotic ecstasy, apparently achieving orgasm at the end of the fantasy going through her

* »John's first post-film school movie *Roman Candles* (66) starred the nucleus of his present company: David Lochary, Mary Vivian Pearce, Mink Stole, and Divine, all friends from juvenile delinquency. ›Divine was still a hairdresser and just a starlet. But it was a start and it did well. We showed it in bookstores and we used to go around puttin' up posters for it in laundromats. It worked too, so we still do it‹.« (from an interview of John Waters by Glenn O'Brien, Village Voice, March 3, 1975).
** »It was about a deranged governess and her lover who kidnap models and force them to model themselves to death.« (same source)
*** »his first feature-length film. Made for $ 2,000,– it was shot on location« (same source).

mind, which we intermittently see: the story of Cinderella. In it, these grotesquely high-society elder sisters of hers in evening gowns and jewelry primp themselves in front of their mirrors, apparently expecting a visitor. She comes down the stairs even more elegantly gotten up than they. They fall on her and in a little sadistic scene of hairpulling, beating etc. tear her dress off her, and she somehow gets away back upstairs. The suitor and his page, approximately in 16th century Spanish courtier costumes enter, he takes a shoe from the open shoe box held by his adjutant, offers it to one of the fluster-ed, pleased ladies, it is too small, then to the other, it is still to small. The Girl comes downstairs again, again gorgeously dressed, but bare-foot. He tries the shoe on her foot, it fits. She comes. The rapist sits back, then slowly gets up and walks away into the woods. She sits up, extending her arm after him, but he keeps going, like Shane. She wanders off through the woods herself, in distress.

We now see this big gorgeous broad, another blonde, in a big open car, the radio blaring rock (throughout the film, at least hereafter, the action is accompanied by various rock hits with texts appro-priately inappropriate to the action of the moment), going down the superhighway, mugging it up, – Divine.* Her moues are grotesque. She is in decolleté, her tits are large, and lamé pants. She notices a gorgeous hunk of masculinity (undressing him in thought) hitch-hiking by the wayside, backs up to pick him up (the one thing always shot well in Waters' films has been the movement of cars, then the camera really clicks), inadvertently backs into the Chick coming out of the woods, gets out to investigate, the Chick is lying there out or dead, limp, sprawled, bloody. She picks her up, stuffs her in the back of the big car, drives off. Parks the car in an empty lot, steals a black party dress in a Hadassah thrift shop, on her way back to the car steals the shoes off a raped virgin (surely) she happens across on the sidewalk, gets into the car with her loot, drives to the laundromat, there changes the Chick's clothes (the Chick is laid out on a table), the one other customer there not worrying too much about it (throughout the movie we never see the Chick naked, have one brief glimpse of a breast), having already sort of wiped the blood off her face, – a girl has to look good, no matter what, – the Chick is still out, seems dead. While there, the Big Broad has her first vision of Mary, Mother of God, a peasant-type virgin in a kind of popular-image wedding dress type dress, and goes into her first fit

* who presumably named himherself for the hero of *Notre Dame des Fleurs*.

of screaming adoration of her and of the Holy Trinity, on her knees begging for the Chick to be made hale or brought back to life. As the whole movie has been very badly synchronised some time after being shot, there is little relation between Divine's mouth movements and the words. She finds a wheelchair to trundle the Chick around in, comes upon the escape of a madwoman and her capture by two men jumping out of a station wagon with butterfly nets, as she leaves the scene is herself, with the Chick, caught by them, stuffed in the rear of the station wagon, taken to a madhouse: a room full of Winter's friends acting mad. It's a madhouse, sexual approaches etc. (no orgy, actually, nothing consumated), there is a great exceedingly clumsy dance on a table by a young girl, naked down to the waist, with extremely beautiful small breasts, – entertainment for the inmates, – something like a rape of the dancer is broached (no additional nudity, she wears black tights), pandemonium, Divine mimicking her shocks at what goes on. The Virgin Mary appears again, Divine and everybody fall on their knees, Divine again asks for the Chick to be fixed up, and does a Holy Roller bit, the Virgin then first materialises an Angelic sidekick, a kind of angel, who slips Divine a switchblade, and then performs the miracle of opening the asylum door. All flee, including Divine and her victim-ward in the wheelchair. Divine phones a doctor from a phone booth, gets an appointment, so the Chick can get medical attention. At the doctor's there is a freak in the waiting room, leering, sneak-looking, and the receptionist is boredly reading *L'Image*. They wait, a half-naked woman, bloody incisions down her front, bursts into the waiting room, the receptionist presses a bell for an attendant, who comes down some stairs, a big man all in leather, and gets a hold of the escapee. In the meantime a young idiot girl of a nurse with a big knife, blonde straggly hair, blood on her uniform has come out of the doctor's office. The attendant and the nurse get the patient back in. Divine is disquieted. After a while it is their turn, the nurse gets the Chick in there, the nurse is all bloody now. The doctor (David Lochary) is giving himself a fix, cheers up, the Chick is laid on an operating table, her feet are sawed off with an enormous hacksaw (it is dull, the doctor has to end up taking recourse to a power saw), chicken feet are substituted (sewn on instead), she wakes up, studies her feet with a modicum of horror (she remains expressionless throughout). In the meantime, a reporter interviewing Divine, accompanied by a photographer getting cheesecake photos of her, has burst into the waiting room, closely followed by the police who want to arrest

Divine, apparently for having left the scene of an accident. (It's not too easy making out the sound and everyone is talking at once and very rapidly.) A fight with knives and guns between the police and everybody else, especially the attendant and the waiting freak, develops, Divine is shot in the belly (blood). The doctor followed by Divine and the Chick get away, they get (voluntarily) into his car, he kicks them out on the open highway near a woods, having on the way tried to pick up, offering her money, a minor leaving school. The Chick half drags Divine through the woods, they end up by a pig farm and drag their way through the pigpen, Divine dying there in the pig shit. The Chick is standing there, her chicken feet all black with pig shit. She makes it down the road into town (developing a funny shuffle of her feet when standing), stands there abandoned, two ludicrous women perhaps waiting for a bus, abuse her to one another in an extended exchange about what she probably is, throwing all the middle-America, hard-hat epithets at her, intermittently simply »she's a slut.«

One review gives Waters' age in 1975 as 28. That would make him 21 or 22 years old when he made *Mondo Trasho*. It is evidently an adolescent achievement. I mean that's the spirit of it. Sound, photography and acting are all lousy, non-existent, really or rather. Divine has not yet come into her own as performer in this film: she is still quasi-acting a part, the glamorous broad: in her adorations of the Virgin she prays for her Divinity to become real, – that prayer was not answered until *Pink Flamingoes*. She doesn't act the Goddess in *MT*. The absence of acting makes these figures very true to life, – the American scene.* What makes them all, victims and bourreaux, appealing is their sturdy forging ahead** according to their characters, i.e. dreams and desires, an unperturbably tranquil living-out-

---

* Perhaps by contrast, because the acting in real movies is designed to hide how we are and give a false picture, which in turn, as far as determinants within the art form as such are concerned, may have come about because the makers, including the actors, of movies presented as representations of real life in fact have been formed by the making of mythological movies, – Westerns, gangster movies. Sturges is an exception, *Greed*, W. C. Field's movies, the early Griffiths . . .

** This is also a quality of the movie: one-thing-after-another, just as in de Sade, or in *Candide*, the style of which goes back to the pre-18th century novel, though it periodically reappears, e.g. Goethe's novels, Stendhal, *Adolphe*, . . . Waters is rapidly telling what happened, giving the salient facts, *Diane Linkletter* still has this beautiful reportorial dryness, thoughtlessness, but then it gets lost. – The cause of it was surely a youthful combination of ineptness and recklessness of Waters'. He had a couple of ideas, a couple of characters, jotted down successive things that he or his friends thought might happen, then just barged ahead with the shooting.

of-one's-inner-self in real life reserved for the dumb, the dumb who also are grosso modo doing what they've been told, who conform, but in these movies leading these people into transgression, the sublimely idiot step into disorder. Plus: dream and desire are mixed here, co-habit, are pretty much close to one another. This gives the spectator a lift: vision of integrity. The subject matter of the movie is the heroine's feet, a neat IDEA of Waters', – ›idea‹, note her consistently unmoved features, her uncrossed legs, the unexposure of her body. Her own dreams and desires focus on her feet. Thus: we do not have to deny ourselves. The movie is trashily made, a throwaway product, comes apart in the viewing of it, disposable, does not impose itself, lets you use it, go on (the better for it).

The Diane Linkletter Story, which I saw during a March 75 Fridays at midnight John Waters series at the Bleecker St. Cinema, a short, straight-out attack on middle-class values, perhaps 20-30 minutes long, describes a tragic event that actually befell a TV talk show host and early investor in Disneyland, Art Linkletter, who put out a 45 with musical background about his daughter's death under the influence of LSD. It features Divine as a teenager, and Lochary (in his screen-appearances a degenerate-looking individual of indeterminate age) and Pearce (who always looks tough and cold, primly sadistic) as her parents. They are waiting up for her to come home, the father just having heard from the mother how the girl is going bad, sitting apart from one another on the couch of a lower-middle class sitting room, in TV-style pretending outrage at all their girl is doing, interrupting one another, seeming to invent their stiff lines, »in desperation«, but actually talking about the daughter's progressing moral deterioration as 2 housewives in a TV commercial might with pseudo-excitement chatter about the excellencies of some household product, though of course indignantly, trying to come up with as many stock phrases as possible. The daughter finally comes home, from a date with ›Jim‹, – no better than an animal,– she loves him, – very fat, in extravagent hippy Indian style clothes, with headband, though also with curlers, they assault her verbally, she cries, defends herself, she's doing her thing, nobody understands her, etc., the father calls ›a doctor‹, the girl rushes upstairs, tosses herself on her little white bedspreaded bedsie, cries and cries, keeps getting up to peer out the window to see if the doctor is coming, finally opens the window and tosses herself out. A long shot of her spread-eagled on the pavement, with blood. – Nothing very bad about the girl comes out: having seen other Waters movies one expects the couple to work themselves into an erotic frenzy by their talk, imagining her evil ways or what fate she might suffer, but nothing like this happens. A clean movie.

Multiple Maniacs is a study in praise of excess. It shows Divine going off the deep end: progressively more maniacal and more homicidal, increasingly homicidally maniacal and maniacally homicidal, she ends up a raving maniac, out of control completely, laughing her head off, in one stolen car after another, driving and stopping, slaying and laughing. Her ascendancy into infinitude is contrasted with the cautiously picayune self-preserving criminality of her ›boy friend‹ (the Baltimore vocabulary is determinedly‹ ₅oies non-hippie, – no ›old man‹ is conceivable here) and business manager, the barker at her freak show, David Lochary.

> »For the love of God, Montressor! For the love of God!« (R. Bradbury, *Pillar of Fire*; and elsewhere.)

John Waters' *Pink Flamingos* of 1972,[*] replacing the ineptly tragic liberalism of *Night of the Living Dead* and the profound nonsense of Jodorowsky as weekend midnight show at the Elgin, is an altogether charming and delightful popular comedy of the utmost vulgarity, by a series of filmed outrages, under the name of »filthiness« celebrating the virtue of transgression without qualm. Its message is that anything goes. Like *Myra Breckinridge*, its subtler, more restrained and less exciting high-comedy relative, it is a joyous movie. Unconcerned with the evil (rape, murder, kidnapping, the sale of heroin to Negro children) and the immorality (incest by cock sucking, exhibitionism in parks, chicken fucking) it brings up, as though they were the hang-ups of yesteryear, it subsumes them under filthiness, as in »a filthy way to act,« »a filthy thing to do,« »he is utter filth,« »how filthy can you get,« – »revolting filth,« – i.e. transgression of taste, disgusting behaviour, epitomized by the concluding shocker of the movie, shiteating. The categories of evil and immorality are absent from this movie. Sex as such is not its concern, and if it incites us to filthiness, it is not by conveying to us the pleasure of being filthy, – not by titillation, – but by an effective beatification of

---

[*] I wrote the following about this movie in 1973, about a year and a half before I wrote the text about his other movies.

transgression, – at its basic level, filthiness. It is by no means a pornographic movie. But it is filthy. By its choice of performers, and by the theme spelled out by its selection of acts to photograph, it recognises that filth is filth, claiming neither (though one might) that a liking for it is natural, nor, pornographic rationale of *Deep Throat*, that it affords sensual pleasures in addition to the delights of transgression. The instances of sensual delight, such as the heroine's when she sashays down the street, pantsless, a raw steak in her crotch under her dress, or munches on the raw thighbone of a dismembered cop, her antagonists', transported by love and mutual footkissing, the heroine's son's, fucking a pick-up by the intermediary of a chicken (at climax inducing a bowel movement in it by cutting its head off), are not exactly mock-acted, but the acting is transparently a gag. Sensual pleasure is not the point. These filthy people, we notice, are quite clean in their person, they wash, take care of their hair, are concerned with their personal appearance. They dress neatly, – the women in the Divine family in a slightly whorish lower class southern suburban chic, the Marbles as business people w/a fashionable touch of affluent hippie. Even the Divines don't live like pigs. Waters, at a reported cost of nearly a thousand dollars,* outfitted their trailer with blonde mahogany, leopard skin contact paper, painted plaster Madonnas, ball-fringe throw rugs, souvenir ashtrays.

There are no barriers in their minds that would make transgression transgression for these degenerates. Neither are they repulsed by the physical aspects of filth (the performers were, of course), nor do they feel at all any taboo attaching to it. Though they are competitive in their filthiness, and publicity-minded (though not out to shock anybody), their primary motivation is not in these areas, but in a delight in filthiness, – and though they specialise, they are not obsessive. In fact, for the most part, – the incestuously voyeurist Miss Cotton is an exception, – they have nothing psychotic about them. Neither compulsive nor fetishist, they are not driven by attachment to any particular form of filthiness. They wallow easy. They are having fun. This makes the movie very clean.

Transgression as such, abstractly and generally, the transcendence of existing even where inoperative barriers is the source of delight, not the self-liberation, but the free movement, not the outraging, but

* Slimy New York Magazine at the end of '74 put its no doubt hallucinatory classification of *PF* as a ›two million grosser‹ into its perspective by reporting its cost as $10,000.

the outrage. Transgression has become a mere idea for these degenerates, but even as just mere idea committing it gives them a thrill.
When she eats the shit, this idealism in the practice of everyday
life shines out in the easy mischievous, big glamorous glorious smile
on Divine's face, huge, bland, obscenely pretty, its eye sockets, under
stiletto brows angled over the pate, grotesquely shadowed by blue-
underlined chalk, bald up to the crown of her head, where the
coiffed abundant tresses of her blonde wig, their roots carefully
darkened an inch or more up, spring. But why filth?

Superficially, to calm reason, filthiness, in its essence perhaps aesthetic
infraction of the taboos ordering segregated excretory* and alimentary practices, perversion, the immoral infraction of sexual
taboos, and evil, the sinful or criminal infraction of taboos ordering
hurtful practices (such as burglary or the betrayal of buddies, the
thrills of which Genet celebrates), form an *ascending* series of the
species of badness or wrongdoing. But not only is the prejudice against
perversion, having always seemed even to the hypocrites professing it
odious, – a kind of ultimate filthiness, – beginning to seem ludicrous,
but to modern feeling filthiness, infraction of *self*-respect, rather than,
as to the Ancients and Christians, criminality, infraction of a Divine
order, and rather than, as to the bourgeois, immorality, infraction of
the social order, *defines* badness and wrongdoing, *the genus*. By
dealing with filthiness as fun, the movie thus denies the badness of
badness. We now-a-days feel that criminals and perverts are *degrading* them*selves*, e.g. the sickies among us do when they put them
down by suspecting them of being sick. When asking ourselves why
treason, murder, sodomy are bad or wrong, more and more among
us are increasingly unable to feel that calling them sins, crimes or
unethical has any meaning: but most will with a shudder feel that
they are dirty things to be doing. A wrong act sullies the doer. Modern sensibility identifies badness as filthiness not just because filthiness, – the unwiped arse, stuffing your mouth, – is ugly, but because
(unlike criminality or immorality) it makes the filthy individual him-
or herself look (or smell) ugly. That weaning and toilet training are
the ontogenetic inceptions of civilised conduct may enter into this. –
Also, in our unaesthetic though polluted culture, the inaesthetic has
the dignity of rebellion, – as compared to the undignified conformism
of ecology-minded reformism, unaestheticism pushed to its limit.

* At the Divines' party, a guest contributes to the entertainment by an exhibition
of arsehole eurhythmics. *Mondo Trasho* ends with Divine crawling through pig
shit.

The movie's style, set by the screechy trash-accents of the unseen narrator, now and then cutting in, is the careless pretension to a low brow capitalised on by Mad Magazine: in spite of the occasional lapses into college vocabulary, as acceptable to low and hi' brow as the phantasy rural regional accents of Dylan's earlier balladeering. There is not a trace of high mindedness in it, nothing like Genet's sacral poetry or de Sade's rationalist sermonising. It intimates commercialism, not moralism. It claims no detachment.

Its photography is a teensy bit arty, a still of a pair of feather-crowned mules, a cleverish following of a walk, – surprising, I would say, mainly in being adequate. The inanimate imagery provides a powerfully real setting, mostly because high-powered cameras if nothing else make it so unreal in most movies. Shot outside Waters' hometown of Baltimore, it is clearly the small town California setting for the performances, i.e. for the making of the movie: but the performers and the movie characters' real life settings are the same. A few striking shots: the artless shot of the pink and black trailer that the heroine and her family live in, showing all of it, out noplace, a pink scummy plaster flamingo dipping into a birdbath on the littered grounds in front of it; the loving photography of the glorious red fire that consumes the trailer, arson having been committed; a shot of a new car parked out in the brush, Mrs. Divine's '58 Cadillac, so still and sleek and new our eye almost supplies the garage, – separate shots show the insigne »Coupe de Ville« and the electrically rising pane on the driver's side as it starts smooth as silk, gliding slow. The photography is careless, meaning it's just to show what goes on. Not the film, but what the actors do is the subject.

The story is that the Marbles (Mr. and Mrs.) are outraged at the media's playing up the Divine family (Mrs. Divine, who to preserve her privacy has assumed the name Babs Johnson, her egg-eating mother Edie, her daughter, Miss Cotton, her boy Crackers, – no husband) as the filthiest people in the world. They decide to go after the Divines, proving their superiority in the process. They send Mrs. Divine a turd for her birthday, hire female spies to get in on the family's movements via Crackers, sick the police on a party celebrating both Divine's birthday and her egg-addicted mother's marriage to the egg-man (the party captures the cops and eats them raw), finally in the Divines' absence burn down their trailer. The Divines retaliate by a visit to the Marbles' nice suburban villa, where they put a hex on the furniture by orgiastically licking it (so the couches throw off the Marbles when they come back), liberate the teen-age girls imprisoned in their dungeon, handing over their guardian, the Marbles' butler, to the girls and capture the Marbles. Before invited representatives of the media, they try, convict and execute the Marbles for the crime of being arseholes, and cheerily depart for Boise, Idaho.

The revenue-sources of the Divines, – the Marbles say they are murderers, – are not specified. The Marbles, united in the holy bonds of matrimony, live off selling to Lesbian couples the babies of kidnapped teen-age hitch-hikers whom they keep chained up in their basement and have their transvestite slave-butler impregnate (when the girls get hold of him they castrate him, he bleeds to death, we see his castrated corpse). They invest the proceeds in porn-shops and in heroin – distributed in the central city elementary school system.

Mrs. Divine, beloved head of her loving family, apparently likes to fornicate. She's a bit of a slut. But we don't see her making it with anybody. She gives her son head at the Marbles', – they are so het up by all the licking, – she defecates on a public lawn, – she makes believe she is going to pick up a hitch-hiker, but when he comes running up, she drives off, laughing her head off, ... Miss Cotton really likes her brother Crackers. She doesn't want him to touch her, but she just can't get enough of watching him make curious kinds of love to his sweethearts. And he really tries to oblige. Mrs. Divine's vast mother is kept – with much love – in a playpen, where she gets all the eggs she wants to eat. The Marbles dearly love one another; they make love to one another's feet. He also has a thing about exhibiting himself to young females in public places, a sausage or other lengthy piece of meat hung from his penis.

The Divines come out ahead of the Marbles morally. This is because they are not business people or on another level because they are not schemers. In a minor way it is an impression resulting from David Lochary's (doing Raymond Marble) not being as good as Divine so that Mr. Marble's transgressions come out a little forced, and from Mink Stole's (doing Connie Marble) doing more acting than Divine, so that Mrs. Marble's viciousness comes out less purely joyous, more »character.« The Divines' criminality is more informal than the Marbles', – the point is, their economics is not to the point, they aren't integrated at all. Also, though the trailer is neat, the Divines live like trash. While the Marbles are motivated by envy, status-drive, the Divines follow a spontaneous heroic drive toward glory: not toward being the filthiest, but toward absolute filthiness. They try to extend the concept. They, notably Divine, exult in what they are doing: it merely satisfies the grim Marbles. Waters has in his corrupt way coupled the Divines' being more likeable with their being less or not vicious. Checking out the respective lists of misdemeanours of the two families, we find that the only nasty thing that the Divines can be credited with is that tease Mrs. Divine pulls on the hitch-hiker, whereas the Marbles are not only meanies but really evil characters. What filthiness!: for the sake of audience-appeal, Waters distorted the whole picture! But fortunately it is too loosely put together for anyone to notice. The series of outrages overwhelm Waters' squeamish separation of nice, harmless filthiness from nasty, evil filthiness. One doesn't care who did what or how far they went.

The lines are as awkward as is much of the acting:* the product is sleazy, Edie's inexpressive hollow delivery of her lines, – she acts like a baby, – is masterly in its patent consistent insincerity. The excellence of John Waters' directing is evident in the poor acting of, say, Edith Massey (doing Edie), Mink Stole, or the girl that does the whining and screaming pregnant slut in the Marbles' cellar. Just because they can't quite pull it off, they show the big-time ideas he gave them for how to do it. Mrs. Divine's and Miss Cotton's soap-opera-nice cajoling of the grandma is splendid, hilarious mimicry. Divine himself is a great performer. It isn't just the sure touch of his mimicry when he impersonates the big easy vulgar slut of a woman, as free of feeling and conscience as of taste, supremely confident of the allure of her overripe flesh, totally indifferent to the opinion of others, but that he enlarges her beyond the human by the gusto of her enjoyment of herself and of her pleasures, perhaps by transmitting to us, – using her as his mask, – his own mocking enjoyment of the impersonation.

The movie celebrates without subterfuge or indirection** all transgression, hence transgression as such, – as source of joy and fact of liberation. The directness of this homage distinguishes it from Genet's

---

* »›They can eat shit‹ – in the words of the dialogue of one of the best scenes in *Pink Flamingos*, the speech in the opening which is marked by a moronic quality that you know at any moment could erupt into filth. This moment is deliciously held back for a few seconds until the ›... you can eat shit...‹ line spews irresistibly from the lips of one of the film's two spectacular leading ladies. From that moment on the dialogue becomes a gilded torrent of filth, the colors become more and more garish as the story unfolds.‹ (Jack Smith in the Village Voice, July 10, 1973).

** I disagree with Jack Smith's turn of phrase when he says that Waters »seems uncannily to have built into the film« a »nausea factor.«

work, for Genet's poetic perception focusses on the ambivalence of transgression both as source of joy and as fact of liberty: the profounder view and the truth, but by its reflectiveness in fact less incisive than the naiver endorsement of *Pink Flamingos,* just as *La Philosophie dans le Boudoir* is a break in the history of expression whereas *Les Liaisons Dangereux* isn't. Nobody could make a saint out of Waters.

Female Trouble, a Dreamland Production, X-rated, from Saliva Films Inc., a division of the New Line Cinema Corp., opened on February 12th 75 at the RKO 59th St. Twin I theatre: an absolutely splendid movie, even technically. Waters must have sunk the loot from *Pink Flamingos* into this production, and may lose his shirt. The photography is now adequate, an adaptation to the extremely careful (and excellent: recalling the interiors of Vuillard) interior decoration and hairstyling, as well as dressing (in a superboutique pimp style, synthesising the ›ethnic‹ with the ›hippie‹ into the near-science-fiction: last flowering of the boom before the depression of 74/5): again and again coming up with breathtakingly luscious stills in which color has been added to the frames of the underground comic strip, the Americana grotesques antagonistically detaching themselves, screen-high, from the wall papers.

Waters' people have all become good actors, too, now, and without any concession to the straight, still absolutely freaks: in a style basically that of television,* the 60s style of acting in soap operas, commercials, talk shows, interviews, the original freak-style of acting, but inspired by the illumination the underground comic strip*

* Whereas the Ridiculous Repertory Company's style derives from the pre-50s movies its members saw on TV when they were kids. While Ludlam and his actors up to *Stageblood* created fantasy figures by caricaturing (exaggerating) the grotesque ideals and the grotesque personifications of evil, of the contemptible or of the degenerate created by the mass culture industry of an earlier, more discriminately class-conscious age, Waters' actors by underplaying the no less grotesque reductions to types of lower middle class people achieved by that industry in a more recent, emphatically egalitarian period, – the TV of the 50s and 60s as distinct from the movies of the 30s and 40s, – model sociological schemata, animated puppets: caricatures of real people. Thus the art of Ludlam's theatre is closer to that of the regular, that of Waters' films to that of the underground comics.

* A San Francisco art form: Motor City Comics, Yellow Dog, Bijou Funnies, San Francisco Comics Book, Insect Fear, Captain Guts, Zap Comics, Young Lust, Big Ass Comics, Slow Death, Skull Comics, Tales of Toad. Not just Spain and R. Crumb, but J. Green, Kim Deitch, Geiser, Larry Wetz, Roger Brand, L. Gardner, Bill Griffith etc. etc.

of the late 60s and beginning 70s cast on those TV productions' peculiar acceptance of the lower middle class personality.*

David Lochary as operator of the exclusive Lipstick Beauty Salon, its clientele limited to whores and genuine horrors of genteel vulgarity, guru-entrepreneur, the hippie-shopkeeper, counterculture profiteer at large, a veritable Timothy Leary of beautification, is plausible: he has given up his woody countenance and jerky delivery in favor of a smoothness more simply according with his wont unctuousness, and his enthusiasms (as amateur of photography), – invoking the belief of the Colonie de Mettray that ›crime is beauty, beauty crime,‹ he for the sake of its enhancements of her beauty in the medium of his snapshots of her crime-flushed countenance gives Divine faith in her hitherto merely natural criminality, – while as unfrenzied and phony as ever, now are naturalistically phony, shoddily suave masculine equivalents of gushery. Mary Vivian Pearce, as his spoiled imperious beauty of a wife, her every wish a command, similarly has gone into the solidly grounded phantastic, presenting a figure of pure nasty, emptyheaded hysteria, as finely grotesque as Madeleine Kahn's campy fiancé in *Young Frankenstein*, but truer to life even in the blurring of its outlines. Mink Stole as Divine's horrid brat Taffy, magnificently standing up for herself, though starved and mistreated giving her mother tit for tat, contemptuously turning down the advances of her mother's luridly crude pimp hairdresser boyfriend (the stud Warren Beatty did in *Shampoo*, but for real and more than real), running away from home to live with her pig of a daddy and butchering him resisting his drunk rape attempt, convincingly plays a 12-year old embodiment of the life force, with no appeal to compassion getting our admiration: a precise, high-intensity reproduction in 2 dimensions of a very hard slum kid. Neither Pearce's classic-bitch/adored wife, ladeda sensitivity, position as sovereign beauty queen of The Lipstick, nor Mink Stole's Taffy's unremitting power of meanness, recalcitrance and hateful resentment (the same power as that of the magnificent heroine with other means created by Fonda in *They Shoot Horses*) fit in with anything else. These are independent blocks, contributing nothing to the story which is that of Divine's career: the two just went ahead and (with

<hr/>

* The toughness and meanness of Waters' world is not unlike that of the characters in the Depression movies of W. C. Fields, – *If I had a Million* and *Tillie and Gus*, w/ Alison Skipworth, *Mrs. Wigs*, w/ ZaSu Pitts, *You can't cheat an Honest Man* and *The Bank Dick*, w/ Grady Sutton. But the Fieldsian lower class is just a notch above the Watersian: does not admit its rank, insists on its respectability; and thus foregoes the all-out hedonism and slobbiness of Waters'.

Waters' help) got the most out of their parts, which beautifully enhances the movie's insane disjointedness. Edith Massey as Ida, Divine's across-the-backyard-fence-enemy, an old Miami Beach/Atlantic City crone, soft-hearted and mean, who thinks heterosexuality is nasty and is always trying to get Divine's boyfriend/husband to abandon this perverse life and find himself a nice boyfriend, has parlayed the moronic infantilism she displayed in *Pink Flamingos* into the whiny-screechy dumb verbosity of a sustained vivacious senility.

And above all, Divine himherself, now camp cult object and a great not merely good actor: in *Mondo Trasho* steadily laying out a dumb background aura of innocence and goodheartedness, but in her moaning and bellowing beseeching adoration of the Virgin making no attempt to be convincing in any perspective, in set outbreaks in *Pink Flamingos*, as bigger than life trailer camp slut-queen projecting the joy of life, outrage in the flesh, but outrageous only (though this is a great deal, as regards acting!) as what comes naturally, and restricting himself to a caricatural but ultimately naturalistic portrayal of the competitive lust for fame, now in *Female Trouble* not only embodies outrageousness and projects the joy of life as well as innocence (though not, except briefly toward the end in a beautifully tender and humane Lesbian cuddle on death row, goodheartedness), but gives a *sublime* performance of passion, of daemonic, – one might almost say, ›divine‹, – Dionysiac – frenzy, far surpassing the performance of needful supplication in *Mondo Trasho*, of vengeful rage in *Pink Flamingos*. Passion, – specifically, again, the passionate hunger to be extraordinary, – in this film has become the substance of the figure. Divine took the virulent evil insanity that rode her into disintegration in *Multiple Maniacs,* and, controlling it as actor, made it the mastered, controlled core-vibration, – passionate nature, – of a duped and victimised, but integral figure, joyful, innocent and life-affirmative as in the movies before *Multiple Maniacs*, retaining its control over its destiny through slaughter and right into death.

She is in a rage from the opening in a 50s high school, one of a small clique of bad girls, sullenly submitting to the teacher, spits rage in the girls' locker room putting her stuff away before the Xmas recess, smoking on the steps, anticipating not getting the cha cha heeled shoes she asked for, flies into a rage Holy Eve, when, after unwillingly mouthing Holy Night, Silent Night with her working-class-square, appropriately though painfully jolly parents, pouncing on the giftwrapped shoebox and tearing off the wrapping, she finds sensible footgear (she slams out, burying her humble mother under the Yule tree, leaving home for good), moans and bellows her passion when the swinish, leering truckdriver (played by Divine also), who has picked her up on the highway, on one of the thrown-out mattresses littering a roadside dump humps her (loving shot of a shit streak on the underpants he doesn't take off), – he gets her pregnant, – but really takes off and keeps climbing, when, after an 8-year or so interval of sustained indignant gusto, working her way up from cocktail waitress to gogo girl to street whore (the energy of this courageously old-fashioned life-history sequence conveys *her* working class push), she finally hits it big, being accepted as customer (others, less outré, are humiliatingly turned down) by the Lipstick Beauty Salon: we see her mainlining on eye-liner.

From this point on, her figure is transcendent: crucified victim, she transcends her mere humanity; and Divine, the actor, does it. The film is about beauty and passion. Since this is America and Waters is nothing if not realistic, the modus operandi is not, as with, say Querelle of Brest, only instinct, but the machination of inspired commerce. The deus is in fact ex machina. Her aesthetician instructs her that her beauty treatments need to be supplemented by crime. Criminal passion makes beautiful. His photographs, – she will model for him, – will make her a star. Up to her meeting with him, her crimes have been merely a way of making a living, – muggings, robberies, receiving, – or excesses of temper, – her mistreatments of Taffy. Only after they start her on her modeling career, – her rapid-motion speedfreak's posing for them, a splendid shimmy, *is* her artform, – she gives her last performance, as special treat, to cheer up her weeping friend on death row, – does she get going as a *vicious* criminal: her rage is no longer outrage, it has become joyous.

During a little party she is giving for her patrons, Aunt Ida revenges herself on her for something by throwing acid in her face, an act enthusiastically photographed by Lochary. The ambiguity of her reaction to her horrible disfigurement (an excrescent scar tissue, bedecking her face like a leproid tumor, – which in a brief scene with the doctor, – one of the inset parts, played straight, from a normal viewpoint, – we see her patrons indignantly refuse to have removed by facial surgery) is one of the beautiful subtleties, – contributing to what I have previously referred to as the crazy disjointedness of this movie, – of Divine's performance. When at the unveiling of her (bandage-swathed) head at the hospital, – the proprietor of the Lipstick Beauty Salon and his Wife, their hair-dressers, Divine's prostitute girl-friends, pressing around her bed with presents to celebrate her new beauty, – she first sees her face, – the celebrants ohing and ahing, – in a handmirror pressed on her by one of them, she is shocked, hesitant, and is only after a beautifully acted moment of repulsion, dismay, – of weakness, – converted to her evil genius' view of her hideousness as beauty, gazes about shyly. She is similarly aware of her supreme ugliness in her exacerbated hatred of Aunt Ida, her disfigurer. When Ida, kidnapped by Lochary's beauticians, is presented to her in a large ornamental white parrot cage, as a pet and as piece de resistance of the tinselly new apartment the couple are giving her, now that she is going to be a star, she chops off Ida's hand (Taffy later presenting Ida with a metal hook replacement). She is ready to go on stage. On her opening night, just before she is to go on, her daughter, now a Hare Krishna freak in Buddhist robe, clean and nice, a true angel, visits her in her dressing room and, shaking her tambourine, merrily teases her, flaunting her salvation. Incensed by her child's indecent purity, infuriated, Divine strangles her, the photographer once again eternalising the beauty of her transports. Her preposterously untalented night club act, – trampoline leaps, frenzied modeling, finally a random shooting of members of the audience (›who wants to die for art?‹), – all done shouting, jumping, laughing like crazy, in a transport of self-adoration, a fever of amazement at her wondrous beauty and brilliance, a joyous ecstasy at being so truly a star, and in a spirit of infinite generosity and good will, she wants to share it all with all of them, with all of them out there, – is the climax of her career of passion and a truly great performance. That this veritable monster, this sucker, this piece of shit, during her court trial, – the slimy snapshot artist and his wife testifying against her with decided moral indignation,* – she can't understand this, how can they lie like that? – and during her stay on death row, warmly loved and

* The fact is that in pretty much all of Waters' movies, the people played by Lochary and Pearce are in conflict with the figure done by Divine, and in pretty much the same way. They are the bad people, I mean really bad, viz. mean, self-righteous, fearful and commercial, and she is all right, viz. generous or giving if not actually good-hearted, reckles and enjoying herself, with a lot of freely flowing energy, not judging herself or others. In one sense or way or another, they tend to put her up to her crimes, and mostly, though not in *PF*, they win or get away with their crimes, while she ends up the victim. The schema is varied and the superficial similarity between the filthy criminal things they do and she does tends to cover it up, especially for people like them (who, however, are not as apt as the others, more like her, to go see these movies). The opposition it's focussed on is sort of

admired by the other female-inmates, ridiculed and roughly handled by the tough slut matrons, becomes a nice person (a good human being, lovable), and not even as a victim, not at all, but, more definite than Harcamone, fully cognisant of this end to her as acme and consummation of her beautification and rise to stardom, quietly settled into the awareness of her greatness and calmly accepting the responsibilities consequent upon her superiority, – in an incredible peroration, strapped into the electric chair, shaved bald (more woman, powerful woman, than ever) for the act, a Martian metal yomulka on her pate, thanking all those that aided her ascent, including, especially, her daughter and those she made famous by shooting them at the night club, – is a true ending: the final shot of her bald head, blue eyes staring, after she has been jolted to death, is one of the greats of film history.*

what Waters believes in or sees, – and me too, – and has been classically stated, in terms of the difference between those judging him and himself, by a clearheaded man of good sense (and good will), Charles Manson. (Manson's statement – of 1970 – to the court was republished in 1973 by David Lee and The Vanishing Rotating Triangle Press.)

* Divine turned out a marvellous female impersonator and actor, one could say actress, on the stage also, in a feeble pastiche by Tom Eyen, *Women Behind Bars* (from the 62 *House of Women*, from the 50 *Caged*, from *Mädchen in Uniform*), feebly directed by another purveyor of trivial vulgarities, Ron Link, that ran on Divine's vigor from April 76 beyond December 76, – it was said she was fired at the end, which is hard to imagine, and that during the next few weeks there were several little fires in the dressing rooms at the Truck and Warehouse Theatre. Sweet William (»for six seasons« one of Vaccaro's performers – *Heaven Grand in Amber Orbit, Lady Godiva*) as Louise, block screw or the like, the Matron's (Divine's) side kick, little pet, vicious victim, etc. was not bad, the others – I missed Repr. Mills' lady friend, Fanny Foxe, who was in the play for a while, – foolish, whether in their posturing or, – one of them, Virginia Barry, acting a little old murderess, – by their professional acting. Louise and the Matron run this bunch of women: two transvestites, that is, a bunch of real women, the prisoners, who are not up to their womanly ways, the casting reproducing the play.

Divine did his part of a bull-dyke jailhouse matron, – with the statuesque agility of a comic strip heroine, – a swish of the flanks cum tail, – a continuous air of tense contempt, – blonde wig cascading, vast pink face, big cheeks, mouth, curved little eyebrows way up, an absolutely cool face, – enormous toothy false jolly laughs – with absolute authority, an enormous figurine, all flesh and girdle. His driving force was the thing, the high points his three or four great monologues, stating his philosophy of contempt for the inmate/losers, done with a grand factuality, sobriety, the hint, perhaps, of compassion, not for them, but for them, him and all of us, his raspy, gleeful, contemptuous, gravelly voice driving forward, riding roughshod over pretense. – He laid out the Matron beyond type, larger than life, an ideal, a male woman, rough and mean, misanthropic, – putting a bit of glee in her, she's definitely evil, but not making her sick, merely able: it's not that she's especially bad, she's just especially tough (and so where she is), – you have

Waters' *Desperate Living* had its American Premiere in the singles' bars' uptown east 50s and in the Village in October 77. Divine wasn't in it, instead a big fat Negro woman, Jean Hill, as maid,

to be tough. At the end he reappears in nun's costume, all sweetness and light, equally vicious. – He holds back, is slow, placing his enormous body and head with intelligent power and precision, – no unnecessary movements, the fine timing of bitchery and sadistic games, – with great simplicity. Most actors are too busy: don't give time. He takes his time as an actor: this creates an area of peace for the spectator. He has a great sense of placing himself in the stage space, in a space, – mark of the good actor, the bad ones (such as the other people in the play) merely putting their body in different postures, but unable to keep in mind where it is, thus not dominating space. Of course, the dominating placements of his big body went with his character, and of course, also, Divine simply – as matron and as star – took center stage, marching right down the middle, – or in the ›intimate‹ scenes, stage-left (the matron's boudoir, pink light), throning in the chair by the table among the knickknacks, made his big body count, threw the stage off-balance. The power came from his straight forward, unabashed lowerclassness of stance and utterance: coming on as definitely a street queen, giving himself no airs, – no device, this, for characterising the jailhouse matron, but the avoidance of devices, – he like the good movie actors merely rendered a natural come on (not necessarily his in private, there is his probable shyness) more forceful and consistent, projected it. Such tough, no-shit accents are of the essence of ridiculous theatre (ballet, film): a proletarian vulgarity, spurning genteelity and ridiculing it, not using it as a weapon. – The curtain calls had been outrageously arranged so as to give an extra good-by-saying playlet to Divine as a finale, shaking and shimmying, doing little rushes and rubbings in her tight shiny ruby dress: in perfect bad taste, the rest of the company getting no time, but having to keep up the pretense of smiling joy and good fellowship.

– In February 1978, Divine reappeared in the upper Broadway Delicatessen district as a former strip teaser and now manager and owner of a burlesque house, in an extraordinarily improvised-looking gay disco, a bare loft, rigged up with graft, beautified by the gross brutality of its hustler promoters scintillatingly penetrating the spontaneous innocences and beautiful sincerities of the competent young gays staffing it, his vehicle another tacky Ron Link/Tom Eyen confection, *The Neon Woman*, unable this time, however, by his energy and control to dompt the too powerfully vulgar pastiches and too degradingly banal camp of these counter-culture merchants. The dormitory cell was now the burlesque house dressing-room, the warden's office to the left of it the madamy owner's office, only the jailhouse corridor had been moved, from the rear to out front, where, along one long side of the disco, it was ambiguously a walk-on stripper's ramp and the corridor leading to the burlesque house stage. The girls fight and philosophize and show their humanity, a young innocent is (again) introduced among them, there are a lot of murders (Eyen, taking his cue from Waters, making Divine their insane perpetrator, finally discovered, but never acting out any mania). Divine's failure, this time, is consummated when, during the final climactic scene, repeatedly and laboriously prepared, he fails to demonstrate that he was once the greatest of the strippers by stripping. This was watched by an audience of hundreds, all more or less cool, young and greedy, seated on the floor. After that, there was the regular dancing.

Elvira, of another Baltimore lady, Mrs. Peggy Gravel (played by Mink Stole as a nasty, pretentious, hysterical bitch). Hill is nice to look at, but lacks Divine's madness, is just a big tough nice dyke, – I didn't think the film was much good. It had a lesbian bias, is mostly about female couples battling one another, – lecherous males are vaguely hanging about, but except for a slob garbage collector, the men are nancies in leather serving the evil/authoritarian whining queen (Edith Massey) as harem studs and police force. This exclusion of the heterosexual syndrome (identifying it, incidentally, as among what's *really* bad) is part of the irrealism dulling the movie's cutting edge, the first of Waters' movies that doesn't seem about the U.S., – the queen's palace has moat and drawbridge, a fairy tale appearance. Waters wanted to make the idea – the implicit moralism – of his earlier movies a little clearer. And Divine is not there to carry the Life Force of Maniac Transgression so the consumption of rats, lapping of jellybellied cunts, playful torture-murders are doubly pointless. Peggy is in fact insane. She and Elvira having murdered Mr. Gravel – Elvira finishes him off by sitting on his face, – flee Baltimore, a flasher cop rewards them for submitting to his unnatural lust for having his lingerie looked at, by directing them to a refuge, Mudville or Mortville, city of criminals, a dump, ruled by the queen, where they board with Muffy (Liz Renay), a voluptuous former stripper à la ZaZa Gabor, and the super-tough Mole (Susan Lowe), – she has moles on her face, – her ›man‹, a former lady wrestler, having a lottery ticket extorted from them in payment. The ticket is a winner: Mole returns from collecting on it with lots of presents for Muffy (the prize one a sex change operation on herself, but Muffy is so repulsed by the prick qua prick, Mole cuts it off) and hand guns serviceable in the later rebellion against the queen. The queen's daughter, princess Coo Coo (Mary Vivian Pearce), is in love with the sanitation engineer, her mother, horrified at the misalliance (but subtextually it's just that she and her daughter are the third lesbian couple) forbids her to see him, she flees, is apprehended with the opportunist Mrs. Gravel's help. The queen, sensing a kindred spirit, adopts Mrs. G. in her stead, condemns her daughter to some horrible death, puts Mrs. G. in charge of the judgment's execution and of an urban renewal project, viz. the citizenry is to be infected with rabies. Mrs. G. joyfully proceeds, picks the princess as the first victim and transmittant, the girl, green slime in her mouth from the rabies, triggers the rebellion, Mrs. G. is shot up the anus (shot of her bleeding arse), the queen bar-B-Q'd for a feast of revolutionary celebration, the liberated townspeople dance joyously in the streets.

Jack Smith, 1975-77.
The horror of sex.

Among the religious ads of the Village Voice of Nov. 15th 1977:

"I would like to get this play in my
safe for one night."
                        Jonas Mekas

MONTY CARLO
IN
"THE SECRET
OF RENTED ISLAND"
by JACK.SMITH

HELD OVER! 8:30 - NOW EVERY WED. to SUN.

AT THE COLLATION CENTER
25 PARK PLACE
(NEAR CHAMBERS ST. W. of City Hall)

964-6528   TDF ACPT. - $2.50

To later ads, Smith added »adaptation of Ibsen's *Ghosts*.« In spite
of the »Held over!,« and tho there exists a handsome poster announc-
ing a Halloween opening, the run may have begun Nov. 10th. It
continued beyond the end of the year.
The Collation Center is an office- or office-cum-lecture-hall complex
above a squash club in the financial district of Manhattan, a lunar
landscape nights.

The first week end,* Ibsen's heroine, Mrs. Alving, played by N.Y.U.
professor and critic R. Argelander, was, mutatis mutandis, the center

* Nov. 14, when I saw it the first time.

also of Smith's adaptation: some old drag queen, – the Monty Carlo of the ad, – in a super market shopping cart, covered over by a face-covering turbulent black wig,* doing her best to act. Smith did her son Oswald, his father's victim the ARTIST unable to art. Regina, actually Oswald's halfsister, Mrs. Alving's servant, a slut, was played by a big pink pig, a toy animal over a foot tall, roses in her hair, – a diadem of roses. Toy monkies, not her size, had been cast for the two secondary male parts. They were on wheels, – the pastor Manders, whose idiocy is so profligate it absolves him from hypocrisy, Engstrand, the alcoholic carpenter, Regina's nominal father, whose cunning greed not even his hypocrisy can hide. Smith is very tall. Mrs. Alving's wheelchair was pulled, whirled and shaken (indicating her emotional upheavals) by a very tall performer, face covered, in the discrete black of Kabuki-manipulators broken out in horny spines. Regina, Manders and Engstrand were pulled into their positions and there sometimes on their lines were moved a little by a girl in a harem outfit, her lower face veiled, very tall. Making clear that the casting had by no means been restricted by paucity of personnel, a very tall (and serious) girl, like the others on high heels; Eva Piet-kiewicz, was on stage most of the time, on a ladder. She was trying to hang a bronze chandelier. The lines, except for Smith's, had all been taped, – more Kabuki. Mrs. Argelander, toward the end, was allowed some viva voce. An electric phonograph, stage-right, provided occasional musical accompaniment: lushly instrumented trashy melodies, contrapuntal to their sound-effect overlay of at first collapsing waves, then rain. It rains persistently and hard during most of the play.

For the longest time, green light, draperies, Moorish arches and items of home furnishing, mood music generate an elaborately, delicately and precisely atmospheric stage. The play begins with this giant masked peasant woman sweeping the stage, a lengthy, finally efficient enough, – some irritability occasionally in the movements, or disaffection, he shouldn't have to be doing this, – it's Smith, – job, but stretched out, interrupted, the accumulating little heap of dust and glitter there for quite a while on the (otherwise) empty stage, and/or the broom, leaning on THE COUCH, while the menial has gone to do something, – something else elsewhere. When the play then has actually begun, i.e. the tapes are running and the animals and the

---

* Smith assumes the heroine caught her late husband's disease, and at the time of the play could presumably no longer walk, nor in decency show her face. The pustulent hag was to reveal her face at the end.

cart are being moved about, Smith, now in a kind of costume (Sheik of Araby as in most of his work), – his costume keeps developing, it seems, perhaps only other romantic layers of clothing being uncovered, Mrs. A.'s son is still vaguely Saracen, tho not much, – is sitting on the couch sifting the sweepings: the dust goes into a carton, he keeps the glitter. There is some economy in this, and also some symbolism, the dust standing for Ibsen, the glitter for Smith, or else the glitter for the scarlet gold of art that before our eyes Smith is panning from a rubbish of ridicule. The couch is where he does most of the play from, i.e. when he isn't in and out.

The tissue of the play was stretched by the taped speech, especially that of the two mannikins' who had been provided with excruciatingly slow and ponderous male voices. Listening to the substitute-father's spaced coarse growl and the preacher's pedantically drawn-out pompous voweling going on and on in the aggressive register of harshness and overbearing, – all low cunning and foolish hypocrisy, – was torture: the experience of a boy exposed to upbringing. The pig spoke in silly, affected accents, in a hollow false voice, the widow, tailed by electronic whines, with fruity theatricality in yelps and squeaks, played so fast you couldn't make out what she was saying, which was appropriate to her hermetic appearance, really just a black ball of feathers, fur or wig, lacy widow's weeds, all scrunched up into a small curved shape at the pushing end of the metallic basket of the cart, something brought in, though then in its furry way very much there, mostly head (hair), and a pair of gesturing hands: the transvestite performer trying to draw on some imaginary repertory, but hemmed not just by the sides of the cart and his generally surely uncomfortable position (where were the legs?), but by his imagination, just a street queen's not into the arts (or an academic's): the small voice went with the small figure and well contrasted with its grandiosity of finery and stymied gesture. Since the lines are the play, and the play is of this NORWAY OF MARRIAGE, A COUNTRY IN WHICH THERE IS NO JOY OF LIFE, but only corruption and hypocrisy, parental country, the reduction of speech to a hairy background did justice to the play, as doing Becket in mime would Becket, and in fact realised Ibsen's verbal intimations *theatrically*, an adaptation, – a necessary adaptation: since now-a-days we expect the better class of people to be low, it takes more than verbiage and plot to bring to mind the system's horror.

Smith himself spoke in a small voice, mostly mechanically reading his lines (or pretending to) from the proof-page-size sheets of the script that, seeing as how the syphilis had corrupted their memories, he and Mrs. A. (tho hers were 8 by 11: he so to speak had the original) had been provided with, – the voice of the sick and timid son of the house, beyond the hope that might lend strength to a voice, – a slightly whiny voice, actually his actual one. He made no attempt to get the lines exactly right. Apart from *being* him, – which gave him license to introduce some of the personal metaphors he has developed (the lobster, uncle fishhook, orchid rot, Atlantis, references to rentals*), – he made no attempt to perform the character. His was the human voice, his presence the human presence. He was the hero.

The stage, serene and chaotic, a performance-space including us in its extensions (the room was small, the spectators sat on bleachers, there was no stage-elevation), tho Oswald's lines and the displacements of the other four characters corresponded pretty well to what Ibsen would have expected, – approached a 1-to-1 relation to it, – was in the main a place for humorous distortion, an oddly silent airless space, in which zombies seemed to be doing an imitation of the Marx Bros. in a running down time which was systematically so distorting their timing that nothing was funny, tho the humor was excellent. Smith kept getting the pages mixed up, losing his place, he was fighting the paper, asking the assistants for page 12 (was provided with it), showing the queen in the cart the right place, – in one sequence this latter gave various lines previously given, you were suddenly in the wrong place in the play, Smith pretending to be lost (»What's going on?!«). The performance, especially in the dramatic third act, under Smith's despairing, exasperated direction, – nobody is doing anything right! – keeps lapsing into work on the presentation, – Mrs. A.'s nurse-manipulator is not wheeling the cart properly into or out of the pink spotlight, – Smith keeps telling him (her) just what to do, – it's so simple! – in between, he puts the skull-mask he is wearing by then back on, says a line (›acts‹) . . . . Something wrong or missing: Smith disappears with nervously energetic steps to see to or fetch it. But of the 8 people there, I was the only one that laughed, – rarely and feebly. Everyone out there was so totally uncommitted to this comedy, – like all good comedy, obvious

---

* The lobster is maybe the system, Atlantis this earthly paradise, uncle fishhooks are critics/exploiters of artists: renting – selling something and even so keeping it or making people pay for *time* – is to Smith, prodigious with time and with what's his, viz. himself, the system's paradigm. Also, Smith had Oswald referring to himself as queer.

comedy, – that you had to *think* to realise it was there: having set it up as something to keep one in stitches, Smith had strangulated it, – presented you with its corpse. No release in laughter. But this sublimation induced a secondary exhilaration: gave you an asphyxiation high.

At the end of the play, Smith is coughing out the glitter (Oswald/ Camille), and Mrs. A., filicidal instrument of his suicide, standing up in her cart, is scattering it over the stage, symbolism of death by morphine. They are both wearing masks, he a large glittering, splendid skull, she a monstrously distorted ulcerously figured pink sow-face.

This careful staging retrieved the classic work.

By the next week end, Argelander had been replaced by a (black-and-white) lady's boot sitting in a crack of the backdrop curtains on a table. This made Oswald not only the hero of the play, but its visual center as well. The Chinese girl that had been selling the tickets was now handling the animals, and for the finale between mother and son did the mother in the shopping cart. The supernumeraries had been amalgamated, the (or a) Person in A Harem Outfit, the on-stage street-queen, adding the sweeping and the wheeling about of Mrs. A. to her chores, and some stage manager taking on the (abbreviated) role of Superfluous Stagehand, the previous performer of which (Eva Pietkiewicz), – whom, years earlier, in Wilson's *Deafman Glance,* nude, I had observed to have one of the most beautiful female bodies I have ever seen, – was now handling light and sound behind the curtains at the other end of the boot's table. When the large bulb for Mrs. A.'s lines went on back there, – to tell us the boot was speaking, – she was visible, a stocking over her face, a masked and shrouded Frankenstein.

The air of the open stage is pink and green, a diffuse light, not too strong, the backdrop a genteelly sedate dark green plywood wall with a broad Moorish gate cut into it, in which hang the two flimsy light green curtains, there are other curtains of the same sort hanging stage-right and stage-left, with elegant negligence and great calculation combatting the office-atmosphere of the place and delimiting the drawing room stage area (still others here and there are suspended up above, short ones, creating an illusion of fly-space), and out in front, at an angle at the left, a saw-toothed little demarcation or wall, a foot or so high, extends a little less than half-way across, here and there encumbered with Near or Far Eastern North African incense burners, suggesting perhaps the oasis fort, Foreign Legion outpost, or a sand castle's bulwark defending illusion from the crude humours of adventitious audiences. It does not quite hide the three floor projectors (two of them trained on the side curtains). At the extreme right, near the door through which Smith and the others have to enter and exit, there is a phonograph. By the back wall, a trunk, upright, that never enters the action, perhaps suggestive of Oswald's arrival from »out there.« A green chaise longue to the left of stage center by its evocations both of elegant lassitude (it has small lion's feet) and romantic love suggests decadence, a potted but plastic palm crowded into the up-stage, stage-left corner, the North's nostalgia for the South. Some ropes have been left dangling, – indicating the artist's preoccupation with the essential has brought with it some unavoidable inattention to detail, concomitantly, as testimony to his confidence in the power of his work, less than tragic. Thus also last night's glitter on the floor and the unlit Moorish lantern, never lit. – Although our host has proclaimed this to be musically the age of Puerto Rico, we are being entertained by the Orientalising airs that came to be written in the wake of certain exhibitions: the sounds of the Casbah are about us, and of Bali, and of Montenegro, . . . – of the dancing-girls.

One of these latter enters, – not a real Oriental, too tall, but with face-veil, and the classic tasseled head-cloth, held by a head-band, flowing down her back, all in green, down to her glittering high-heeled shoes. If there was a flaw in this production, it was the absence of kohl around her eyes, but perhaps Smith didn't want to overdo things. She starts sweeping. The north wind has begun to howl above the string-sweetened horns, the sensuous dancing rhythms of the south. The houri's brisk handling of the broom makes it difficult to submit to the seduction of the scene, set as it is for spiritual whoring, – for unspeakable, e.g. financial, orgies. (Theatrically, this opening of *Ghosts* may be considered an inversion of Y. Rainer's opening with the vaccuum cleaner, tool of revery.) During a momentary abatement of the storm – delicate tinkling of ankle bells! – taped paroxysms of eery laughter offend us. The cleaning woman, baring one socked leg, – the ankle sock is not pulled tight, – to its knee, has, seated on the chaise longue, begun to sift her collection of dust and glitter, but has to get up, setting her carton of sweepings aside, to help a stage-hand, making some last-minute arrangements, with his ladder. Both of them having had to leave, the stage, except for the illustrative music and the winds, is empty, but then she reappears wheeling in an extensive tho, in the dark, unidentifiable collation, which she abandons somewhere over to the right, as, fortuitously to a tenor saxophone solo, a stooped-over small geisha, her broadly striped kimono supplemented by a utilitarian fur boa fitted over her rounded back, a tiny handbag dangling from her arm, scuttles in like a little harlequin to retrieve the SCRIPT OF THE PLAY from underneath the dust-carton. The well-worn sheaf of proof-size pages, left on the couch, had in fact, tho inobtrusively, been the center-piece of the stage-setting. It is about half her size and she leaves with it. The harem maid reenters and after some fussing with the tray (she has had her instructions) with a scanty but discernible ceremony of gesture offers us refreshments; leaves for coffee; comes back in with a Turkish coffee pot. There are two or three takers, – the audience doesn't quite believe in the thing, – a plastic container of dried dates, – the refreshments, – is passed, she waits, leaning against the wall ignoring scattered belated demands for coffee, waits for the little cups to be emptied. She gathers the cups and leaves as a heavy rainfall starts on the tape.

From our rear the geisha enters (still bent double, she stoops throughout the play), carefully pulling – script in hand – the pert silver-turbaned toy-monkey standing on its four-wheeled cart, leaves it standing in front of us, leaves, returns by way of the front side door, – no: stops, retreats, it's the wrong door, – leaves by the rear door, comes back in through it with another toy animal, but has to take it back out. Some mistake has been made. Mysterious light signals from behind the curtain. Another aborted entry of the geisha's. – Consultations with the Indian cleaning woman, who, having lit the incense sticks, is now in the obligatory Lotus position, or at any rate, with her legs under her, squatting by them. The geisha trips in, bends over the little monkey, on a little instrument makes 3 sounds. Smith is from the couch watching this ceremonial consecration of the first character, Mr. Engstrand. More light flashes from behind the curtain. The little Oriental, a rich mess of garments, pulls in the garlanded pig, more richly decked out than she. More flashes.

The tape starts, – act I, Regina keeping her nominal father out of Mrs. Alving's house. He wants her for a whorehouse he is planning, reminds her her mother was a whore. The little assistant is busy, Kabuki-fashion, with the monkey, – Engstrand is speaking of »temptations« (thunderclaps and lightning from behind the curtain). Regina refuses to go with him. The assistant, following developments in her script, is back and forth between the two characters, daintily, a little fussily, – she was superb, – repositions each a little as it talks. Thunder and lightning again as the pig mentions the Alvings have been to court. Smith is fanning himself with a large straw fan. Splashing sound of rain (»Through the glass wall a gloomy fjord landscape is discernible, veiled by steady rain.«) The very very quiet grotesque ceremonial out front on the floor makes the nasty dialogue more horrible. The old crook is thrown out, the assistant leaves with the monkey, returns with another, even more exotically splendid, aglitter in violet, bearing a basket of glittering gifts on its back, – pastor Manders, – and pulls it over to the pig. They face one another. The pig is huge compared to the men-monkeys.

small table
w/ coffee
machine

Pastor
Manders

Regina

The assistant moves the monkey's arms when he talks, rocks him, – turns a page in the script, – tenderly budges the pig on its lines. The pastor wants her to go live with her »father,« Regina angles for a housekeeper's job with him, with some »real gentleman,« someone she »could feel affection for and look up to as a father.« The two ornate junk-objects, the assistant's bent back, her ratty fur, dense black wig make a compact, rich, confusing ensemble on the bare floor. Smith is vaguely, tho voluptuously, reclining on the couch, fanning himself, his bare knee showing, an enigmatic, undefined figure as yet, neither man nor woman. Regina is to fetch Mrs. Alving for the pastor. Smith leaves, the assistant takes out the pig, returns to reposition the reverend by the stage-back curtains between which the boot has appeared on the protruding corner of the table. The monkey addresses himself to the boot, rises to it, — stands on the table, glittering basket on his back. The assistant moves him. A light turns on behind the curtain, – Mrs. A., ununderstandably, but clearly a lady, speaks, behind her, momentarily, the masked mummy. The Hindu cleaning lady enters to remove the Turkish coffee can. The minister is rendering hommage to Mrs. A. (»if such a thing as art were to dull the natural affections,«) who responds with a brief yelp. He goes into the money matters, – »the interest isn't very attractive, – 4 % with 6 months notice of withdrawal ...« The cleaning lady is back in, cup of coffee in one hand, the other on her hip, she sits down on the table, next to the boot, unquietly, – leaning into the curtain, in her grey and green veils an interesting supplement of vulgarity. The money talk, – the torturously slow, rough voice, – goes on and on. The monkey licks the boot, strokes its calf. The cleaning lady is fiddling with the curtains, – goes here and there. There is a glimpse of a glove, of peacock feathers between the curtains. The reverend is talking Mrs. A. into not insuring the orphanage they are instituting in honor of her late syphilitic scoundrel of a husband. The reverend is fully insured himself: but what would people say if he had this God-dedicated enterprise insured? Smith enters in a magnificently handsome Sheik outfit, knotted handkerchief on his head, burnouse etc. (»Oswald Alving, in a light overcoat, with his hat in his hand and smoking a big meerschaum pipe, enters through the door left.«), changes the record. Hawaiian music replaces the rain (Mrs. A. is happy). The Hindu sweeper picks up the dustbox, resumes filtering the dust. Pause, no dialogue. Smith has picked up a script, approaches the table with the monkey and boot, and, as the assistant, by the turntable, turns down the volume, standing awkwardly behind the couch, falteringly, ›ill at ease‹, reads Oswald's lines in response (the tape going again) to pastor Manders' (». . . You must not think I condemn the artistic profession out of hand ...«). The pastor talking again, he has put the script down, his turn comes, he starts in, – »well, . . .,« has to pick up the script, – »I haven't done much acting lately ..« He takes off his striped Benjamin's coat, – under it he is wearing a dashing Douglas Fairbanks explorer's uniform, – folds it for a pillow for himself, – Oswald is in a bad way, – reclines on the couch. The assistant is still beautifully manipulating the pastor's painful little naggings. The light behind the curtain goes on for a replique of Mrs. A.'s. Smith with an irritated expression goes over to turn up the almost inaudible phonograph. Another pause in the dialogue, – the assistant takes out the pig, forgotten out front, – and Smith veers into Oswald's defense of the free life of artists, attack on the immoralities of »our model husbands and fathers«, – »Someone has to pay for all that humping, to pay for the lobster, lucky landlord of Baghdad, those beliefs which are put into the world by all the uncle fishhooks, . . .«, in a lame, lost, weepy voice speaks of married people's envy of »what the queer goes out at night and does,« they »only dream of it.« He leaves for his »turn in the garden,« hand on crotch.

The Hindu cleaning woman rekindles the incense. Smith wanders in and out looking for something. Pastor Manders is droning on. »Seven days in Waikiki:« the assistant, walking backwards, pulls in the grandly decorated pig, – »Shall it be white port or red port, Mr. Oswald?« The pig is carried out, Smith leaves with it to help it uncork the bottles. To a sentimental ballad from the phonograph, Mrs. A.'s faggoty voice is telling the pastor how she caught her late husband with Regina's mother, »putting his sausage in her oven.*« Off-stage squeak from Regina (Oswald's pass at her), sound of the bottles. Smith reenters with glass. He and his Oriental counterpart, the cleaning lady, keep coming and going. She's fanning herself on the couch. He is changing the record. The dialogue is continuing. The assistant keeps the pastor gesturing softly but grandly as he declares

* Smith rewrote the play. Making cuts and changing the wording, he condensed each character's lines, especially where they did not refer to ongoing action, into lengthy monologues, expositions of character. E.g., Mrs. A.'s lines here:
»I went back – it was only the business in connexion with the orphanage that obliged you to come and see me. My husband died as great a profligate as he had been all his life. I have suffered a good deal in this house. To keep him home in the evening – and at night – I have had to play the part of boon companion in his secret drinking bouts – in his room up there. I have had to listen to his ribald senseless talk, have had to fight with brute force to get him to bed – then jerk him off and then – before I could wash my hands, sitting up the rest of the night counting money, going over rent receipts, nursing Oswald. (THUNDERCLAP). He was only a baby then and scrubbing toilets. All the increase in the value of the property, all the improvements, do you suppose my husband troubled himself about any of them? I had always before me the fear that it was impossible that the truth should not come out. That is why the orphanage is to exist – to silence all rumors!«
We see here not only Smith's persistently splendid crudity in interpreting the morality of the bourgeoisie, but his amalgamation of Ibsen's heroine, – e.g. in Ibsen she speaks not of rents and money, but of »additions to the estate, all the improvements, all the useful innovations,« – into the crowd of money grubbers. His radicalisation of Ibsen's play is exemplary for how a living theatre must deal with the handed-down dramatic literature: and not only because it in fact is faithful to the original author's spirit. The elimination of the »naturalistic« dialogue-in-snippets is characteristically modern.

his proper sentiments of horrification at his hostess' after dinner reve-
lations, – how Regina's mother, – »that intimacy had consequences,
Mr. Manders,« – impregnated by captain A., with a dowry provided
by Mrs. A. bought herself Engstrand for a husband, . . . From time to
time, Manders' drone while the monkey delicately floats up and down
next to the boot deteriorates into screeches that compete with the lush
baritone off the record player.

Smith, the assistant, and the cleaning lady out, Smith back in with a
large coffee machine, the little assistant solicitously with Jacob Engstrand, who is placed in front of the table on his little red wheels,
looking up to Mrs. A. and to the pastor, – they are not of the same
social class. He proposes an edification inaugurate the orphanage,
after the assistant finds her place in the script rises up to the table to
mollify the pastor.

The distension of the speech of the two old fools, – conniving man
of conscience, the conniver, – gives it the gigantesque horror that
his nice Christian natal land inspired in Ibsen, but that his now
totally unbelievable, naive story-book dialogue, with a low cunning
akin to his compatriots Manders' and Engstrand's twisted by him to
create their characters and render plausibility to the really quite
crass story, but really to serve his rage, could no longer inspire:
Smith's staging is honest where the old-fashioned play is, as such,
dishonest, the playwright's conscientiousness a hypocrisy.* Smith
makes the cadavers speak out of their whitened sepulchres. The scene
meanwhile is generally quiet, – nicely lit, – with Smith, drink in his
hand (Oswald is guzzling at this point), and the tall Oriental loosely
in and out, and the small assistant with infinite care manipulating
her puppets, her fur-packed back curving over them under the curve
of the green arch, the music hardly interfering, a detaching intimation of a better world. No pressure, no hurry, no urgency, – an
infinitely slow, almost pointless, but quite necessary ceremony, –
theatre. Smith addresses some direction to the assistant, picks up the
script, reclines on the couch, fans himself. The pastor agrees to do
some edifying at the orphanage, the assistant wheels out Engstrand.
The light goes on for Mrs. A. (she and the pastor are taking leave of

* The naturalist playwright's creation of individual characters is not only qua
mask of his self-centeredness dishonest, but embarrassing, – *penible*. There is something unpleasantly petty about it. – Ibsen's dishonesty is revealed by a comparison of the *grotesqueness* of the play's story, – Ibsen's *real* concern, – with his no
doubt sincere feeling that the play is about Mrs. Alving, is almost a glorification
of womanhood.

one another), goes off as the pastor is hopped off, – Smith, »no, it should blink off and on« (it does), – pause. The record-player is turning more and more slowly, Smith, disgusted, weary, turns it off (glass in hand), – »Mother, may I sit on the couch beside you?« He pulls the couch over to the table protruding from the black crack in the curtains, sits, »now I must tell you something,« – drinks, – the light goes on, an affirmative faggoty squawk, – the mother is apprehensive. Smith, following the text more or less, tells her, exhausted, of his illness, – »I'll never be able to memorise lines again!« – he collapses on the couch. »No, no, it isn't true! How did this frightful thing happen to you?« He sits up, with many dry coughs, the pauses *very* wrong, milking the speech for flatness, emoting lamely, goes into the grand confession, – his syphilis, the doctor's remarks about the sins of the fathers, how he defended his father to the doctor, reading him his mother's beautiful letters about what a wonderful man his father was. He is reading the speech from the mangled stage-script, can't see, has to get into the light to read the text, – reads it, in his weepy voice, hanging off the end of the couch, but otherwise quite comfortably extended on it. There is a brief rejoinder from the mother (Smith fanning himself).
The pastor, still Haroun al Rashid, but now blue and gold, is trundled back in, Smith, glass in hand, is back by the phonograph, – Chinese music – the pastor's drone recommences. Smith pauses briefly in an errand involving the Turkish coffee pot to respond, is gone, reappears: »What can be the matter? What is that glare?« (shine from behind the curtains, behind which Smith has passed to give the mummy there instructions). Vibes on the phonograph, rear light one, Mrs. A., in fruity tones, »The orphanage is burning!« The two monkeys enter, carriages locked, front to front in an embrace, caressing one another, as on the tape Engstrand, the arsonist, pretending to have seen the pastor start the fire, blackmails him into transferring to his whorehouse, – to be named in honor of Mrs. A.'s late husband, a substitute for the orphanage, – the funds that were to have subsidised this latter. Smith is on the couch, not listening, drinking and watching uninterestedly, – lights the incense (the cleaning lady taking over on the couch, fanning herself). The fire is still flickering on the rear curtain. We can smell the incense. The monkeys are removed.
The rest of the play is about Oswald and his mother, Smith having, for a simplified dramatic line and an emotionally more intensive third act, – wiping out some of Ibsen's pettifogging structure, – trans-

posed to after the fire Oswald's champagne party in celebration of
his telling his mother he is taking Regina, this »healthy« girl, so »full
of the joy of life,« to Paris with him. In the pauses between his and
his mother's speeches we hear the pretty tinkle of the phonograph.
The Hindu street queen watching from the door, he stands stiffly,
facing us, script in hand, proposes champagne. The little geisha
takes the place of Mrs. A., her legs and script replacing the boot,
which, however, at a direction from Smith – »no, stay on the table,
mother,« – is kept up on the table also. Smith is leaning over the
table, back to us, close to his mother, his handkerchief falling over
his suit-jacket's collar, – »Mother, have you noticed how everything
I've done is concerned with (very loudly) THE JOY OF LIFE? (he finishes
his drink, – it's coffee, –) Always, always, the JOY OF LIFE (a grand,
vague, sweeping gesture) . . . a holiday feeling . . .« As on the phono a
concert piano plays a grandiosely solemn theme, the street queen and
the stage manager by the door pull up a large dripping bundle to an
over-head line and haul it across, – Regina the pig on a vast bag of
goodies and magnums. Smith, poking the pig in the arse, removes one
of the bottles as the bundle stops overhead center-stage. He leaves,
comes back in with two champagne glasses in one hand, the bottle
in the other, stands drunkenly, the street queen (she has a young girl's
voice) asks, »Shall I open the bottle?«. »No thank you Miss Engstrand, it has already been opened.« Pause. The package is dangling
overhead in the green, blue and orange light. Smith (it is, after all, a
party) is at the phonograph considering a record, – »I wonder if I
should do my tap dance now, – or at the end . . ., – at the end.« He
gets rid of the bottle and glasses between his mother's protruding
motionless legs on the table. The light goes on for Mrs. A.'s confession:
she didn't have the joy of life, drove her husband, who did, to his
profligate ways . . . Smith, »You mean, Regina is my half-sister?!«
Delicate Chinese music from the phonograph. The wet but glittering
overhead package, – the joy of life, – is being pulled out, but
Smith holds on to it, stunned, to his mother's cold Ibsenian lines,
leans his head against it sorrowfully, sniffing. Package out. (Regina
off to her adoptive father's brothel.) Hand to his head, he mimicks
shock, – dropping pennies out of his pocket, dripping champagne on
the script (extremely sentimental music). »Goodbyeeee.«
He leaves, returns with cartons of casein envelopes (decks) and sifted
glitter (he seems dissatisfied there isn't more of it), asks the cleaning
lady houri who has handed him a script-page to fetch something. To
lively music from the phonograph, she brings in the shopping cart.

Mrs. A., the little Oriental girl, a heavy black veil over her face indicating her lack of joy of life, covering up the ravages of the dread disease (reference to the departed Regina's callous »No, I am not going to stay out here in the country and wear myself out looking after invalids«) climbs into it off the table, the stalwart houri pushes her (script in her lap) over next to Oswald on the couch. She gestures grandly, – a splendidly irrelevant gesture, – to her typed lines, – »Oswald, my dear, has it been such a great shock to you about your father?« Smith is filling bags with glitter, there is a pause, before, consulting the script, he answers »that he died of Orchid rot of Atlantis?« He is holding a large plastic hand, a white mask she is wearing is partly visible under her veil.

Mixing in a barrage of patient, long-suffering stage-directions to her and to her keeper, – where to move, where to put her hand, – continually losing his place in the script, – interrupted by repeated whinnyings and unexpected whoops from her, – consultations between them as to whose turn to speak it is, – putting in long pauses, – he speaks of his father's queerness, about his father's pipe (reference, transposed by Smith from act I, to a nasty trick the captain played on little Oswald), about »softening of the brain« (soft low music from the phonograph), about »cherry-colored velvet curtains.« His voice is affecting. The cleaning lady is standing, holding the cart, in a sentimental pose, head inclined sideways. He pulls the carton with morphine envelopes out from under the couch, »Do you see this, mother? – Guilt flakes, – I have saved up 12 of them ... 14 ...« She is pushed forward, hand to her face gives a scream, he coughs heavily, »Have you a mother's heart and can bear to see me suffering? This unspeakable horror ...« A squeak, »You mean, you will ...?« While he drinks some coffee, her faggotty voice off the tape: »You have just imagined these dreadful things, Oswald. You've imagined it all. All this suffering has been too much for you. But now you shall rest. At home with your own mother, my own dear, blessed boy. Point at anything you want and you shall have it, just like when you were a little child ... do you see what a beautiful day we're going to have? Bright sunshine.« Mrs. A. in the cart is being wheeled about. Consultations between her and the Indian lady wheeling her. Oswald on the couch is putting on a death-skull mask, sits, hands dangling from knees, puts his head on his knees, – »mammie, put on the ...« in a very slow, dying-down voice, interrupted by her taped, squeaky »What did you say?« »... put on the ... Doris Day ...« To Day's *Once I had a Secret Love*, by a passion-twisted path, driven to and fro by conflicting impulses, – the Hindu queen wheeling her mechanically, – she makes it over to the couch, picks up one of the little envelopes, is about to scatter the seed of eternal forgetfulness, but the spot isn't right, the dying man keeps having to redirect her, – »no, not there, there, in the middle of the spot-light,« – at last gets it right. He picks up two of the envelopes, stands, lets glitter drop from weak hands at his side, – the mask frightening, – goes over to her to give her another envelope, dropping glitter: her veil is up, her white face-mask is showing. He walks slowly over to the stage-left wall, leans his head against it, – some more glitter.

By the third week end, Smith was doing the show himself, tho Eva, masked, in a hospital attendant's jacket was still behind the curtain, and her mother and a good-humored, beer-drinking young fellow were lending a hand back-stage, i.e. out in the lobby. Mrs. Pietkiewicz was also selling the tickets. Smith was being evicted.

The inanimate performers were very splendid now. Regina, besides the garland of roses from which dangled blue and green necklaces, had flowers all over her and a green gauze-scarf draped over her snout. She pulled a tiny straw-barrow loaded with glitter and a spool of thread. Pastor Manders, a very smug expression on his face, wore a blue and silver fakir's turban with a peacock feather in it and a violet glitter-jacket, and there was shiny red paper on his wheels and on the wheels of a basket-carriage he was pulling, charged with silver and red christmas-tree garlands. Jacob Engstrand had a silver turban on.

One of the projectors was trained on the pert-snouted Engstrand, center-stage, his turban glittering, and on the mysterious appearance of Regina further to the right and a little more up-stage: glittering splendidly, but invisible behind her veil. She was bathed in pink thanks to the red paper tied to the bulb in the ceiling above her.

Smith is working. He has taken off his striped wool coat and is arranging the figures, beer can in hand. He experiments with extending the Engstrand-Regina diagonal* by a candle in a Moorish candle-stand. The tape is going for the Regina-Engstrand dialogue. The dialogue over, he takes out Engstrand.

* Having done away with the Kabuki form of the show, the handling and the handler of the figures, Smith has to put them in just the right – semi-permanent – positions. His beautiful solutions of this formal problem of static theatre miraculously emerges from the ridiculousness and terrible (willful) chaos of the production.

To the sound of splashing water, he promenades Regina around in a circle. He goes to get pastor Manders, leads him in, but then takes him entirely apart, – takes him off his platform, the basket spilling, ... puts him together again. Something had been wrong with him. He waits on the couch while the pastor has his dialogue with Regina, – water has been splashing during all this sofar, – but after the dialogue he kneels down by him again, calls for help, – weakly, – »please, couldn't someone ...‚, – all he needs is a tiny little nail, ... if it isn't done right, it will never be right.« His bushwhacker's Sahib suit is green and is cut a little like a fatigue suit. Mrs. Pietkiewicz and the young fellow come to help out, they are all three out there repairing the pastor. It is raining. Mrs. Pietkiewicz takes some pictures. The two Hare Krishnas in the audience leave. The man behind them is asleep, or at any rate is resting his head on the row in front of him. There is no one else left, but then a hatted blond fellow that had left earlier comes back in.

A long stretch with no dialogue while the pastor is being repaired, – tape stopped. Now (Smith has just brought in a small step-ladder) the dialogue continues. – The pastor greets Mrs. Alving: whose leg appears between the curtains, white, draped over a carton, a stuffed white stocking in a black shoe. – Smith lights the Moroccan lamp hanging down over center-stage, or tries to, but its bottom falls open, – he proceeds with the show.

He's been drinking beer, but by his stare, when, as often, he stops whatever he is doing and just stands, seems stoned. He gets the broom, sweeps a little. ACTUALLY, all of Mrs. Alving is built up over that leg, behind the curtain: a black mass of hair and such. The statuesque hospital attendant behind the curtain, – Eva in red tights and red and black wool stockings, – briefly enters to put the needle on the turning record: but there is no music, only the rain. The broom is on the floor, Jack is standing, a little unstable, hand to his head, shirt open over his chest, a big ring on the small finger of his left hand, an abbreviated tasselled burnouse on his head, an enormous red handkerchief in his breast pocket. His shirt is very colorful, – blue with shiny spots in other colors.

The pastor is up on the table now, the leg is off the carton, replaced by a big glittering basket of gifts, Mrs. A. qua libidinal investment. With the pastor's voice droning on, to Smith, a kind of OM, hypnotic, and only Smith out there, and behind the curtain the unmoving white masked figure, occasionally lit, and with the state Smith is in, it's like a wake (for traditional theatre; for the play; for what Smith might have been, Errol Flynn in a boudoir.)

The sweeping is unfinished. The broom is center-stage, leaning against the couch, but Jack is disturbed by the absence of a spot light on Mrs. Alving – the basket, – asks his stage manager for assistance, gets the tall ladder, proceeds to climb it, but has forgotten to spread its legs, – he and the ladder fall, he lands on the couch. The ladder has been set up, but the tape is already up to where Oswald is supposed to talk about the depravity of decent citizens. From the top ot the ladder, putting the spot on her, he explains to his mother who the uncle Fishhook is in whose columns, according to the pastor, he has been favorably mentioned, – »... a magazine-writer ... (long pause) ... luring baby film makers to leave their film in his safe for one night ... in this way, Jonas Mekas has built up a priceless collection of art of a certain sort ...«* His mother glows in the pink spot, previously useless on the floor downstage. The organdy curtain is a rich salmon color. He's back down on the floor, the young fellow has taken out the ladder. He is wearily discoursing on all the guilt in marriages, in well regulated homes, guilt for all the humping, somebody has to pay for the humping, – »all day long *they* are thinking about what the queer goes out at night and does.« He gives this speech haltingly, standing stiffly, arms at his sides, »thinking« with his eyes (the tortured soul) in traditional theatre-manner, then staring straight out. As – his hand under his jacket, – he says he'll go into the garden to take a turn, being so tired from his journey, glitter is falling in a thin stream from his crotch. The little silver rivulet is sinister and elegant. He has returned with a new can of beer (Regina's voice, »Dinner is ready. Will you have white or red port, Mr. Oswald?«) His lines always come a little late, – he has to remember them. »Both, Miss Engstrand. I may as well help you with the bottles.« Off with Regina.

Mrs. A. is telling the pastor all. The bandaged, Frankensteinian monster behind the curtain, in the glare of the naked bulb is manip-ulating Mrs. A.'s head, a silvery wig, from side to side. The scene on the table and behind the curtain is a terrible mess, – indefinitely out of a horror movie, – the carton, the leg, black and silver things, the basket and its contents, unidentifiable objects hanging down obscurely from the lamp that Eva has on much too much of the

---

* Mekas is a Lithuanian promoter of the independent art film. Smith's charge is sort of symbolic: Mekas has been making a living, but isn't getting rich. He's made a position for himself.

time, – the lighting scheme, light *on* for Mrs. A.'s speeches, has broken down. Mrs. A., »I saw him put his sausage in her oven. That intimacy had consequences, Mrs. Manders.« Jack is finishing sweeping the glitter. A small *golden* heap of glitter. He interrupts his sifting to light a stick of incense. On his knees, sifter in his hand, he poses for a shot by Mrs. Pietkiewicz. Additional spectators have arrived in the lobby. The stage manager enters, wants to know can they get reduced rates, Smith still on his knees, facing us, says to let them in for $2.–. Mimicking inquiry to the audience, he proceeds to reposition Engstrand (he's been there all the while), has him, with his head way back, looking up at the pastor, who's on a stool below Mr. Alving on the table, and looks out into space over Engstrand's head.

Eva is trying to make the coffee-maker behind the couch, – which Smith has found has been on all the time, but not making coffee, – work. She looks grotesque. Does her job gravely. Jack asks to sit beside his mother, – »of course, dear boy,« – he shuffles over to the end of the couch near the table, having pushed the couch in that direction, asking for the script is told it is »the legal papers« (that the pastor brought Mrs. Alving in his gift basket), gets it there, – gives his confession, with it beside him, consulting and reading, and playing horribly with the white leg.

On the, due to the steady, subdued colored lighting, *very* still stage, humor and infinite depression are being equated. Smith's high-pitched, low-energy voice is by now keeping the performance going very *steadily*. The continually unraveling tissue of the play has miraculously established itself as form, a medium of failure and continuation.

The first music of the evening. Oriental fifes and a rolling piano salute Regina's final entrance, as a vast heavy white package with her on top hoves into view. Jack has to throw some water on it after it enters, this apparently having been omitted by his assistants, – he does want the rain-soaked effect. It dangles there, green, red and sparkling in the light, misshapen, a blob. He struggles to get the big bottle out of the net, stands there forlornly with it and with the glasses. Music off on Regina's exit (»Goodbyeeee.«), – the bundle dangles out. »Here I am with queerness from my normal parents as well as orchid rot of Atlantis from my married parents. Mommie, we must have a little champagne!« – briskly off behind the curtains, back out with the shopping cart in which the head and wig tumble down. He sits fingering a plastic hand, the shopping cart behind him.

Gets up, drops the hand in the cart, goes to pick up the morphine envelopes, puts on the death mask, »Mammie, play the Doris Day record. Mammie. Play the Doris Day record. Mammie . . .,« – masked face on his knees, in a superslow, draggy low voice, lugubrious. The record is put on, »Once I had a secret love that lived within the heart of me/ all too soon my secret love became impatient to be free/ . . .« He thrusts the cart with the black mummy aside, scatters the glitter with the plastic hand, – gets more glitter, stands, arms hanging, drops it, lets it run through his hands, pours it over the black mess in the cart, with feathery paretic step walks about the stage, scattering it, goes out, comes back with the envelopes, tosses them into the air, throws the remaining ones into the cart, slowly, the Doris Day still on, walks over to the wall, gloved hand in crotch, glitter dripping from his crotch. Lights out. Record out. Lights back on. Triumphant music. Smith exits with the cart.

The show had started out an hour and a half, two hours long. The third week end it was 3 hours long. At its last showing, some time in January, it was apparently 5 1/2 hours long.

Early in December, Jack told me he had only just found the key to *Ghosts*: he has to introduce Engstrand, – is now taking him out of his (Oswald's) trunk, the trunk that had stood unused behind the couch, and putting him by the record player. *Scheherazade* brings him to life, he is placed next to a bell and rings it, arriving chez les Alvings and starting the play. Oswald is playing with his dolls.*

* Smith at this point was planning to reduce the play to a slide show, – that way he could do it by himself, wouldn't need any assistance. This unadvertised slide show early in February (1977) in its first half at least, which was all that I saw, turned out a variant of the 1 1/2 hour *How can Uncle Fishhook have a Free Bicentennial Zombie Underground?* done, the city and Little Italy in particular exploding all around it, at the Artist's Space in Soho, Independence Day of 1976, which was itself more or less a permutation/combination of the 3 hour *Horror of the Rented World* slideshow he did at the Collective for Living Cinema, after he returned from Rome, on the midnight of Halloween 1975, which according to a friend, Mel Andringa, to a Hawaiian accompaniment, against a background of Roman ruins and modern buildings on Jack's slides looking like Maya cities, golden, and of a Roman park, its foliage seeming tropically luxurious, told the tragic story of Jack's affair with a toy penguin, Inez, and of Inez's abduction by the green witch. Jack's slides are an assembly kit, his one-time-only, do-it-yourself movie. They are beautiful. I believe I saw the trunk from *Ghosts* in the 77 movie, open, overflowing, Jack – a sheik, – taking something out of it, – the only reference to *Ghosts* I noticed, and I am not sure of it. I noticed no penguins in the 76 movie. It had a park, i.e. Valley of the Nile or Oasis, a Sidewalks of New York, and a freakshow or Melanesian Stone Age section, the first two of

Syphilis is a representation of the horror of sex: of the adolescent's
fear of a union of opposites in which two become as one, and the
adolescent an adult; and of the fearsomeness this fear attributes to

which were linked by a lobster dance, and were the story of a Man (Smith) and
a Woman, a story of Romantic passion and despair. Selectively:
We see Him first (in this 76 movie), walking down a path, – i.e. he is *there*
(Smith composes his movies by the industry's classic conventions. Now and again
the image poses briefly as convention). – He as that Egyptian Deity, classic
profile, body frontal, elbows at his side, lower arms out sideways, – in a park
landscape, its shrubbery by Rousseau. – Lurking, nails in mouth, bloodshot eyes
glitter-ringed, expression anguished, puzzled. – »Lo, what do I see!« – SHE
appears, belly-dancer in her prime, the proud queen with the face of a performer,
picnic basket on her arm, – opening a soft drink (throbbing tango), breasts
(chastely covered). – An etc. of close-ups, jewelry, flesh, make-up, emotion writ in
the face, ... the stalking game. – Her ringed fingers withdrawing a flowered paper
napkin. –·Lush Oxodol commercial, – keeps white white eternally. – Him in the
underbrush, worried, balled fist near face, blue sun glasses. – (Fireworks detonating
in the streets were the constant accompaniment: behind the church of St. Anthony,
the Italians each year underpaint their Roman candles (remnants of the underground
fireworks traffic from Chinatown through Little Italy) with a sidewalk-level St.
Anselm's fire of giant fire-crackers tossed from the roof.) – The announcer sums
up the (Oxodol) story sofar: she doesn't know if she loves him, she likes, admires,
respects him, – but love? – The black basket on a pink rug spread on the green
grass. – A gas-station, trade-in tires stacked. HE's putting gas in a car, – misty
head-gear, Merlin's cape, a giant, red lobster claw in his right. – Decaying neigh-
bourhoods, laundries at night, parked cars, – the eroded ad of collision specialists.
– Floating images of neon signs. – HE with poster, »Select Now A Deposit holds
Your Selection,« a mad grin of commendation on his face, a small boiled lobster
holding on to his outstretched right, – the cape. – A cape dance of drama poses
to Andalusian songs of sadness, – his shirt, jacket and pants loose, all patterned
in large patterns, different ones: against a flat yellow firewall ... His face, its left
side carmine, made up a Japanese mask, his arms curved up, the lobster over his
head, a figure tilted in space ... In a pose of exhaustion, a joke-shop chicken in
his arm, clutching the poster, the little lobster. – Palms. – SHE, debonair in white
in the mean streets. – HE and SHE, together in innocence, behind »Comet Hotel«.
»Vincent's Clam Bar«, glowing red. – A wrecked building over a tragic pose, cigar
store display window full of open cigar boxes over another one. – (Intermission.)
Wireless lecture on the prophet with a purpose. Wanting to break new ground, he
brought breasts to the screen. Howard Hughes. The lecturer's gush as lush as the
slides. – Slides of dressed-up, no-talent weirdos, feeble cripples, Mario Montez, a
mild Negro. – Pearls, tattoos, feathers, shells, lace, satin, grotesquely alluring
poses, weak gesturings, vapid expressions, bloated faces, »For Rent«, »telephone
service interrupted«, »no loitering between this point and the poll«. – Voice
talking about Russell's breasts. – Montez sideways, nude torso, unclear face as on a
drowned man floating just below the surface, photo of a non-existent male. – An-
thropological natives, heap of dolls in an old drawer. – Lecture on sex stressing its
benefits. The condom rejected, diaphragm better, woman may lose a beautiful
experience. – Magic images, a golden doll in the mouth of a cave, church interiors,
jewels, blood, shimmering stairs. – Two diaphragms, to be worn alternately, avoid

it, a sociability of the flesh that kills the spirit, as spirochaete the brain. In Smith's phrase, the price of humping. *Ghosts* makes it an emblem of marriage, Smith's adaptation, the emblem of fucking. *The Secret of Rented Island* hereby makes manifest the essence of queer art.

> »Loathsomeness waits and dreams in the deep, and decay spreads over the tottering cities of men.«
> H. P. Lovecraft, *The Madness from the Sea* in: Weird Tales, Feb. 1928.

disturbing waits. – A dead crab, a crushed can of Crush, compositions of refuse, in exquisite colors, exquisitely composed.

The movie is a manifesto, opposing to sex, an anxious duty, QUEERNESS, life as theatre by ironic self-immolation transmuting into beauty (flower of the imagination in a world of trash), – part I, the ideal; part II, living like a freak.

Smith does not confront heterosexuality with any other kind of sexuality: sexuality is identified as heterosexuality; it is opposed to sublimation; and sublimation proves immolation to the grotesque, a thronging forth of death. Homosexuality is a substitute, and Smith's art is not homosexual but transvestite.

The queerness of queerness is that it is asexual. It is an adoration of art so absolute it would make life art. It ends up making art of this unachievable ideal, perforce ironic art. Ironic, not only because the ideal is suicidal and – worse – unrealizable, but because the lover's *daring* conduct, the art of seduction, tactic of the war between the sexes, language of an act of the imagination, love, turns out the only artful way of life natural to or devised by man. This art, animated by the high tension between the opposing sexes, the masked dance of penis and vulva, is precisely the art rejected by the queer, and rejected in the name of art, but it is also precisely the art that for its uniqueness as art of life he sees himself forced to counterfeit in artistic reproduction, transvestivaly.

The original theatre of the City of New York.
From the mid-60s to the mid-70s.

Book 1. The theatre of visions: Robert Wilson.
Book 2. Queer theatre.
Book 3. Richard Foreman's diary theatre. Theatre as personal phen-
   omenology of mind.
Book 4. Morality plays. Peter Schumann's Bread and Puppet theatre.
Book 5. Theatre as psycho-therapy for performers.
   A. Joe Chaikin's Open Theatre. The Becks' Living Theatre.
   B. Richard Schechner's Performance Group. Andre Gregory's Man-
   hattan Repertory Company. With notes on Grotowski and Andre
   Serban.
Book 6. The 1970s hermetic theatre of the performing director. Jared
   Bark. Stuart Sherman. John Zorn. Melvin Andringa. With ap-
   pendices on Ann Wilson, Robert Whitman and Wilford Leach.
Book 7. Theatre as collective improvisation. The Mabou Mines.
Book 8. Black theatre and music. With notes on the Duo Theatre and
   M. van Peebles.
Book 9. Dance. Merce Cunningham, Yvonne Rainer, Meredith Monk,
   Douglas Dunn. With a note on Ping Chong.